About the Author

Angelina Bennet is a chartered occupational psychologist and is the Director of I Potential Ltd. She has a broad and varied experience of applying occupational psychology in a variety of organisations and at all levels.

Angelina has a BSc in psychology with languages and an MSc in experimental methods in psychology. After several years working for the NHS as an assistant clinical psychologist, Angelina attended Cranfield University where she gained an MSc in applied psychology. She is currently completing a professional doctorate in occupational psychology. Additionally, she is a qualified hypnotherapist, accredited coach, and has been trained in the Enneagram and in psychosynthesis techniques.

Angelina has a depth of expertise in working with personality models, particularly Jungian typology and the MBTI®. She is also on the board of the British Association for Psychological Type (BAPT).

The Shadows of Type

Psychological Type Through Seven Levels of Development

Angelina Bennet

Lulu 2010

Front cover photograph by Roland Atkins
Total Solar Eclipse – Turkey, 29th March 2006

Quotation on page 5 cited from J. Campbell (Ed.) (1976), *The Portable Jung,* Viking Penguin p.463. Originally from C. G. Jung, *The Spiritual Problem of Modern Man, CW Vol. 10:*. © 1970 Princeton University Press. Reprinted by permission of Princeton University Press.

Jung, C.G.: *Psychology and Religion, CW Vol.11.* © 1969 Princeton University Press. Jung, C.G.: *Aion: Researches into the Phenomenology of the Self, CW Vol.9.* ©1969 Princeton University Press. Jung. C.G.: *The Structure and Dynamics of the Psyche, CW Vol.8.* ©1969 Princeton University Press. Jung, C.G.: *Psychological Types, CW Vol.6.* ©1971 Princeton University Press.

Reprinted by permission of Princeton University Press.

® MBTI, Myers-Briggs Type Indicator and Myers-Briggs are registered trademarks of the Myers-Briggs Type Indicator Trust in the United States and other countries. OPP® Ltd is licensed to use the trademarks in Europe.

© 2010 by Angelina Bennet
All rights reserved

ISBN 978-1-4457-4167-3

"So long as all goes well and all our psychic energies find an outlet in adequate and well-regulated ways, we are disturbed by nothing from within. No uncertainty or doubt besets us, and we cannot be divided against ourselves. But no sooner are one or two channels of psychic activity blocked up than phenomena of obstruction appear. The stream tries to flow back against the current, the inner man wants something different from the outer man, and we are at war with ourselves."

C.G. Jung

Contents

Preface	9
Part One – The Shadows of Type Theory	11
Psychological Type and the MBTI®	13
Limits to Using Type for Developmental Coaching	21
Psychological Type and the Psyche	35
Psychological Type and Psychosynthesis	48
The Levels of Ego Development	60
The Developmentally Levelled Type Descriptions	85
Part Two – Practical Applications	181
Practical Applications of the Shadows of Type Model	183
Techniques for Working With the Dynamics of Psychological Type	191
Techniques for Working With Different Parts of the Psyche	202
Techniques for Working at Particular Ego Development Levels	211
Afterword	217
Appendices	
Appendix One: Glossary of Terms	218
Appendix Two: Ego Defence Mechanisms	223
References	226
Index	229

Preface

When I first discovered psychological type it provided me with so many answers: why two people would react so differently to the same situation; why they would approach the same task from completely different angles; why something would appeal to one and repulse the other; how they could completely misunderstand what each other was saying. However, after this initial enlightenment came the questions. Why are some people flexible and adaptable with their type, while others are trapped and restricted by their type? Why are some Extraverted Feeling types caring and considerate while others are self-centred and prickly? How can a person with a preference for Extraverted Thinking be fair and objective on one day, then condescending and judgemental on the next? The type descriptions say ENFPs are inspiring, creative and insightful, yet the 360° feedback report is describing a person who is unfocused, novelty-seeking and hypersensitive – why? What is it that makes a person a "good INTJ" or a "bad INTJ"?

This led me to start thinking about how well we use our types and what factors have an influence on our expression of type. My search first led me to explore the effect on type from the other aspects of the psyche - the ego, the persona, the shadow, the "light" shadow – and I realised that people who are not using their type "well" are often unconsciously trying to defend their sense of who they are – their ego image. Moreover, they tend to operate on "autopilot" without considering why they behave as they do. This causes them to habitually restrict their behaviour and judge others according to their own ego image. This was interesting and enlightening, however, it did not answer why some people were victims of their ego images while others were free, flexible and effective.

I found the answer in ego development theory. People have different perspectives on themselves, on others and on the world. Some people can only think in black and white, some can think in shades of grey, and some can use the entire spectrum. These different perspectives influence how adaptable we can be in ourselves and how accepting and understanding we can be towards others.

In this book, type is taken back into Jung's original context of the whole psyche, and the influence of the different parts of the self on the expression of type is considered. Jung's psyche is then "upgraded" to Assagioli's psychosynthesis model which provides more clarity regarding these influences on type. Type in its context is then set into ego development theory, leading to developmentally levelled descriptions of each of the 16 psychological types. These detailed descriptions deal, not only with the "dark" shadow that traps and restricts us, but also with the "light" shadow; the part of ourselves that is full of untapped potential. From these descriptions we can identify what is going on in the psyche, where the inner conflicts and tensions lie, and how this effects the expression of type. The descriptions also provide a "route map" of the potential developmental path for each type. The last few chapters will suggest practical ways of using and working with this developmentally layered model.

This book is intended for those who are interested in psychological type for their own personal development and for coaches who wish to work with type more extensively and in more depth. As psychosynthesis is a key part of the model and the associated techniques, this approach can also be a useful resource for practitioners of transpersonal coaching. It is not, however, a comprehensive account of Jung's theory, a complete guide to psychosynthesis, a full account of ego development theory, or a coaching manual. All of the relevant information that forms part of the final theory and model is included, as are suggested practical uses for the "Shadows of Type" model, however a degree of skill in type use and coaching are assumed.

I hope that by reading and using this book, you too will find some of the answers to your questions.

Part One

The Shadows of Type Theory

Chapter One

Psychological Type and the MBTI®

During his lifetime the Swiss psychologist, Carl Gustav Jung (1875–1961), developed a vast array of theories about dreams, spirituality, symbols, religion, and synchronicity, to name but a few. Amongst these, one of his most popular works was his theory of psychological types. Jung's typology was mainly developed from his observations of people and from reading literature about characters from history, mythology and fiction. Whilst many other existing theories of personality are based on observable behaviour and characteristics, Jung's theory was based on the flow and balance of psychic energy within an individual.

Jung's first attempt at developing a typology identified the difference between people who were predominantly Introverted (internalised energy) and people who were predominantly Extraverted (externalised energy); he called this pair of energetic orientations the *attitudes*. He later added in the *functions* which are the different ways that people take in information (Sensation or Intuition) and make judgements (Thinking or Feeling). Combining these attitudes and functions resulted in a typology of eight psychological types – Introverted *or* Extraverted Sensing *or* Intuition types, and Introverted *or* Extraverted Thinking *or* Feeling types. As the characteristics he ascribed to the different types were based on observations of his patients, they tended to be somewhat negative and concerned with the poor development or imbalance of the psychological types. His book on the subject, "Psychological Types", was published in 1921 and the English translation was first published in 1923. Jung's work can be notoriously difficult to follow, however his theory of psychological type has been modified and further developed to make it more accessible to a wider audience by Katherine Briggs and her daughter, Isabel Briggs-Myers.

Following the Second World War, Briggs and Myers believed that Jung's typology, if adapted to describe normally functioning people rather than those with psychological problems, could be useful in helping people to identify the kind of employment they would be best suited to. They looked for a questionnaire that would help to identify an individual's Jungian type and, when none could be found, they began their work on the development of the Myers-Briggs Type Indicator® (MBTI®), a self-report questionnaire designed to help an individual to identify their psychological type. The first edition of the MBTI was published in 1962. By 1998 an estimated 3.5 million MBTI questionnaires were being administered per year and the indicator was available in over 30 languages (Briggs-Myers, 2000).

In addition to creating the type indicator, they further developed Jung's theory by adding in another attitude pair that related to how people deal with their external environment – Judging or Perceiving – and introduced the term "preference" to describe an individual's most naturally used attitudes and functions. This new attitude pair helped people to work out which of the psychological functions was the most dominant for them. They also suggested the inclusion of a second predominant or preferred function for each type to provide support and balance to the main dominant function. This led to there being 16 different types, and the possibility of denoting the type using a four-letter abbreviation (e.g. ESTJ – preferences for Extraversion, Sensation, Thinking and Judging). There are several other type models and instruments based on Jung's original typology, but the Myers-Briggs® model is one of the most popular and well-known.

The Myers-Briggs Model of Psychological Type

The Myers-Briggs model of type has four dichotomies or "preference pairs". These relate to where individuals focus most of their attention (Extraversion-Introversion), what type of information one is most drawn to and trusting of (Sensing-iNtuition), the process used to make decisions and judgements (Thinking-Feeling), and, in addition to Jung's original attitudes and functions, how one deals with the outer environment (Judging-Perceiving). The definitions of these functions and attitudes are shown in Table 1.

Attitude: Where you focus your energy and attention	
Extraversion (E)	**Introversion (I)**
Focus attention outwards Energised by interacting with others and from taking action Develop ideas by talking them out Have a broad range of interests and "friends" Expressive Do not like to spend much time alone Like interacting with large groups	Focus attention inwards Energised by thoughts and taking in experiences Think through ideas before discussing them Have a smaller yet deeper range of interests and "friends" Contained Content to spend a considerable amount of time alone Like to interact with small groups
Perceiving Functions: What type of information you prefer to use and trust	
Sensing (S)	**Intuition (N)**
Prefer to attend to and trust tangible and real information Like to have the details Want to see a practical use for ideas Are focused on the present Trust past experience Like to verify information Tend to remember details and facts Observant Realistic	Prefer to attend to and trust ideas and inspiration Like to see overall patterns Like theories and ideas Are focused on the future Trust inspiration and vision Like to try out ideas Will remember details if they form a pattern Tend to see the big picture Enjoy using imagination
Judging Functions: How you make decisions or evaluations	
Thinking (T)	**Feeling (F)**
Use logic: cause and effect, pros and cons Tend to step out of a situation and look at it objectively Have a sense of detachment from tasks or situations Can appear "tough-minded" More likely to criticise than praise Like to find solutions Task-focused Implement "fairness" by treating everybody equally	Use values: what is important to them Tend to step into a situation and identify with it Have a sense of attachment to tasks and situations Can appear "tender-hearted" More likely to praise than criticise Like to empathise People-focused Implement "fairness" by treating everybody as individuals
Attitude: How you deal with the world around you	
Judging (J)	**Perceiving (P)**
Tend to organise and structure things Energised and satisfied by getting closure Like to be organised and planned Can be seen as decisive Stressed by last-minute rushes Tend to compartmentalise and order things Methodical	Tend to want to experience life as it comes Prefer to leave options open Feel constrained by plans and structure Can be seen as casual or laid-back Energised by last-minute rushes Tend to see things as open-ended Spontaneous

Table 1: Definitions of the functions and attitudes

In the Myers-Briggs process, clients are asked to complete the MBTI questionnaire; this is followed by a discussion with a qualified MBTI practitioner to assess where they think their preferences lie. This is known as the self-assessment process. The information from the questionnaire (reported type) is then added into the process and a four-letter "best fit" type for the client is arrived at. The 16 Myers-Briggs types are described in Table 2. It is important to note that the MBTI questionnaire is only designed to provide an indication of one's possible psychological type and only forms a part of the overall Myers-Briggs process. Although the questionnaire has good evidence for reliability and validity, there are a range of reasons why an individual's reported type may not be their actual best fit type.

The four-letter type has a hierarchy of functions as per the theory of "type dynamics". Type dynamics gets closer to the Jungian type categories, in that it combines the Extraversion-Introversion attitude with the clients' most dominant preference (e.g. Introverted Thinking or Extraverted Thinking) and with the other functions of their type. These "function-attitudes" are described in Table 3. The Myers-Briggs theoretical model postulates a four-function model where there is a dominant function (the most developed function), an auxiliary function (the second most developed and supportive of the dominant), a tertiary function (not often used and not one of the preferred functions) and an inferior function (the least used, most unconscious and opposite in both function and attitude to the dominant). For example, the type dynamics hierarchy for an ESTJ would be:

Dominant Extraverted Thinking (Te)

Auxiliary Introverted Sensing (Si)

Tertiary Intuition (N)*

Inferior Introverted Feeling (Fi)

The "Car Analogy" is a good way of describing the positioning and interaction of these functions. The dominant function is the driver of the car; it sets the direction and has ultimate control of the car. The auxiliary function is the front passenger; reading the map, helping to spot signposts and generally offering assistance to the driver. The tertiary function is the teenager in the back seat; sometimes helpful and

---

Note: In the Myers-Briggs model the tertiary function is not attached to an attitude. In some other developments of their type theory it is, but there are differing opinions as to whether it is introverted or extraverted for any one type. Most theorists suggest that it will be in the same attitude as the dominant function.

good company, and sometimes immature and irritable. Finally, the inferior function is like the infant in the baby seat. Although the baby is usually asleep and unnoticed, sometimes it will emit offensive odours and unpleasant substances, and the boot of the car may be full of baby baggage. However, when the baby wakes up and screams, the

ISTJ	ISFJ
Reserved, systematic, logical, dutiful and dependable. Like to do their research before acting and look for efficiency. Tend to stay within their comfort zone and change only when they see it as necessary. *Can become inflexible and anxious when faced with ambiguity or the unknown.*	Quietly supportive and very loyal. Conscientious and have a sense of duty to others in a work place. Tend to find it easy to remember details about others and take notice of anniversaries and traditions. *Can become anxious about being seen to do the right thing by others.*
INFJ	**INTJ**
Look for meaning and purpose in what they do. Like to have a vision about how things should be and aim to gently relate to others according to this. Enjoy creativity and thinking about what makes people tick. *Can become stressed and withdrawn when the world does not fit their ideal vision.*	Like to think of and implement new, goal-oriented ideas. Tend to see connections between things quickly. Enjoy theorising and strategising. Independent-minded, logical and questioning. *Can become intolerant of others' "interference" with their ideas and plans.*
ISTP	**ISFP**
Quiet observers with a tendency to go with the flow until there is a logical problem to solve, then they spring to action. Practical, analytical, observant and independent. They like to understand how things work and are often mechanically-minded. *Can become impersonal and unaware of their emotional impact on others.*	Considerate, kind, sensitive and gentle. Committed to their values but generally unlikely to force these on others. Loyal to those who are important to them and true to themselves. Playful and spontaneous in life. *Can become oversensitive, be a push-over for others, and become self-doubting.*
INFP	**INTP**
Values-driven and idealistic about the world. Seek a life that is congruent with their values and beliefs. Quietly accommodating, yet tough when their values are threatened. Supportive, good listeners. *Can become judgemental, and be dogmatic and unrealistic about their beliefs.*	Enjoy logical problem solving and can see beyond the usual limits of thought. Analytical and sceptical, they will take their time to get to the best solution. Enjoy gaining expertise in their area of interest. *Can become detached, emotionally and physically, and try to fit logic to everything.*

ESTP	ESFP
Realistic, flexible, logical and practical. Like to take practical action, particularly in a crisis. Live for the moment and get bored with long processes and boundaries. Often fun-loving and good company. *Can become hedonistic and create crises for fun, and unaware of consequences.*	Outgoing, flexible, lively and life-loving. Tend to be entertaining company and caring and loyal towards those important to them. Bring fun and common sense to situations. Willing to take risks. Action-oriented. *Can become impulsive and thrill-seeking, and can over personalise situations.*
ENFP	**ENTP**
Energetic, imaginative and constantly scanning for inspiration and possibilities. Enjoy the process of having ideas and creating a vision. Tend to be optimistic and enjoy being part of a team. Excited by change and ideas. *Can become blind to negatives and realities, or constantly seeking the ideal.*	Actively look for new opportunities and novel solutions to problems. Enjoy innovation. Look for logic and enjoy the challenge of debate, sometimes playing "devil's advocate". Sociable, yet selective with closeness. *Can become easily bored, argumentative and unaware of others' needs or feelings.*
ESTJ	**ESFJ**
Action-oriented and striving for efficiency and completion of tasks. Tend to be rule-conscious and have a good eye for the details. Firm yet fair in dealing with others. Approach life with consistency, precision and logic. *Can become too focused on tasks at the expense of people and enjoyment.*	Find practical ways to help others and maintain harmony. Enjoy organising things for others and like to be appreciated for their efforts in return. Quick to mediate during conflict. Loyal, dutiful and thorough. *Can become too focused on helping others than helping self, leading to resentment.*
ENFJ	**ENTJ**
Seek to inspire others and help others to develop and grow. Enjoy working in teams with shared values and aspirations. Caring, helpful and empathic. Try to see the good in others and focus on the positives and the future. *Can become intrusive to others, and have feelings of being undervalued.*	Enjoy taking the lead in groups and getting the best results. Critically evaluate and seek improved ways of doing things. Forthright with their views and decisive. Seek challenge and new opportunities for progress. *Can become dominating, forceful and condescending, and have a "my way or no way" style.*

Table 2: Descriptions of the 16 Myers-Briggs types

car's passengers, and in particular the driver, is sent into chaos until the baby's needs are met.

Extraverted Thinking	**Extraverted Feeling**
Extraverted Thinking types are energetically action-oriented and enjoy setting direction and improving efficiency. They are task-oriented, enjoy results, are motivated by taking on a challenge, and place a high value on competence and responsibility.	Extraverted Feeling types enjoy doing things to help or please other people. They enjoy creating harmony and reaching consensus. They are motivated by values-led environments and place a high value on mutual support and genuine relationships.
Extraverted Intuition	**Extraverted Sensing**
Extraverted Intuitive types scan the outer environment to inspire them to have new ideas and see possibilities. They enjoy exploring options and ideas, are enthusiastic and enjoy change. They prefer initiation to maintenance and value discussing future possibilities and their visions.	Extraverted Sensing types enjoy living for the moment and being action-oriented and adaptable. They enjoy direct experience of the external world, are fun loving and enjoy and seek variety. They are responsive to immediate demands and place a high value on personal freedom.
Introverted Thinking	**Introverted Feeling**
Introverted Thinking types enjoy problem solving and attempt to find perfect solutions and absolute truths. They are logical and thoughtful. They enjoy complexity and are motivated by intellectual pursuits. They place a high value on objective truth and logic.	Introverted Feeling types live life guided by their personal values. They are ideals-oriented, seek honesty, and are motivated by supporting and making a difference to others. They place a high value on living in congruence with their values and creating harmony.
Introverted Intuition	**Introverted Sensing**
Introverted Intuitive types quickly see the connections between things and use these to create new concepts. They enjoy theories, innovative ideas and making connections. They are motivated by implementing original ideas and value inspiration and originality.	Introverted Sensing types are reliable, dependable and stable individuals with a strong sense of wanting to do the right thing. They enjoy taking in and processing information, are capable of vivid recall of memories, and enjoy stable and structured environments. They value tradition and loyalty.

Table 3: Descriptions of the function-attitudes

Other type theorists, for example Lenore Thomson and John Beebe, have suggested models that contain all eight of the functions in a hierarchy for each individual, and these eight-function models are currently gaining in popularity. In fact, Jung's theory states that we have all eight functions as part of our overall psyche, however some are less accessible, desirable or conscious than others.

Myers and Briggs have made Jung's typology easy to understand and very popular, and they have created descriptions of each type that emphasise the positive attributes. However, Myers and Brigg's development of Jung's typology, whilst enabling the theories to be more accessible, has also been criticised for contributing to the over simplification of psychological type theory and for placing too much emphasis on the positive aspects of type.

Chapter Summary

- The theory of psychological types was developed by Carl Jung and further adapted by Myers and Briggs.
- The theory suggests that there are two opposing styles for
    - Where we focus our energy or attention
    - What information we prefer to use and trust
    - How we make decisions and evaluations
    - How we deal with the world around us
- We have a natural tendency to prefer one style over the other.
- Operating in our preferred styles requires little energy and effort.
- Operating in our non-preferred styles takes effort and can be de-energising and de-motivating.
- The preferences can be denoted in a four-letter "code".
- Our preferences have an order or hierarchy.

Chapter Two

Limits to Using Type for Developmental Coaching

Originally, the Myers-Briggs® typology was mostly used in counselling settings, however it is now mainly used in organisational settings by occupational psychologists, coaches and management consultants. In fact, Scoular and Campbell (2007) suggested that the MBTI® was the most commonly used and well-known psychometric employed by coaches, and this has recently been confirmed by research by McDowall and Smewing (2009). In a survey of the use of psychometrics in coaching, they found that the MBTI was, by far, the most used, with 49% of the sample of coaches reporting using the MBTI in their work.

The available Myers-Briggs resources for coaches focus on the strengths, development needs, stressors and coaching styles that each of the 16 types will tend to have. The development needs for each type tend to be confined to helping the client develop and access their non-preferred functions. With regard to potential dysfunctional behaviours, the literature about type development warns against becoming one-sided and rigid in one's use of type in older age if opportunities for development are being missed, however there is little mention of the issues that a particular type can encounter when overusing their preferred styles on an everyday basis. Therefore, coaches who want to work with clients on personal development using the Myers-Briggs may be limited to helping clients to gain awareness of their preferences and the opposites. Additionally, the resources available for coaching and development work are likely to overemphasise the "gifts" and positives of their type and overlook the negatives. So, for example, how can a coach integrate a client's positive Myers-Briggs description with a 360° feedback profile that clearly states that the client is displaying negative behaviours? Conversely, how can a coach use the Myers-Briggs information to facilitate the development of further potential beyond type awareness in their clients?

In a survey that I carried out recently, the applications of the Myers-Briggs that most coaches were aware of were leadership development, change, communication and relationship difficulties, and these were also the applications most used by coaches. This is not surprising as they tend to be the focus of many coaching interventions, and they are also the main application areas covered in the Myers-Briggs training and literature. Of the more "negative" applications, most of the respondents believed that the Myers-Briggs could be useful in working with stress, however very few were aware that type could be used to address dysfunctional behaviour, inauthentic behaviour, inflexibility or entrenched behaviour. Addressing the latter four areas can be vital for developmental, transformational and psychological coaching.

Coaching work places a large focus on maximising the strengths of an individual and focusing on the positives and it would appear that the current applications of the Myers-Briggs are most frequently being used in this way. However, for coaching that focuses more on developmental or transformational work, there is a need to look for the blockers, negative behaviours and "traps" that the client is prone to; these are usually a function of one's own personality. Additionally, developing further potential tends to be limited to helping the client to "flex" into the non-preferred functions, with little guidance on how to further develop a client's actual preferred functions. Clearly, there is something missing from the popular models of psychological type that can make it difficult for developmental and transformational coaches to work with the more negative aspects of an individual's functioning, or to explore ways to develop further potential beyond addressing the typical type-related blind spots.

Is There a "Missing Element" in the Popular Models of Typology?

Critics of current type approaches comment on the oversimplifying of typology, the potential to use it for labelling, the positive bias of the descriptions, and the separation from the context of the wider psyche. Myers and Briggs, for example, were keen that their version of psychological type maintained a positive focus and, as a result, the types are described in most of the resources in a positive light, with only a brief mention of their potential pitfalls. These pitfalls are usually concerned with the potential for people to use one of their preferences out of balance with the other (e.g. overusing the preferred Perceiving function and not adequately using the preferred Judging function), to neglect the styles that are related to their non-preferred functions, or to manifest some slightly negative aspects of their type if they do not find a suitable outlet for their preferences.

Myers and Briggs made it clear in their writings and teachings that their theory of psychological type did not tell the whole story about an individual's personality. Type is a broad brush approach to personality and is overlaid by traits, environmental and genetic influences, experiences, and individual characteristics. Myers and Briggs also emphasised that psychological type cannot be used to predict behaviour, as people are at liberty to behave how they like, but that behaving in a manner that is not congruent with one's preferences will require more effort and energy and be less motivating. In fact, it could be argued that the Myers-Briggs theory of psychological type is not a theory of personality, but rather a theory of cognitive processing as, broadly speaking, it is about one's preferred mode of gathering and using information. However, as it is conceptualised as a personality theory, comparisons have been made with other theories of personality and, consistently, the Myers-Briggs model is seen as missing an element. Exactly what this "missing element" is varies somewhat from theorist to theorist, however it seems to be broadly concerned with how well somebody uses and expresses their type – "psychological health".

The "Big Five" Approach and the "Missing" Neuroticism Element

Since the early part of the 20th Century, researchers have been attempting to measure and categorise personality. Numerous studies have gathered data on personality traits and have consistently found that five independent broad factors seem to make up personality (aka the "Big Five"). Although many researchers have been involved in the discovery of these five factors through a variety of methods, the names most frequently associated with the five-factor model are Costa and McCrae, as they also created the NEO-PI™ questionnaire for measuring these factors. Their names for the five factors are Extraversion, Openness, Agreeableness, Conscientiousness and Neuroticism, the first four of which have some relationship to the Myers-Briggs' Extraversion, Intuition, Feeling and Judging preferences respectively. Although the five-factor model is a trait approach, for research purposes McCrae and Costa (1989) correlated scores on the NEO-PI™ with scores on the MBTI and found that Extraversion, Openness, Agreeableness and Conscientiousness correlated as expected with the MBTI scales of Extraversion-

Introversion, Sensing-Intuition, Thinking-Feeling and Judging-Perceiving respectively.

The MBTI has no dimension to assess mental health or wellbeing and, in the above study, as expected, Neuroticism was not significantly correlated with any of the Myers-Briggs preferences. However, it is the absence of a measure of Neuroticism that some believe to be the "missing element" of the MBTI. Scoular notes this as one of the main criticisms of the MBTI by coaches, stating that,

> "Critics of the MBTI note the scientific consensus that there are five major personality scales making up the key components of individual difference, and the MBTI only has four." She goes on to say, "This criticism is entirely valid, the fifth scale is indeed missing in the MBTI, and there are indeed clients where coaches think to ourselves, "is something else the problem here?!"(p.3).

Some type instruments, for example, the Golden Personality Type Profiler (GPTP), have attempted to include a Neuroticism element alongside the type preference information. In the case of the GPTP this scale is called Tense vs. Calm. The idea of interpreting the type preferences alongside a measure of Tense vs. Calm is that, if a person is reporting as tense, it is likely that this will have a negative or distorting effect on how they are expressing their preferences, whereas if they report as calm, they are likely to express their preferences in a reasonable and productive manner. This is a reasonable assumption and provides useful additional information for the client and coach; however it is subject to the skill of the coach to work with the information effectively and sensitively, and subject to the coach's knowledge of distorted or defensive expressions of type-related characteristics. In addition, as it is a questionnaire-based measure, the client's responses to the Tense vs. Calm scale are likely to fluctuate over time and in different circumstances and should therefore be treated as a possible measure of their current state rather than as a definite stable trait.

"In the Grip"

Naomi Quenk's "In the Grip" theory, developed in the early 1980s, brings some aspects of the unconscious, the non-preferred functions, and the dynamic nature of the psyche as an addition to the Myers-Briggs theory. Quenk's work focuses on the role of the inferior function in times of stress and bridges the gap between Jung's overemphasis on the negative aspects of the inferior function and Myers' understating of its negative attributes. The theory is based on

Limits to Using Type for Developmental Coaching

the dynamic energies of the psyche and, in particular, the principles of equivalence (trying to obtain balance) and entropy (energy invested in one aspect will create equal potential energy in its opposite). As her work goes back to some of the original Jungian concepts, Quenk uses the phrase "Jung-Myers theory" to describe the theoretical context of her work.

In brief, the theory states that in times of stress we invest more energy in our preferred functions, pushing the non-preferred functions further into the unconscious, thus becoming polarised. Eventually, under extreme or prolonged stress, the conscious energy is expended and the potential energy that has built up in the inferior (and sometimes the tertiary) function causes the inferior function to erupt into the conscious realm, resulting in the person being "in the grip" of their inferior function. This inferior function is out of conscious control and, by its nature, undeveloped and primitive. Therefore the individual's behaviour will be maladaptive or unproductive and very unlike their usual self. Nevertheless, it is a mechanism employed by the psyche to prevent complete burnout or psychosis. Her theory has been developed from looking at the dynamics of the psyche as per Jung's model and through observations of clients in her work as a therapist.

Quenk's theory has a valid role in describing and explaining some of the maladaptive behaviours that individuals can display under pressure, and also explains why, when extremely stressed, people report behaving out of character and feeling "as if somebody else was working the controls". The theory is relatively easy to use with clients and there are good resources to help coaches and therapists to work with "The Grip". However, it mainly focuses on the inferior function and situations of extreme stress or pressure. It does not include the everyday role of the inferior function and its influence on our everyday personality. Her work also describes how an individual's preferred functions may become overplayed and unproductive, but again the focus of this is the individual under stress. The theory does not account for how highly effective people may experience a reduction in functioning that may not be evident to others, or how ego defensiveness, immaturity or environmental circumstances can affect our personality balance. Additionally, the theory only addresses the dysfunctional end of the spectrum, and is not concerned with maximising individual potential. Nevertheless, aspects of her theory have a place in the final model being proposed in this book.

"Survival Games"

Another attempt to explain "undesirable" behaviours in relation to type is the "survival games" theory which comes from Keirsey and has been further developed by Eve Delunas. This theory suggests that the different temperament types (types divided into groups of SP, SJ, NT and NF) will engage in particular defensive behaviours, driven by unconscious energy. These "survival games" are self-protective coping strategies used to deal with stressful circumstances or times when we are not getting our fundamental needs met. The games can be played out at a very mild level through to extremely severe levels. The severe end of the continuum involves psychopathology, mental illness, criminality and serious physical dysfunctions. Although all of the games will cause issues for both the individual and for others involved, some games are more detrimental than others.

There are four factors that contribute to the potential onset and style of the survival games that a person may become engaged in. These are temperament, unresolved traumas, level of development and current environment. The temperament will determine the core needs and stressors of each type, and how they are likely to respond to a perceived stress or threat. Any unresolved traumas may make a person more vulnerable, less resilient, or prone to environmental triggers, therefore making them more likely to engage in unconscious survival games. The level of development that a person has reached or is operating at will influence how defensive and adaptable they are and, in turn, how unconsciously motivated they will be to engage in survival games in an attempt to defend their sense of self. Although some people who are at a defensive level of development and have unresolved trauma may actually create environmental stressors that perpetuate their engagement in survival games, others who have a predisposition may have the onset of a survival game triggered by changes in their environment.

SPs (aka Artisan or Improviser) place a high value on freedom and gain self worth by being able to impress others with their ability to achieve the seemingly impossible. They are stressed and de-valued by boredom, constraints, external control, losing and having no opportunities to impress. They engage in a game that Delunas calls "Blackmail", in which the SP takes actions that threaten to take something away from others (property, comfort or themselves) unless their needs are met. To do this they will take excessive risks, perform rebellious acts, engage in exciting compulsions, or be destructive towards themselves or others. At the extreme end of the spectrum this can involve activities such as illegal drug use, vandalism, theft, violence and self harm. At the less extreme end they may engage in selective use of the truth – telling others what they want to hear or not telling the whole story, pushing rules to the limit, and taking extreme advantage of their circumstances. The aim of their game is to excite themselves, punish others or hide their own failure.

SJs (aka Guardians or Stabilisers) need security and stability and gain a sense of self-worth by taking responsibility and doing the right thing. Therefore, they find insecurity and chaos stressful and will feel devalued if they are not needed or if they are excluded. They will also be stressed by feeling that they have too many responsibilities and by others who they perceive to be shirking their responsibilities. They indulge in the "Complain" game, where they will attempt to gain pity or involvement from others by complaining of illness, anxiety, depression and fatigue. At the extreme, these games can lead to serious psychosomatic complaints, physical disability, dependence on medication and depression. They can also get into relationships that enable others to take advantage of them in order to make themselves feel needed and have a role. The less extreme forms of the Complain game are complaining about illness or being overburdened, or being harshly critical and judgemental about others. The purpose of these games is to provide a reason why they cannot carry out their responsibilities (i.e. they are too ill), to hide their selfish motivations or negligence, or to draw others in to them. Unfortunately the Complain game often has the opposite effect of making others avoid them.

NTs (aka Rationals or Theorists) place a high value on competence and achievement, and therefore they get their self-worth from being competent and reaching successful outcomes. They indulge in the "Robot" game, designed to distract themselves and others from their failures or ignorance. This game involves compulsive thinking or acting as if they are operating according to an emotionless computer program. At the extreme end, NTs will develop pointless compulsive behaviour leading to obsessive compulsive disorder, have recurrent horrific thoughts or develop illogical superstitious behaviour. They can also become emotionally cut-off and overuse rationalisation, intellectualisation and logic. The less severe manifestations of the Robot game are extreme arrogance, believing they are superior to others, having a know-all attitude, or being excessively critical. They can also develop perfectionism paralysis, where they are unable to complete anything because they are compelled to keep changing or tweaking it until it is perfect.

NFs (aka Idealists or Catalysts) place a high value on authenticity and integrity and gain self-worth from having a sense of meaning or purpose in life. They become stressed when they are not true to themselves or when they are in environments that they perceive

The Shadows of Type

to be unethical or abusive/demeaning towards others. They will feel devalued if they are betrayed or deceived by others as relationships are very important to them. NFs indulge in the "Masquerade" game. This game involves keeping themselves and others from becoming aware of their self-centredness or lack of integrity, by manifesting other problems as a distraction. These can be unusual physical complaints such as the loss of a sense, sudden fatigue or the development of tics and twitches, or mental issues such as forgetfulness or paranoid beliefs. They can also become martyrs; giving up their true selves to make someone else happy. Another variant of the Masquerade game involves sudden changes of subject to avoid talking about anything that is shameful or painful. At the extreme end this can result in serious unusual physical complaints such as blindness or paralysis (medically known as conversion disorders), seizures, narcolepsy, fugue or paranoia. At the milder end of the spectrum they may develop unusual physical complaints that doctors cannot fathom out, or they may imagine that others are thinking negative thoughts about them. They can display resentful and passive-aggressive behaviour towards others, and they may tend to tell lies, both to themselves and to others.

Each of the games has several variants depending on the other type preferences, the situation and the other "players". Some of the variants of the games can be linked to Quenk's "In the Grip" theory, others could be seen as extreme distorted features of the type preferences, and some are purely pathological. Aspects of the milder manifestations of the survival games feature in the new model that is to be proposed in this book.

Eight-Function and Archetypal Models

Other theorists have looked for typological explanations for problematic behaviours by adding to the Myers-Briggs four-function model. For example, Lenore Thomson (1998) suggests a model containing all eight functions where, sandwiched between the dominant and auxiliary preferred functions and the tertiary and inferior non-preferred functions there are the other four functions; two of which can provide a different but useful perspective for the personality, and two which can be disruptive and lead us away from our best ways of working.

John Beebe, a Jungian analyst, also proposes a model that contains all eight functions, however he has assigned an archetypal influence to each function in an attempt to explain how it helps or hinders the personality. Beebe's eight-function model is summarised in Table 4.

Function	Example ENFJ	Archetype M/F	Archetypal influence
1. Dominant	Fe	Hero/Heroine	Strong. Welcomes challenge, reliable.
2. Auxiliary	Ni	Father/Mother	Guide, good parent.
3. Tertiary	Se	Puer/Puella	Immature and vulnerable, eternal child.
4. Inferior	Ti	Anima/Animus	Shame vs. Idealism. Potential to mediate the tension of opposites.
5. Same as 1 with opposite attitude	Fi	Opposing Personality	Paranoid, avoidant, passive-aggressive. Primary source of defence.
6. Same as 2 with opposite attitude	Ne	Senex/Witch	Arrogantly judgemental, change-resistant.
7. Same as 3 with opposite attitude	Si	Trickster	Double bind others as a defence.
8. Same as 4 with opposite attitude	Te	Demonic/Daimonic Personality	Undermining oaf or beast.

Table 4: Summary of Beebe's eight-function archetypal model

The eight-function models are thought-provoking, however the roles assigned to each function are somewhat prescriptive and limiting. For example there is no accounting for a poor or distorted expression of the dominant function, or a skilful expression of the tertiary function. What is useful, however, is that the functions referred to as the Opposing Personality and the Demonic Personality are often areas of difficulty or conflict for individuals and can be the most difficult, along with the inferior, to integrate into one's own personality or to accept positively in others. The Opposing Personality can cause us irritation when we see it being expressed by others, and the Demonic Personality can sometimes be useful and accessible and at other times be baffling or clumsily expressed. The influences of the Opposing and Demonic Personalities are included in the model being proposed in this book.

Combining Psychological Type with Other Psychometrics and Models

It seems that none of the adaptations and expansions of the models of psychological type described above completely account for the "missing element" that would enable coaches to work with their clients on matters regarding everyday problem behaviours and blockers to potential. Additionally, none of the models explicitly consider the development of untapped potential. In her criticisms of the limitations of type models, Scoular suggests that to deal with the "*something else*" that is missing, other psychometrics and tools are needed. Several type theorists are combining psychological type with other psychometrics and theories to try to account for this.

The Enneagram

The Enneagram is a personality type system that suggests there are nine basic personality types. In the Enneagram system, a personality structure develops around a particular innate ego desire or need. The individual develops defences and characteristics aimed at getting these ego needs met. Although there are some strong correlations between certain Myers-Briggs types and Enneagram types, there is not a perfect connection between the two models. In comparing psychological type with Enneagram type, Flautt and Richards (1999) describe psychological type as being about consciousness and cognitive behaviour and the Enneagram as being about motivations.

Flautt and Richards summarise the potential complementary use of the two models as "*How* does a person behave?" (Myers-Briggs), and, "*Why* does a person behave in a certain way?" (Enneagram). They suggest that the Enneagram and psychological type can be used together effectively, particularly in work on personal development or in-depth exploration of relationships. Using the two together would provide a depth of information about the individual's motivations and needs with a psychological type overlay as to how their cognitive process may be operating and how they may go about meeting these needs. Using the Riso-Hudson (1996) model of the Enneagram can show how an individual's Enneagram type will operate from its highest potential through to detrimental behaviours. However, to use both models together would require a considerable amount of time, and as Flautt and Richards themselves note, it may not always be pragmatic to use both tools together.

The Hogan Development Survey (HDS)

The HDS (Hogan and Hogan, 1997) is a self-report questionnaire that measures 11 characteristics. These 11 characteristics are personality traits that, when used in an appropriate manner, are often seen as strengths for the individual, but when the individual is under pressure the traits can become exaggerated and problematic. The HDS was based on the official medical descriptions of personality disorders and has been adapted to measure these tendencies as they manifest in normal populations. The questionnaire is designed for use in organisational settings with a view to assessing potential career derailment factors.

There is no established direct theoretical connection between the HDS traits and psychological types, however one might expect certain patterns to emerge. The HDS may be useful to introduce into developmental coaching as it would cover some of the gaps in the psychological type models regarding potentially detrimental behaviours. However, while the two models could be used together in a coaching session, the HDS adds *more* information rather than addressing the "missing element" in type theory, or indicating an individual's level of psychological health or resilience. The growing popularity of the HDS in coaching is, nevertheless, indicative of the need for a way to address negative behaviours in coaching interventions.

Emotional Intelligence

Using measures of emotional intelligence (EQ) with psychological type can provide some insight into how well an individual may be functioning and how effectively they may be applying their type. The two approaches are completely different, in that EQ is about competence and can change over time, while type is about preference and is constant, however, as stated by Maddox (2006) *" ... type will influence the development of EQ; ... EQ will influence the development of type."* He goes on to explain, *"EQ influences the effectiveness with which type is applied, and type influences the ease with which different aspects of EQ are learnt"* (p.10).

EQ has both intrapersonal and interpersonal aspects to it, and Maddox suggests that introverts may be more oriented towards the intrapersonal side and extraverts to the interpersonal side. There are also elements of self-management, stress tolerance, relationship-management and problem solving encompassed within EQ. However, the main benefit of using EQ with psychological type is that together they provide an indication of how individuals may manage their personality, what their pattern of type development may be, and how, according to their type, they can best apply our EQ. Individuals with well-developed EQ will have a good level of self-awareness and be able to adapt their behaviour according to different situations. Therefore, they are unlikely to display their type preferences rigidly or in a habitually dysfunctional manner. Again the use of both tools will require adequate time during coaching, however it would appear that one's EQ will have an impact on how one uses their type and is an important part of the overall picture of an individual's functioning – possibly a large part of "the missing element".

Horizontal vs. Vertical Development

In considering the limitations of psychological type, a key criticism of the theory is its lack of a "vertical" dimension. Cook-Greuter (2004) describes personal development as being both horizontal and vertical; horizontal development is the acquiring of new learning, new skills and new knowledge, whilst vertical development (also known as ego development) is concerned with changing how we see the world, being able to expand our cognitive capability to make meaning of the world, and taking a broader perspective. She comments that being aware of one's personality type is horizontal development, as it is acquiring new information and knowledge, however using this information for the development of self-understanding, understanding others, and expanding one's perspective, would be vertical development.

She notes that, in terms of type, some individuals are able to read others' styles and respond appropriately and skilfully, and that this can be explained in terms of their level of emotional intelligence – a concept closely related to the vertical developmental levels. She adds that, in her view, the developmental stage that an individual is capable of operating at is as, if not more, important as their personality type. Ken Wilber (2000) comments that one should realise that each personality type can exist at each of the main vertical levels of development, and goes on to suggest that if a typology can be combined with each of the developmental levels *"you can start to see what a truly multidimensional psychology might look like!"* (p.54). This suggests that typologies such as the Myers-Briggs model would benefit from the inclusion of a vertical dimension.

From this brief look at the different ways in which researchers, type users and coaches are attempting to accommodate the "missing element" in psychological type theory, be it a measure or theoretical addition of Neuroticism, derailment potential, emotional intelligence, etc, it would appear that there are issues or limitations with each approach. The recent coaching research indicates that increasing numbers of coaches are moving into developmental and transformational coaching, with transpersonal coaching also gaining in popularity. Therefore it is becoming increasingly important to find effective ways of addressing everyday detrimental behaviours and, for the transpersonal aspect, to find ways of maximising one's potential using type, and so expand on the current applications of the Myers-Briggs and other models of psychological type.

Perhaps the "missing element" in popular psychological type theories such as the Myers-Briggs – be it Neuroticism, balance, emotional intelligence, psychological health, or self-awareness – can be found by re-visiting Jung's original work on type. Jung's typology has as its core the idea of the dynamics of opposites; Jung postulates that, although an individual will have predominant or preferred functions, the opposite functions will be attempting to come to the fore, thus creating constant dynamics and tensions within the individual, and that personal development comes from acknowledging, exploring and managing these tensions. In relation to this, Angelo Spoto (1995) sees the Myers-Briggs model as being concerned with the *"problem of differences"* in its treatment of the preference pairs (i.e. how does one person differ from another), and neglecting the *"problem of opposites"* (i.e. how is an individual's type working within them), thus losing some of *"the heat and passion"* of Jung's original work (p.7). Spoto states that *"... because Jungian psychology itself is psychodynamic, keeping typology connected to the larger model makes typology infinitely more interesting and useful."**

The next chapter will aim to "go back to the source" and place typology in the wider context of the psyche according to Jung.

---

*Personal communication with Angelo Spoto, September 2009.

Chapter Summary

- The MBTI® is the most popular psychometric used by coaches.
- Coaching is becoming less about goal attainment and more about personal development.
- Personal development coaching requires the exploration of an individual's issues, detrimental behaviours and blockers to maximising potential. Type theories do not provide much guidance in this area, indicating that they may have a "missing element".
- Some developments of type theory account for aspects of detrimental behaviour, however none of them comprehensively address everyday maladaptive behaviour. Additionally none of them consider how to further develop one's preferences to maximise potential.
- Some coaches are combining psychological type with other psychometrics and models to try to account for the "missing element".
- A criticism of type theories is that they lack a "vertical" developmental dimension.
- Placing type theory back into the context of Jung's original theory may account for the "missing element".

Chapter Three

Psychological Type and the Psyche

Jung's theory of personality types is only a small part of his entire body of work, yet it is one of his most important contributions to modern psychology and it is also one that Jung himself greatly valued:

> *"I would not for anything dispense with this compass on my psychological voyages of discovery. This is not merely for the obvious, all-too-human reason that everyone is in love with his own ideas. I value the type theory for the objective reason that it provides a system of comparison and orientation which makes possible something that has long been lacking, a critical psychology".* (Jung, 1990, p.541).

However, as Spoto points out in his comments on the current use of type and the Myers-Briggs®:

> *"I am not sure how Jung would have felt about all this. My guess is that he personally would have been critical of or at best concerned about the speed in which his typological theory has been disseminated through the "tests and measurements" approach."*

He goes on to add:

> *"At the very least one would suspect that he would have warned us about making too much of typology outside the context and intentions of his work as a whole".* (p.10).

Fortunately Spoto is not implying that we should be considering typology in the context of Jung's entire life's work and theories, but that we just need to view it in the context of Jung's theory of the psyche. In itself, Jung's theory of the psyche is fairly complex, so this chapter will only include exploration of the aspects of the psyche that are relevant to working with type.

The Psyche

The psyche, according to Jungian psychology, is the total personality through which psychic energy flows continuously in various directions; inner to outer, conscious to unconscious. The dynamic movement of this energy is an outcome of conflicts and tensions present within the psyche. Jung saw the psyche as an entity that operates according to the principle of opposites, and highlighted the duality inherent within people. Jung believed that the psyche operates according to some of the fundamental laws of physics; namely the principles of *equivalence* and *entropy*. This means that any energy expended in one direction will bring about the same amount of energy in the opposite direction, (i.e. for every action there is an opposite and equal reaction), and that any psychic processes that are out of balance will constantly seek, but never achieve, balance. A simplified map of the psyche is shown in Fig.1.

The Ego

The ego is the centre of the field of consciousness and an important aspect of the psyche, often described as the unifying force within the psyche. Theoretically, when we are born the personality is whole and undifferentiated and full of potential. As we develop it begins to separate and becomes differentiated; the ego develops and becomes conscious as we begin to have a sense of "self", meanwhile, some parts of the whole self split off from the conscious ego and go into the unconscious. This results in individuals having a conscious ego image of who they are and what they are like, and an unconscious part of the ego containing the aspects of themselves that they are unaware of and would not identify with.

The ego is particularly important in relation to type as it is the source of our conscious identity; who we are, what we like and dislike, how we prefer to be. When a person is asked to describe themselves, they tend to report what is in their conscious ego. This is where the individual's identification with the positive aspects ("gifts") of the type function preferences lies. As can be seen in Fig.1, although most of the

Psychological Type and the Psyche

ego is in consciousness, some of it is unconscious and lies within the shadow. This accounts for the parts of ourselves or personality characteristics we may have that we are not always aware of, but, when we see them in others, we are judgemental and critical (this is the ego defence mechanism of projection).

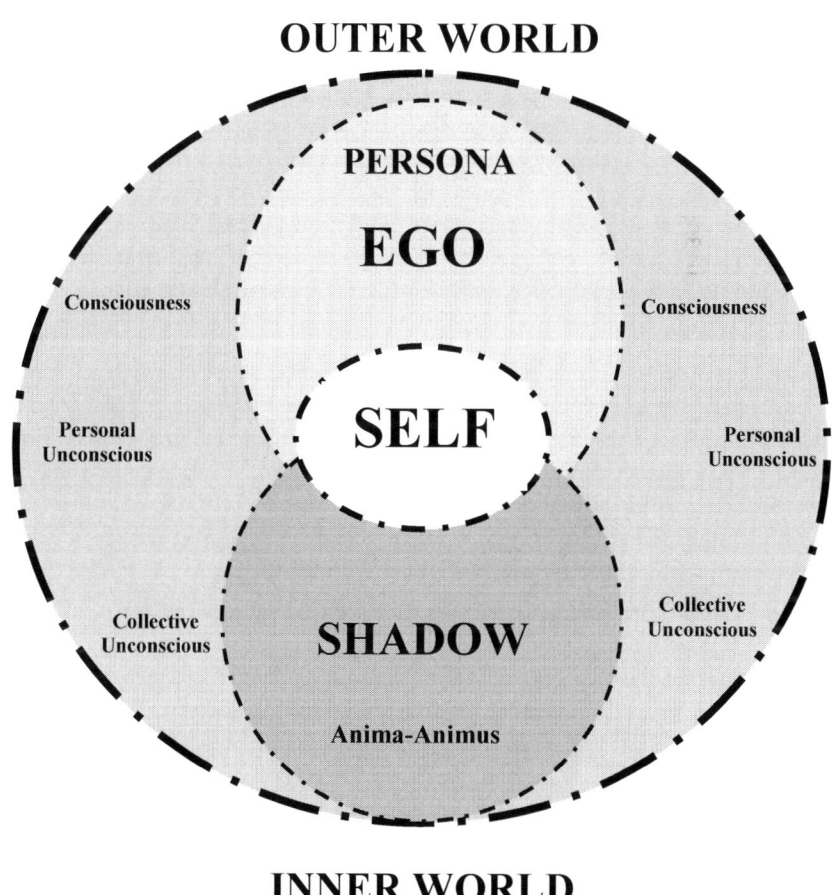

Fig.1: Simplified map of the psyche

Typically, when a type practitioner is working with a client or coachee they are only addressing the conscious part of the ego. The shadow aspects of the client's preferences are rarely addressed, yet this is where the problem characteristics and blocks to potential often lie. As these characteristics are in the shadow, the client may not be aware of them. The non-preferred functions also exist in the ego and are theoretically positioned on the periphery of the unconscious. Relevant to the work of using type in coaching and development, Spoto states that:

> *"When an individual's consciousness becomes restrictive or complacent, i.e., when personality development is too one-sided ... the overall functioning of the personality becomes negatively affected; the balance and flow of psychic energy are upset. The elements of the personality which have been neglected go into conflict with ego-consciousness".* (p.121).

This is to say that when the conscious ego or self-image is the driving force in the individual's personality and is the only aspect of their self that they are aware of, they will need to consciously or unconsciously defend this sense of self, resulting in problematic behaviours, extensive use of ego defence mechanisms, and inner tension.

The Persona

Part of the ego, and the part that faces the outer world, is the persona. The word "persona" comes from the Roman word for an actor's mask. It was used by Jung to describe the mask we wear in order to interact with others according to expectations, social convention and inner motivations. The persona is an essential part of the personality for aiding integration with society as it helps the individual to adapt their personality to suit different environments. A healthy persona will be an adaptation of the individual's real, authentic personality. "Too little" persona can result in a person being seen as a rebel or social misfit, and "too much" can result in falseness, a permanent mask, poor personality development and, ultimately, inner psychic conflict.

When an individual has difficulty in identifying their preferences they often talk about how they behave in different situations, or say that they are adaptable and comfortable with both styles. This can be the result of their inability to differentiate between their core ego and the persona aspect of it. This identification with the persona can be due to habituation, social pressures, influences from childhood, defensiveness, or anything that has given the individual a message indicating that the character of the persona is a preferable or more acceptable way to behave. The persona can have connections to archetypes via the collective unconscious (discussed later), and we may behave in a certain manner or fit into certain roles according to archetypal expectations.

In a "typically developed" psyche, the dominant preference is recognised by the ego as the "right" way to be in the world, and the inferior function is seen as being somehow wrong or undesirable. This is often the state that individuals will be in when they have not undertaken any personal development work or self-reflection, and when their natural preferences have been approved of or been useful in their lives. This lack of appreciation and integration of the opposite style results in one-sidedness and severe imbalance within the psyche. Conversely, an individual who has somehow had it reinforced that their preferences do not fit or are unacceptable, for example by family, work role or environment, may even have their inferior function as a persona. However, theoretically this will still be filtered through to the outer world via their natural preference and may therefore appear odd, incongruent or false. These non-preferred type-related personas can be very interesting to explore with clients in coaching or during the best-fit stage of the type feedback process, and particularly when the reported type from the questionnaire is different to the client's self-assessed type.

The Unconscious and the Shadow

As previously mentioned, when the ego and persona are being developed and certain desirable characteristics of the self are being pushed more into consciousness, other aspects of the self will fall into the unconscious. In Jung's model of the psyche, and indeed in psychodynamic psychology in general, the unconscious is often depicted as being much larger than the conscious area. In Jung's model, the unconscious has two areas, however the boundaries between them are not fixed; these are the personal unconscious and the collective unconscious. The personal unconscious lies on the cusp of consciousness and partly covers the ego. It contains forgotten or unnoticed experiences that are not brought into conscious awareness because they were either lacking intensity or significance for some reason, or they were unpleasant in some way and the ego has defended itself from bringing them into consciousness. It is positioned near the conscious area as it is possible to bring some of its contents into consciousness via therapy, coaching, hypnosis or deliberate effort.

The collective unconscious, according to Jung, resides in the deep unconscious and is a store of memories and attitudes from our existence as humans. It consists of inherited instincts and archetypes that can often affect our beliefs, expectations and behaviours. Jung describes it as *"... a deposit of world processes embedded in the structure of the brain and the sympathetic nervous system [which] constitutes, in its totality, a sort of timeless and eternal world-image which counterbalances our conscious momentary picture of the world."* (1981, p.376).

The shadow represents the undeveloped, unconscious and inferior part of our psyches. The aspects of the personal unconscious that contribute to the shadow are rejected experiences or impulses, our non-preferred functions and the negative aspects of our ego and persona. In exploring Jung's theory, Murray Stein (2004) states that every ego has a shadow and that this shadow is opposite to the persona in that it contains aspects of the individual's personality that they would not like to be associated with or seen by others, or that they may deny to themselves. The contents of the ego's shadow, being unconscious, are not experienced by the ego but are projected onto others by the ego.

Projection is one of the major ego defence mechanisms first made explicit by Freud and readily acknowledged by Jung. Typically, projection is the attribution of one's own undesirable characteristics onto another person. These characteristics may be the undesirable aspects of one's own type preferences, their non-preferred functions, or any other aspect of their unconscious. For example, if a person who pushes themselves hard to achieve at work is extremely irritated by and critical of a colleague who they describe as lazy and unconscientious, despite the fact that the colleague is actually achieving all their objectives, has a good work-life balance and a relaxed attitude to work, then this could be a projection from their shadow. The individual's laid-back and relaxed side has been pushed into the unconscious, influenced by the negativity of the shadow and therefore such behaviour is seen as negative. The more the person pushes themselves and feels stressed or pressured, the more the unconscious relaxed side will be fighting for expression and the stronger and more negative the projections will be. Sharp (1987) adds that:

> "... the shadow and the persona function in a compensatory way: the brighter the light, the darker the shadow. The more one identifies with the persona – which in effect is to deny that one has a shadow – the more trouble one will have with the unacknowledged 'other side' of the personality". (p.95).

As previously mentioned, the non-preferred type functions are theoretically positioned on the cusp of the conscious and unconscious, however there is common consensus in the literature that the inferior function lies fully in the unconscious. The inferior function can erupt from the unconscious during times of stress or when the individual has been overusing their dominant function. As mentioned in the previous chapter, there has been considerable work carried out on the role of the inferior function and stress by Naomi Quenk. However, the inferior function, even when not making an active "Grip" appearance, influences our perceptions of others and gives rise to negative projections. The identification of these projections can be essential in working with individuals on their personal development.

Some aspects of the collective unconscious may also have an influence when working with type. The collective unconscious contains archetypal images that can influence the development of the persona. Archetypes can be personalised, for example the idea of mother, father, God, hero, damsel in distress, etc, and the characteristics associated with these are often seen in myths and fiction. So in a coaching situation, for example, a person who becomes a manager in a business may draw on his "archetypal image of a business manager" (direct, efficient, emotionally detached, decisive, uncompromising, etc) and create a "manager" persona based on this which may be unlike their true self. Other archetypes can be more abstract, for example light symbolising good, darkness indicating evil, femininity being associated with gentleness and masculinity being associated with strength. Our archetypal images may also cause us to predict other people's behaviour on the basis of very little information about them, or to stereotype people. For instance, we may have an archetypal image of "mother" as caring, kind, nurturing, sacrificing, etc., and this may affect our expectations and perceptions of mothers we encounter in reality. If we see a mother behaving firmly and objectively with her child, we may react strongly and negatively about it because it does not fit with our internal archetypal image.

Two of the major archetypes are the anima and animus. These are our internalised images of the female and male gender respectively. These gender role archetypes can have an influence on how the different genders relate to the Thinking-Feeling dichotomy as these are closely linked to the male-female archetypes.

The "Light Shadow" and the Transcendent Function

It must be noted, however, that according to Jung the shadow is not all negative but can contain untapped potential. Sharp (1987) describes this as follows:

> *"The shadow is potentially both creative and destructive: creative in that it represents aspects of oneself that have been buried or that might yet be realized; destructive in the sense that its value system and motivations tend to undermine or disturb one's conscious image of oneself".* (p.95).

Therefore, exploration of the shadow is not all about acknowledging one's negative aspects, but is also about identifying and releasing hidden potential. Jung does not seem to have given a distinct name to this "light" shadow, but acknowledges its existence:

> *"If it has been believed hitherto that the human shadow was the source of all evil, it can now be ascertained on closer investigation that the unconscious man, that is, his shadow, does not consist only of morally reprehensible tendencies, but also displays a number of good qualities, such as normal instincts, appropriate reactions, realistic insights, creative impulses, etc.* (1978, par.423).

This unconscious potential is partly made up of aspects of ourselves that do not fit with our ego image. For example, a person who will not dance at a party, despite wanting to, because it does not fit with who they think they are or how they think they should behave. The creative shadow may also contain positive characteristics that we "put away" during childhood due to messages from parents or teachers that they were undesirable (e.g. "stop showing off", "be seen and not heard", "stop being soppy"). These are all aspects of the self that may have been repressed and therefore become unconscious.

It is via the unconscious that Jung suggests the transcendent function can be accessed. When there is a tension of duality between the conscious and unconscious or between two seeming opposites, a third option may arise via the transcendent function. This third option is usually a union of the two opposites and, according to Jung, often appears in some type of symbolic form or dream. Jung describes the transcendent function as follows:

> *"... the transcendent function, 'function' being here understood not as a basic function but as a complex function made up of other functions, and 'transcendent' not as denoting a metaphysical quality but merely the fact that this function facilitates a transition from one attitude to another. The raw material shaped by thesis and antithesis, and in the shaping of which the opposites are united, is the living symbol".* (1990, p.480).

The transcendent function is most likely to be experienced when people are not forcefully looking for a solution and occupying their conscious minds to the extent that there is no space for anything else to enter. Some individuals experience the transcendent function when meditating, relaxing or after "sleeping on" a problem.

Psychological Type and the Psyche

The Self

The self is distinct from the ego and may be thought of as the final goal of our psyche's striving for balance and integration. Theoretically, at birth we are whole beings without ego, shadow or persona, *"... the unity of the person as a whole"* (Jung, 1990, p.460); this is the self. During our development our ego and other psychic structures develop, resulting in the divisions and disintegration of our psyches as described above. Although it would be impossible to ever return to this pure state, Jung's ideas about development centre on the attempted reintegration of the psyche.

Sharp (1987) explains that the process of psychological development that Jung referred to as "Individuation" involves disidentifying from the persona (i.e. becoming aware that it is not your true self) and consciously assimilating the shadow. However being able to acknowledge both the persona and shadow requires adequate ego strength as it will involve having the ability to live with the resulting psychological tension. Individuation leads to the resolution of our inner conflicts and the disidentification with the ego. This does not mean that we lose our personality or sense of self, but that we are not inhibited or restricted by it.

Progress towards integration and the discovery of the self can often be seen in people during the period that Jung called mid-life, when they become more open to the other aspects of their personalities, ideas and experiences that would have previously been in conflict with their egos or self-images. For some, the development of the self is seen as a spiritual journey and can be characterised by experiencing feelings of being at peace with oneself and of having a sense of connectedness to all other people and all aspects of the universe.

In summary, most of the aspects of the psyche are important in getting a deeper understanding of one's psychological type and putting type into context. The workings of the psyche as a whole, the dynamics of the energies, the striving for balance and the effect of entropy can help us to explore the "problem of opposites" within the individual as well as the "problem of differences"; a key part of type work, as emphasised by Spoto. Preferences lie within the ego, but part of these preferences may be in the shadow of the ego, and gaining awareness of these shadow aspects is essential to personal development. It could be argued that this should be part of any developmental work involving type. In Psychology and Religion (1970), Jung states:

The Shadows of Type

> *"Unfortunately there can be no doubt that man is, on the whole, less good than he imagines himself or wants to be. Everyone carries a shadow, and the less it is embodied in the individual's conscious life, the blacker and denser it is. If an inferiority is conscious, one always has a chance to correct it"*. (p.14).

This statement suggests that it may be necessary for a coach to determine how self-aware their client is before embarking on shadow work.

Standard use of psychological type theory focuses mainly on the conscious ego part of the psyche and on identifying an individual's preferences *(see Fig.2)*. The dark grey shading illustrates the area of the psyche addressed during a typical feedback session.

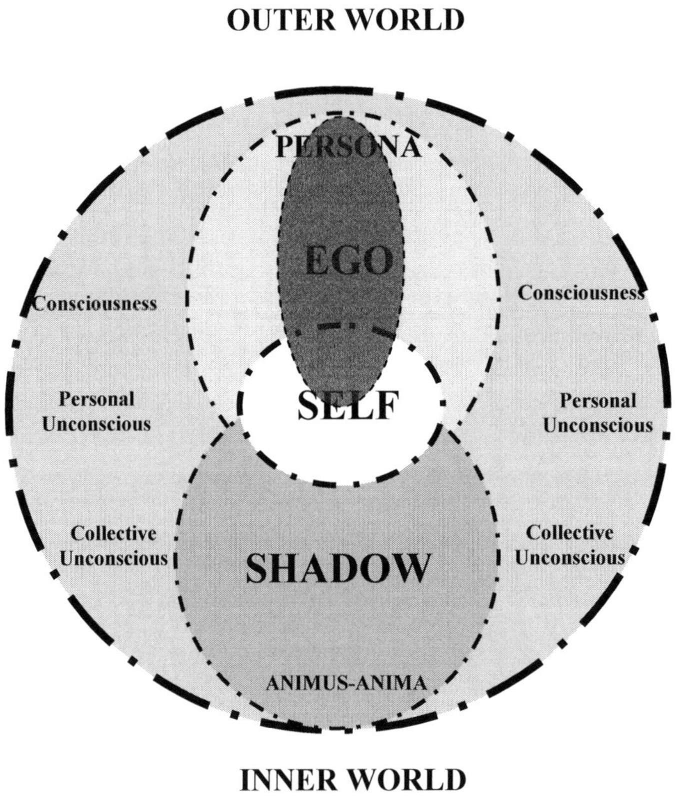

OUTER WORLD

INNER WORLD

Fig.2: The area of the psyche addressed during a typical MBTI® feedback session

Psychological Type and the Psyche

Whilst this is a valuable first step to self-understanding and, in certain circumstances, a valid stopping point, there is a lot further that one can go in working with type, particularly in developmental or transformational coaching. As Sharp states:

> *"Modern technology has provided us with many useful tools, quick and easy ways to accomplish what would otherwise be onerous or time-consuming tasks. The process of understanding oneself, however, is not amenable to short cuts. It remains intractably linked to, and enriched by, individual effort".* (p.100).

By working with type in the context of the psyche, i.e. exploring the ego, persona, shadow aspects of the ego, and "light shadow" aspects of the self, more of the individual's psyche can be brought into conscious awareness *(see Fig.3).*

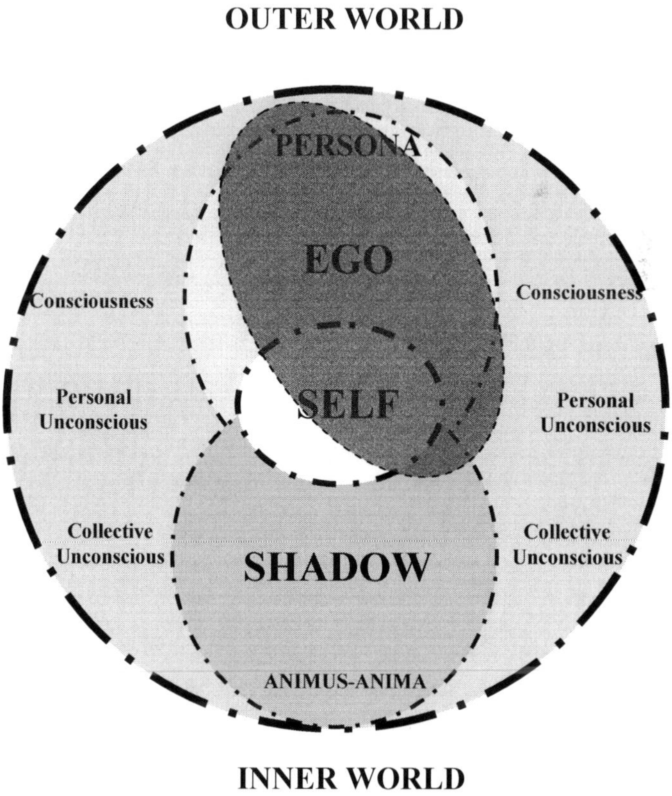

OUTER WORLD

INNER WORLD

Fig.3: The area of the psyche that could potentially be addressed when using type in context for coaching

Working with type in the context of the whole psyche as Jung described it, and attempting to connect with the true self can also comfortably lead coaches into working at the transpersonal level. Transpersonal coaching is increasing in popularity and considered by some, for example, John Whitmore, to be the next evolution in coaching; moving from emotional intelligence to spiritual intelligence. He states, *"Transpersonal coaching skills will be more and more in demand as time and collective psychosocial evolution progress ... "* (2009, p.220).

Jung, together with Roberto Assagioli, are often referred to as *"the fathers of transpersonal psychology"* (D.Whitmore, 2000). Assagioli (1888–1974), an Italian psychiatrist, took Jung's model, and along with several other prevalent models, developed the theory and methods of psychosynthesis, a form of transpersonal psychology. Aside from its potential for enabling coaches to work at a transpersonal level, the design of Assagioli's model provides clarification of and further development of Jung's ideas and more explicit insights for working with psychological type. Additionally, the psychosynthesis approach has accompanying practical interventions for exploring the psyche and increasing awareness and integration.

Chapter Summary
- Placing psychological type back in the context of Jung's model of the psyche can help to explain the "missing element" in type theory.
- Working with type is mainly confined to working with the conscious ego, however, part of one's type is in the unconscious. It is by working with these unconscious aspects of the ego that development can really occur.
- Other parts of the psyche may have an influence on how one expresses their type.
- The less self-aware a person is, the more difficult it can be to work with the shadow. Coaches need to assess where a client is in terms of self-awareness if they are considering working with the shadow.
- There is also a "light shadow" full of untapped potential and good qualities.
- Transpersonal coaching is becoming more popular and can enable coaches to work with the "light shadow".

- ❖ Assagioli's psychosynthesis model can be considered to be an "upgrade" of Jung's original work. It can make it easier to work at the transpersonal level as well as with other aspects of the psyche.

Chapter Four

Psychological Type and Psychosynthesis

Roberto Assagioli, like Jung, was trained in psychoanalysis under the guidance of Freud. In a similar way to Jung, Assagioli was particularly interested in the positive potential of individuals and the spiritual aspects of life, rather than the problems and negative aspects of the psyche that Freud mainly focused on. He suggested that an individual's need for meaning and purpose in life was essential to their wellbeing and that problems in life should be seen as opportunities for learning and growth. Assagioli drew from the work of leading psychiatrists, psychologists and philosophers and was most heavily influenced by the work of Jung and Abraham Maslow; from this he founded psychosynthesis.

Psychosynthesis is an approach to self-realization and the development of potential reached by gaining a conscious awareness of one's personality. It is considered as one of the major forces in the field of transpersonal psychology. To place this in the historical context of psychology, traditionally there have been three commonly recognized forces or paradigms in psychology: behavioural, psychoanalytic and humanistic. Transpersonal psychology emerged in the 1960s and is often referred to as the fourth force in psychology. Although it has its roots in psychodynamic theory, transpersonal psychology is a developmental rather than pathological approach and includes attention to the individual's striving for meaning, purpose and transcendence. Psychosynthesis combines the psychodynamic, humanistic and transpersonal approaches by dealing with the whole person; *"As well as the "basement" of the past, we also have an "upstairs" of potential, of future possibilities. So he (Assagioli) put them together and formulated psychosynthesis."* (Parfitt, 2003, p.12). As coaching is not usually concerned with pathology, but with the enhancement of an individual's potential, Assagioli's model is an attractive theory to work with in developmental coaching.

In his famous lecture, "Jung and Psychosynthesis", (1967), Assagioli stated:

> *"Among psychotherapists, Jung is one of the closest and most akin to the conceptions and practice of psychosynthesis. But the body of his work is so large, his range covers so many different fields, that a complete examination of it would require a sizeable book. I shall thus have to limit myself to a comparative survey of some of the fields that are more directly concerned with psychosynthesis: that is, the structure of the psyche of the human being: the dynamics of the psychic energies: the methods of psychological therapy and education".* (p.1).

Likewise, this embedding of Jung's theory of psychological types into the psychosynthesis model will only focus on the relevant aspects of each theory. Assagioli's full theory of psychosynthesis is vast and includes a huge emphasis on the psychological drives he calls Will and Love, his own "Seven Ways and Seven Rays" typology, and there is also a major focus on spirituality. This work will focus on the areas that Assagioli himself believed were more akin to Jung's work: the structure of the psyche, the dynamics of psychic energy and the methods of therapy.

Assagioli's Model of the Psyche

The so-called "egg" diagram *(see Fig.4)* is Assagioli's map of the human psyche, or as he refers to it *"a conception of the constitution of the human being in his living concrete reality"* (1975, p.16). He himself acknowledges that it is overly simplistic to represent the psyche in this way, and states, *"It is, of course, a crude and elementary picture that can give only a structural, static, almost "anatomical" representation of our inner constitution, while it leaves out its dynamic aspect, which is the most important and essential one."* (1975, p.16).

All of the lines in the diagram are broken, not solid, to illustrate the fluidity of the boundaries and that the different parts of

The Shadows of Type

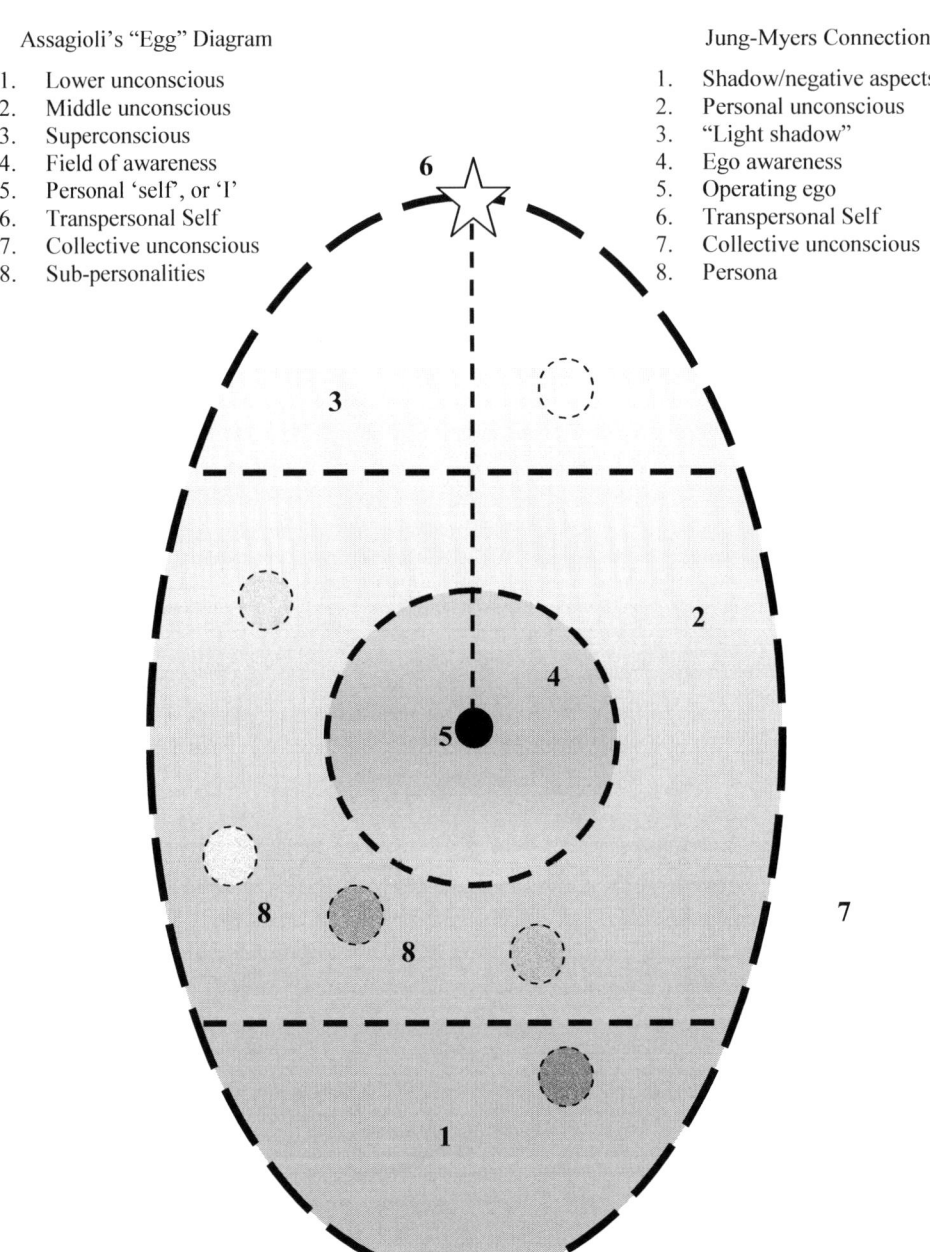

Assagioli's "Egg" Diagram
1. Lower unconscious
2. Middle unconscious
3. Superconscious
4. Field of awareness
5. Personal 'self', or 'I'
6. Transpersonal Self
7. Collective unconscious
8. Sub-personalities

Jung-Myers Connections
1. Shadow/negative aspects
2. Personal unconscious
3. "Light shadow"
4. Ego awareness
5. Operating ego
6. Transpersonal Self
7. Collective unconscious
8. Persona

Fig.4: Assagioli's "Egg" model – connections to Jung's model of the psyche

Psychological Type and Psychosynthesis

the psyche will blend into each other and change shape and size depending on the dynamics of the psychic energies.

The components of the egg model are as follows:

1. The Lower Unconscious

The lower unconscious, according to Assagioli, contains the psychological aspects of the activities that direct and coordinate the functions of the body, and the fundamental drives and urges. These elements are similar to Freud's notion of the Id. Other aspects of the lower unconscious are forgotten memories and experiences, the complexes, some of which are there as a result of ego defence mechanisms, and pathological aspects such as phobias, obsessions, compulsions and delusions. Assagioli suggests that dreams and imaginations with a negative aspect to them, and uncontrolled parapsychological processes also form part of the lower unconscious. In these latter aspects, his theory of the lower unconscious is similar in nature to Jung's concept of the shadow. Exploration of the lower unconscious is usually beyond the realm of coaching and is an area more relevant to and safely accessed in therapy.

2. The Middle Unconscious

The middle unconscious is an area of the psyche that contains information about ourselves that we can bring into conscious awareness, either when we choose to, or with some effort or personal development work. This is the area where one's personality preferences tend to reside before being brought into conscious awareness through, for example, a Myers-Briggs® feedback session. Individuals may know implicitly what they are like and what they are not like, but go through life on "autopilot" without giving conscious awareness to their preferred and non-preferred styles. The middle unconscious is the part of the psyche that coaching work is most likely to be accessing – bringing parts of the client's functioning into consciousness and, in turn, providing them with choice, options and the ability to attempt to consciously control or change themselves. Whitmore (2009) confirms this; *"The middle unconscious is readily accessible by good coaching. It is the more recent and the more present time, and it is where the majority of workplace coaching takes place"* (p.215). The middle unconscious may also contain memories that can be recalled with some prompting but that may otherwise have become largely forgotten. This is similar to the accessible part of Jung's "personal unconscious".

3. The Superconscious or Higher Unconscious

The superconscious is similar to Jung's idea of the "light shadow". It is an area full of positive aspects of ourselves that we may not be in touch with, including untapped potential, creativity and qualities. Assagioli suggests that *"urges to humanitarian and heroic action"* (1975, p.17) are also aspects of the superconscious, as are feelings such as altruistic love, aspects of potential genius, and spiritual energies. Parfitt (2003) refers to the superconscious as our "evolutionary future", explaining that it is the area that we need to explore when we are ready to progress into our futures.

4. The Field of Awareness

The field of awareness is the part of our personality that we are directly aware of. It is constantly changing depending on our state, however in general it is the part of us that is aware of our sensations, thoughts, feelings and desires. Whitmore (2009) suggests that most coaching work is concerned with expanding this area to bring more of the middle unconscious into conscious awareness. So, for example, following some work with an individual on their psychological type, their preferred functions may still be on "autopilot", however the individual has the ability to "switch on" and consciously make use of the preferences as they are now within the field of awareness. The more individuals can expand their field of awareness, the more ability to self-monitor and adapt they will have.

5. The "I"/Personal "self"

Assagioli describes the "I" as *"the point of pure self-awareness"* (1975, p.18). This is different to the field of awareness in that the field of awareness is conscious of the sensations etc that the individual is experiencing, whereas the "I" is the one that is experiencing it. The "I" is at the centre of the field of awareness, however it is often something that we may not be aware of. Again, coaching work can help to bring the "I" to the surface. For example, individuals may be aware of some tension between themselves and others in the workplace, and be able to describe it and talk about it from the field of awareness, but by seeing it from the point of view of the "I", clients in this situation will become more aware of the impact that the situation is having on them, their deeper feelings about it, their role in it, etc, and generally where they really are in the situation. The idea of the "I" being like an observer of the personality is an essential part of the process of psychosynthesis, as it helps individuals to

Psychological Type and Psychosynthesis

disidentify with aspects of their personality, i.e. not be controlled by it. This is also known as "witness consciousness" and is a key differentiator between individuals with poorly developed egos and well-developed egos.

6. The Transpersonal or Higher Self

The Transpersonal Self is the connection to universality and spirituality. Assagioli suggests that *"This Self is above, and unaffected by, the flow of the mind-stream or by bodily conditions"* (1975, p.19). The Transpersonal Self is often referred to as the soul, as our true essence; it is ourselves without damage or "baggage" and it is both individual and universal. The goal of transpersonal work and of psychosynthesis is to connect with the Transpersonal Self, although it is acknowledged that these connections are not only difficult to make but are often brief glimpses or sensations known as peak experiences. The personal self or "I" has a connection to the Transpersonal Self and the egg model considers the "I" to be merely a reflection or projection of the Transpersonal Self.

Note: The Transpersonal Self has a capital S, the personal self or "I" is lower case.

7. The Collective Unconscious

Assagioli's ego is taken directly from Jung's idea of the collective unconscious. It represents our connectivity to the universe, our history, other beings, primitive ideas and higher abilities. The aspect of the collective unconscious that is important for this work is the archetypal content. We all hold archetypal images of people and what they should be like and how they should behave, and this can often be manifested during personal development work. For example, managers may describe themselves as people-oriented, empathic and subjective, yet say they are different to this at work because at work they are a "manager". It is likely that they are trying to live up to their archetypal image of a manager which Jung and Assagioli would claim is information from the collective unconscious.

8. Sub-personalities

Assagioli suggests that within our psyche, but not necessarily within our field of consciousness, there exist several sub-personalities. These are different personas that we assume in different situations and are theoretically similar to Jung's idea of the persona, but Assagioli suggests that we have several differentiated sub-personalities. Jung probably did not intend to imply that we only have one outward-facing persona, but used this term to describe the adaptations of ourselves that we show the outer world. Assagioli makes this more explicit in his model and, to some extent, this can make working with sub-personalities in therapy or coaching a little easier. Some sub-personalities are conscious, some are unconscious, some operate from the lower unconscious and some operate from the superconscious. In terms of working with the Myers-Briggs, the theory of sub-personalities can be useful in exploring differences between reported and self-assessed type, or an individual's lack of clarity regarding their preferences. Sub-personalities are necessary and useful for social adaptation, however in a healthy personality they are recognised and under the conscious control of the individual.

Assagioli's egg model provides a more simplified and comprehensive map of the psyche compared to Jung's and, in addition, it provides a conceptual image to help "visualise" which parts of an individual we may be accessing or seeing when we are working with them in coaching or therapy. Holding this diagram in mind whilst working, coaches can be more conscious of the fact that they are aiming to expand the field of awareness, bring the "I" into conscious awareness and access aspects of the middle unconscious. If they are working transpersonally, they may actively and more consciously try to access the superconscious, and if they are working on issues of identity and authenticity, they may more directly work with the concept of sub-personalities.

Psychic Energy and the Will

Assagioli put forward a similar idea of dynamic psychic energy to Jung in terms of the entropy and equivalence forces within the psyche, however his psychosynthesis theory places a large focus on two types of energy that can be both consciously controlled by the individual and unconsciously at work within the individual. These are Love and Will. Although Jung's typology is also based on the flow of energy, Assagioli is clearer on his definitions of this energy and on how it is expressed. Love is concerned with being, receptivity, nurture, support, inclusion, and the idea of the "mother" archetype, whilst Will is about activity, direction, change, and the idea of the "father" archetype. There is also some recognition in psychosynthesis theory of the fact that, whilst people are likely to use both of these energies, one will tend to dominate resulting in "Love types" and "Will types". It is

Psychological Type and Psychosynthesis

worth noting that there is some fundamental and archetypal similarity between Love and Jung's Feeling function, and Will and Jung's Thinking function.

The Will can be compared to the energies of self-determination, the drive to take action, and, ultimately, the drive for self-actualisation. Piero Ferrucci describes it as *"the capacity of an organism to function freely according to its own intrinsic nature rather than under the compulsion of external forces."* (2004, p.72). The more self-awareness individuals have, the more they can use their Will to direct their lives, recognise their choices, and realise their potential. Assagioli describes different aspects of the Will; Strong Will, Skilful Will, Good Will and Transpersonal Will. Assagioli suggests that a well-functioning individual will demonstrate a combination of these different aspects of the Will, balanced with each other as appropriate to the situation. The positive qualities of the Strong Will are determination, assertion, direction, endurance, persuasion and protection, however it can be distorted if used in isolation or in inappropriate circumstances resulting in domination, crudeness, violence, force, oppression and bullying. The Skilful Will is concerned with the deliberate and mindful directing of our functions and comes with self-understanding and self-awareness. The Skilful Will can result in compromise, co-operation, care towards others, creativity, imagination, diplomacy, and efficiency, however inappropriate use can lead to manipulation, abuse of others, deceit, exploitation and confusion. The Good Will is concerned with consideration for others, acting for the greater good, enjoyment of service to others, patience, empathy and understanding. When the Good Will is used in an appropriate balance with the Strong and Skilful Will, individuals can direct their actions to effectively work towards the improvement of themselves and others. The Transpersonal Will is not experienced by many people. It is the part of the Will that functions through ultimate values, self-actualisation, cosmic awareness and synergies and it channels the qualities of the Transpersonal Self. It is similar to the notion of being "in flow".

Assagioli related Jung's model of the preference functions (Sensing, Intuition, Feeling and Thinking) to his theory of the functions of the Will, i.e. the Will is expressed through these functions. This is similar to Jung's idea that using the functions requires energy to be directed towards or away from them. Assagioli also added two more functions; Imagination and Impulse-Desire and depicted this in his "star diagram" *(see Fig.5).*

The Shadows of Type

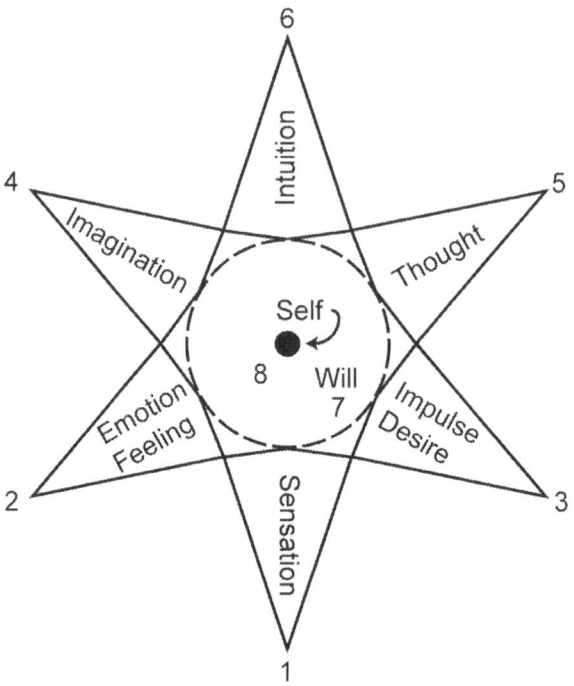

Fig.5: Assagioli's "star" diagram showing the functions of the Will

Assagioli considered the lack of "Imagination" as a function to be an omission in Jung's theory, however he explains this by noting that Jung believed that *"imaginative activity can evidence itself in all the four other functions"* (Assagioli, 1967, p.2). He goes on to say that it seems impossible that fantasy or imagination can be manifested in the Sensing function, however I consider this to be a misinterpretation of the nature of the Sensing function; those with a Sensing function can have active imaginations and often have an image in mind of how they expect (or remember) something to be in order to meet their need for certainty and avoidance of the unknown (SJs in particular). In his inclusion of the function of Impulse-Desire in his model, Assagioli explains that he views it as different to the Will as it is externally focused (i.e. the desire for something), and the Will has to work in conjunction with, in opposition to or under the influence of these desires. Impulse-Desire, however, is not a function in the Jungian sense, although it would have a place in the dynamic energy of the psyche according to Jung's model; like Imagination, it can work through the other four functions. Therefore, whilst the functions of Imagination and Impulse-Desire have a place in the dynamics of the psyche and are useful functions to bring to conscious awareness during therapy or coaching, they are fundamentally different to the original four functions suggested by Jung, in that they are not distinct cognitive styles.

Assagioli suggests that these six functions interact with each other, and through more deliberate and skilful use of the Will the individual is able to more consciously use these functions to their best advantage. He writes:

> *"The will can and should make skilful use of the other psychological and bodily functions and energies existing in the personality: thinking and imagination, perceptions and intuition, feelings and impulses, as well as the physical organs of action. To employ an analogy from the theatre, the will is the director of the entire production but normally he is not himself one of the actors."* (Assagioli, 2002, p.139).

In his model, Assagioli places the Will close to the self as it is the appropriate use of the Will that integrates the personality and brings the individual closer to their true self.

Assagioli's "methods of therapy and education"

Although Assagioli spoke in terms of "therapy", we will consider only those aspects of both his and Jung's theories and techniques that can be applicable to coaching. Assagioli believed that Jung's aims and methods of therapy were akin to those of psychosynthesis, in that they focused on the integration and synthesis of the different parts of the personality. The psychosynthesis approach is a useful addition to working developmentally with type, not only because it is a further development of Jung's original ideas, but because psychosynthesis has a range of existing practical applications that can be applied in coaching, whilst some of Jung's methods were more abstract (e.g. dream interpretation, drawing of mandalas) or required long-term therapy.

Parfitt suggests that it is useful to conceptualise the actual process of psychosynthesis in two parts; personal psychosynthesis and transpersonal psychosynthesis. Personal psychosynthesis falls more into the realm of developmental coaching in that it is concerned with developing the personality to the point that it is effective, aware and free from obstacles. Transpersonal psychosynthesis takes this further and attempts to develop the self of the individual to the point where the Transpersonal Self can be realised, bringing with it a sense of clarity, purpose, connectedness and universality.

The Shadows of Type

The process of psychosynthesis has four stages according to Assagioli: a) gaining a thorough knowledge of one's personality, b) being able to exercise control over the various elements of the personality, c) realising one's true self, and d) the "psychosynthesis" itself which is the reconstruction and synthesis of the personality. Again, unless one is working at the transpersonal level, the first two stages of this process are the most useful for use in developmental coaching.

The process of gaining a thorough knowledge of one's personality can begin with taking clients through a type exploration process, such as a Myers-Briggs® feedback. Further sessions may then attempt to expand their fields of awareness further by exploring their non-preferred functions, the persona or sub-personalities, the dynamics of their opposing functions, their existing motivations and use of Will, and gaining an awareness of their shadow sides. The second stage, the ability to exercise control, can be seen as working on how they use and direct their Will through the psychological functions in order to get the best out of themselves. This process needs to happen in stages and be at a level appropriate to the individual's path of development. Later chapters of this book will address the practical applications for coaching

Although including the other aspects of the psyche such as the persona/sub-personalities, shadow, ego, field of awareness, the Will, true self, Transpersonal Self and collective unconscious can contribute to the "missing part" of current psychological type theory, it does not address the issue of what level of development a client's psyche may be at, i.e. how much is already accessible to their field of awareness. Therefore, placing type in the context of Jung's original model of the psyche and "upgrading" this to Assagioli's model of the psyche only goes part of the way to identifying the "missing element". There is a need to identify what "state" somebody's psyche is in (i.e. their level of ego development) to enable the coach to work at an appropriate level with their client.

Psychological Type and Psychosynthesis

Chapter Summary

- ❖ Assagioli's psychosynthesis model helps to clarify certain aspects of the psyche:
    - o We can have several sub-personalities that can be conscious, unconscious, adaptive or maladaptive.
    - o A separation between the areas of the unconscious into middle, lower and higher.
    - o The idea of an individual's field of awareness.
    - o The difference between the I and the Self.
- ❖ The concept of the Will helps to define the nature of the energy that the individual is using to direct their functions.
- ❖ Placing type in the context of the psyche and the psychosynthesis model has identified the parts of the "missing element" but does not address what "state" an individual's psyche may be in.
- ❖ Information regarding the individual's level of personal or ego development is needed to help the coach to work appropriately with the client.

Chapter Five

The Levels of Ego Development

Setting psychological type back into the context of the psyche has identified the components of the "missing element" from current type theories. We now know that the expression of type is effected by our level of self-awareness, the extent to which we are identified with and defensive of our ego image, and our use of the Will. However, what we do not know at this point is how self-aware or ego-identified a person may be. To work appropriately and safely with type in context, information regarding the individual's level of personal or ego-development is needed. Theories of ego development map out the developmental stages of individuals and their journeys from basic to complex meaning-making in life, beginning with a child's basic cognitive development through to the potential realisation of the Transpersonal Self.

Loevinger's Theory of Ego Development

Jane Loevinger (1976) suggested that ego development takes place in a sequence of stages across the lifespan. The first stage of development is the Presocial (or Autistic) stage, during which the infant cannot distinguish between animate and inanimate aspects of its environment. This is followed fairly quickly by the Symbiotic stage, characterised by the child being able to distinguish its mother from the environment, but not itself from the mother. It is following these two early stages that Loevinger believes that ego development begins. It starts with the stage that she refers to as the Impulsive stage, during which children

The Levels of Ego Development

are aware of their separate existence and exercise their own will. It is at this stage that the child sees others as sources of supply to be exploited.

The stages that follow the Impulsive stage are those that adults, who are capable of later stages of development, may find themselves reverting to under certain circumstances, or they may have their development halted at one of these stages. Loevinger's Opportunistic stage, usually seen in very young children, is characterised by the need to "win" and maintain control. Adults at this stage are manipulative and concerned with getting the better of people. They will obey rules, but only because they do not want to get caught, indicating a poor level of moral development.

The next stage is the Conformist stage, where individuals will relate well to certain groups and follow the norms and rules of those groups, however they will show a lack of understanding of and prejudice towards other groups. This is a stage often seen in older children and teenagers. If development continues, individuals will progress to the Conscientious stage where they are less concerned with trying to get acceptance from groups and fit into norms, and more concerned with achievement, morals and ideals.

According to Loevinger, few people move into the next stages which she calls Autonomous and Integrated. The Autonomous stage is characterised by inner conflict caused by the different opinions and views the individual can hold as they no longer see the world in terms of absolutes. Their awareness of the "shades of grey" and multiple perspectives can make them question their own viewpoint. They are focused on individuality and self-fulfilment. The Integrated stage is the final stage in Loevinger's model and this is where individuals have the ability to resolve the conflicts experienced in the previous stages and have a sense of identity that is integrated.

Adaptations of ego development theory for use with adults

Loevinger's theory of ego development has been adapted by several other researchers and authors for application to the adult developmental process and to leadership development theories (e.g. Kegan 1982; Wilber 2000; Cook-Greuter 2004; Torbert 2004; Eigel and Kuhnert 2005; Joiner and Josephs 2007). Their versions of the developmental stages are fairly similar in nature; it is mainly the names given to each of the stages and the number of stages in each theory that differ. Some of these theories also have roots in Jean Piaget's renowned child development work.

The different theorists' models of the levels of development are shown below in Table 5.

Loevinger	Cook-Greuter/ Torbert	Kegan	Wilber	Joiner and Josephs
Impulsive	Impulsive	Impulsive	Body/ Preconventional	
Opportunistic	Self-Defensive/ Opportunist	Imperial		
Conformist	Conformist / Diplomat	Interpersonal	Mind/ Conventional	
	Self-Conscious/ Expert			Expert
Conscientious	Conscientious /Achiever	Institutional		Achiever
	Individualist		Vision Logic/ Post-Conventional	Catalyst
Autonomous	Autonomous/ Strategist	Inter-individual	Systems View	Co-Creator
Integrated	Construct Aware/Magician			Synergist
	Unitive/Ironist		Unitive View	

Table 5: Comparison of the stages of development adapted by different theorists

This levelled model of personal development is often referred to as a "Vertical" approach to development (Cook-Greuter 2002; Wilber 2000).

Ego development progresses through the stages in sequence and, although an individual may get the occasional sense of the higher levels, they will habitually view the world from the level that they have reached developmentally. The levels of development that are below the one that the individual is capable of will still come in to play when the individual is under pressure, being defensive, feeling threatened, lacking energy, experiencing stress, etc, or, in fact, when they are with people that they feel extremely at ease with. Individuals capable of operating at higher levels may also revert to the styles of the lower levels when certain situations require it, however this will be done with consciousness and deliberation. Therefore, the level that one may be operating from at any given moment is not always fixed at their most advanced level of development and will fluctuate according to their circumstances. However, the theory states that the limit of one's functioning is set by the level they have reached, i.e. somebody who has not developed beyond Cook-Greuter's Expert level may get some brief flashes of the Achiever viewpoint, but will not be able to operate from this perspective.

Development from one level to the next comes from being able to move from the subjective nature of each level to the objective; that is to say that when individuals are at a certain level, it is subjective in that they are identified with it and may find it difficult to step back (disidentify) and look at their attitudes and behaviours objectively. When one is subject to a given level, they have very little concept of there being anything else beyond their current perception. Once they have moved out of a given level, they have the ability to reflect on it from their new perspective and see it objectively. Transition between the levels occurs when the truth or logic that an individual is operating from at a given level begins to fall apart or become questionable. Therefore, before developing into the next level, individuals may go through a period of fluctuation or confusion as the logic of their current level fails and they begin to see the viewpoint of the next level. On moving to the next level of development, there is often a period of instability while individuals attempt to fully understand their new perspective.

A good analogy for transition through the levels is the "forest" analogy. If a person were to live deep in the forest and never emerge from it, their reality would consist of trees, plants, a few animals etc. They would have no idea that anything else could possibly exist other than their own reality. Supposing one day, they climb to the top of the tallest tree in the forest and catch sight of a snow-capped mountain in the distance. Suddenly their existing concept of the world being made up of trees, plants, etc is no longer true. With some trepidation they may leave the forest and travel towards the mountain, learning about the new terrain as they go. From here they can look back on the forest and see that it is only a part of the entire landscape after all and realise that their previous perspective was somewhat narrow and basic. At some point they may decide to climb the mountain and, at the summit, they look out in a new direction and catch sight of the ocean. Once again, their existing reality no longer explains everything. Their journey may take them on to deserts, jungles, cities, polar caps ... With every step their perception of the world is broadened, they can cope with more complexity and, eventually they will realise that the world is one co-dependent eco-system.

These transitions can occur naturally with age, as more complex situations and relationships become part of life, or as a result of difficult experiences, or following deliberate personal development (e.g. coaching or therapy).

Cook-Greuter provides a summary of various studies that she has carried out regarding the distribution of the developmental level in the general adult population (see Table 6). Developmental level was assessed using the Leadership Development Profile (LDP) which is a sentence completion survey tool based on the work of Loevinger and developed by Cook-Greuter, Dal Fisher, David Rooke and Bill Torbert for Harthill Consulting. From this data it would seem that the Expert level of development is where most people operate from, followed by the Achiever level.

Developmental Level	535 managers and consultants in the UK	497 managers and supervisors in the USA	4510 USA mixed adult population
Ironist	0.9	<1	0.5
Magician	5.6		1.5
Strategist	13.5	1.4	4.9
Individualist	23.4	5	11.3
Achiever	33.5	34.8	29.7
Expert	21.1	47.8	36.5
Diplomat	1.7	8.2	11.3
Impulsive and Opportunist	0.4	2.2	4.3

Table 6: Distribution of the levels of development (%)

Cook-Greuter notes that the difference in the UK distribution compared to the US distribution is thought to be a result of the sample being volunteers for the study, and that those who are at higher levels are more likely to volunteer for such research: *"Active interest in developmental measures and theory is in and of itself an indication of Achiever or later development".*

Personal communication with Susan Cook-Greuter, December 2009.

Applying the Vertical Development Approach to the Myers-Briggs®

As previously mentioned, both Cook-Greuter and Wilber note that the absence of a vertical dimension is a significant limitation of typologies such as the Myers-Briggs. In Cook-Greuter's work, she notes that the current Myers-Briggs model comes under the heading of "Different, but equal" in that all types are equally valid and what matters is the fit between an individual's style and the context in which they are operating. She suggests that, *"... another way people differ from each other, the developmental stage, is as important and sometimes more so than how they differ in personality type and preferences"* (2004, p.276). It follows that if an individual of a given type is operating at a low level of development, he or she may not be able to adapt and flex their style to meet type-challenging situations, whereas an individual at a higher level of development will be more able to adapt his or her behaviour to suit different situations. Therefore, combining the developmental level with psychological type can add a whole new dimension to understanding individuals, how their types may be expressed and what their further development needs may be, using psychological type as a platform for coaching and developmental work.

Joiner and Josephs comment that those who are familiar with typologies such as the Myers-Briggs may see certain type characteristics as being connected to certain developmental levels. Indeed, when one first reads the generic descriptions of the levels, one might see the Opportunist level having some connection to a poorly functioning SP temperament; concerned with action in the present with no concern for consequences; the Diplomat level having some of the qualities of the SJ temperament; wanting to belong and conform; the scientific nature of the Achiever having some of the "scientific" qualities of the NT temperament, and the Individualist showing the inspirational and collaborative aspects of the NF temperament. However, Joiner and Josephs go on to say that from their research they have found that level of agility (development) and personality type are completely unrelated, and that every personality type can be found at every level. As previously noted, Wilber also believes that each type can exist at each of the major levels of development.

Considering how the theory of vertical ego development applies to type, the following adaptations of Cook-Greuter's versions of the developmental levels have been created. Note that only the levels from Opportunist to Magician have been used, as it would be difficult to apply actual Myers-Briggs types to the levels above and below these. Importantly, the names given to each stage and the language used in the descriptions have been changed to try to move away from any association with any particular type. For this type applicable model, the levels are named as follows: Power and Control, Social Identification, Personal Identity, Determined Action, Considerate Individualism, Integration and Authenticity, and Magician. The correspondence between these type applicable level descriptions and the Loevinger and Cook-Greuter models is shown in Table 7.

Bennet Type-Applicable Levels	Loevinger	Cook-Greuter
	Impulsive	Impulsive
Power and Control	Opportunistic	Opportunist
Social Identification	Conformist	Diplomat
Personal Identity		Expert
Determined Action	Conscientious	Achiever
Considerate Individualism		Individualist
Integration and Authenticity	Autonomous	Strategist
Magician	Integrated	Magician
		Ironist

Table 7: Correspondence of the type applicable levels to other theories

For the description of each level, the type-related aspects and dynamics of the psyche are provided. The leadership capabilities for each level – cognitive agility, ability to learn, motivation and emotional intelligence – have also been noted for two reasons; firstly, the leadership capabilities include emotional intelligence and cognitive capacity which are some of the capabilities that change as one develops through the levels, and, secondly, because one of the main coaching applications for this work is likely to be leadership development.

The Levels of Ego Development

Level of Power and Control

General Description of the Level of Power and Control

Adults who function at this level are largely ineffective and are likely to have disrupted or dysfunctional relationships. They are operating from the point of view of survival of the fittest and see every situation or interaction as something they need to win or protect themselves in. They can only see the world from the perspective of their own needs and they are incapable of psychological insight into themselves or other people. They have little-to-no awareness of the needs or motives of others and will not understand the benefits of compromise or consultation. They are often manipulative and exploitative towards others and have a strong need to be in control. They look to blame other people or circumstances for any problems they encounter, and this will occur fairly often as they frequently have problems, particularly with interpersonal relationships. As they accept no responsibility and have no insight into themselves, they have little to no sense of remorse. Individuals at this level are likely to show a false outward persona to mask their anxiety, lack of real self-confidence and vulnerability. They will have an underlying fear that others will be trying to control or dominate them. The positive aspects of this style are that they can be tenacious sales people or willing to take physical risks, however in general they are ineffective in the workplace.

At this level individuals will make use of unconscious ego defence mechanisms. The most common defence mechanisms used at the level of Power and Control are fantasy, acting out and projection. These individuals tend to use simple language and often describe things in dichotomies (e.g. good/bad, right/wrong, fun/boring).

Individuals who are normally capable of operating at higher levels of development may revert to this level if they feel threatened, stressed, frustrated or vulnerable, or if they are not getting their fundamental needs met.

Type-Related Aspects

At this level the use of preferences is one-sided and often forceful. Preferences are mainly used on "autopilot" with no conscious awareness or deliberate direction. Any glimpse of non-preferred styles or differences to the ego image are repressed or denied. Therefore, individuals at this level may have frequent outbursts and self-control issues. Using the Myers-Briggs with individuals who are developmentally stuck at this stage can be challenging.

Dynamics of the Psyche

The field of awareness at this level is fairly small as the individual has very little self-awareness. The use of Will is strong, often unconscious, and with little use of skill unless engaged in the manipulation of others. They are likely to have an outward persona (bravado) but little-to-no skilful use of sub-personalities or persona. Sub-personalities are likely to be very disintegrated and unlike their true selves. This can make the person seem very changeable depending on their mood, the situation and who they are with.

Leadership Capabilities

Cognitive capacity: They will see things in concrete, absolute, black and white terms with no tolerance of ambiguity. At this level they will have no insight into others' viewpoints and only see things from an egocentric perspective.

Ability for learning: They are unable to use feedback for learning and would view feedback as a personal attack. At this level their actions are eventually likely to produce results that are the opposite of their values and desires, however rather than recognise this they are likely to continue to do the same things with more force to try to get their needs met.

Motivation: The overarching motivation at this level is self-preservation. Therefore there will be a strong need to win, defend oneself and deflect any blame onto others or the environment.

Emotional Intelligence: Individuals at this level are unaware of why they do what they do or that there may be different ways of being. Different ways of being are considered to be "wrong". They have no awareness of their potential impact on others. They try to defend against others, prove themselves right, and get their own way. They are likely to use others to meet their own needs and have little time for those who are of no benefit to them. Nevertheless, they are usually able to manipulate others to get their own way; sometimes this manipulation will be carried out unconsciously and will involve the replaying of learned childhood patterns of behaviour.

Level of Social Identification

General Description of the Level of Social Identification

For individuals at this level their identity is defined by their relationship to the groups they belong to and their adherence to the norms or customs of those groups. These can be family, friends, work groups, sports groups etc, or impersonal "groups" such as cultural genres (e.g. music, fashion, lifestyle), interests, beliefs, attitudes, political affiliations etc. Others who are not part of the group or who do not fit the norms are rejected and criticised, thus there is a clear "in-group – out-group" dynamic. The norms or rules are accepted without question and they will base their judgements of others on superficial information such as their appearance, their car, their status etc. They can become materialistic and use symbols (e.g. clothes, cars, collections) to illustrate their identity and their aspirations may revolve around obtaining the material possessions that are owned by others who they admire. They are sensitive to the opinions and evaluations of others because being accepted is of utmost importance, and shame is the dominant feeling they experience if something goes wrong for them. They have little or no real understanding of those who are different to how they see themselves.

On a positive note, adults who function at this level are often people-pleasing, helpful and conflict avoidant. They may have fairly smooth social relationships with the people and groups they choose to associate with, however they may not be in touch with their real selves. They may suppress various aspects of their personality in order to fit in and will run their lives according to their beliefs about social norms and/or the beliefs that they have had instilled in them from childhood.

If they gravitate towards groups who are similar to themselves, they are likely to become more entrenched in their preferences and less balanced. People at this level who find themselves with groups and norms that are unlike their real selves may end up in situations where they never feel comfortable, have a sense of being a misfit, or where they have a sense of incongruence.

The defences used most often by individuals at the level of Social Identification are projection (think that others all think like they do) and introjection (accepting others' norms and rules). They will also use suppression to push aside any feelings or needs that do not fit the norms. In communication they tend to give others advice, sometimes unwanted advice; however they evaluate others according to their own preferences or norms so the advice will be in the form of what they have experienced or what they think is the right thing to do. They will use "shoulds" and "oughts" frequently, and they also tend to use a lot of clichés and set phrases.

Individuals usually capable of operating at higher levels of development may revert to this level when they are in a new situation, trying to fit in, or when they feel insecure or lacking in self-confidence.

Type-Related Aspects

If their chosen norms and in-groups are in line with their preferences they are likely to experience less inner tension, however this may lead to them being more entrenched and one-sided in the use of their preferences. If they choose norms that are incongruous with their type (or other personality characteristics such as values) they may feel somewhat unsettled as they unconsciously repress and consciously suppress aspects of themselves in order to fit in. Aspects of this level may be implicated in cases where an individual has different reported and best-fit MBTI® types. Working with individuals at this level can be difficult as the persona will be heavily guarding their ego and they can be somewhat self-deluding about who they really are.

Dynamics of the Psyche

The field of awareness at this level may be a little larger than the previous level in that the individual may have an idea of what they are like and so seek out similar people or interests. If they are in dissimilar groups, they may have interference from the unconscious and, if they develop on from this stage they may have a sudden insight into what they are actually like. They will make use of strong and skilful (yet immaturely skilful) Will to direct the functions that are perceived to be the "right" ones. They will have an idea of what type of person they want to or should be and attempt to cultivate that image or persona. Use of sub-personalities and personas may be both conscious and unconscious, but are likely to appear inauthentic or ineffective if they are incongruous to the real self. Individuals at this level may also turn on different personas or sub-personalities according to who they are with or what the situation is.

Leadership Capabilities

Cognitive capacity: At this level, individuals are able to think in abstract terms (i.e. what might be). This can inform their behaviour as they will have hypotheses about how they are expected to behave and what others may think of them. The individual can see the value of belonging to a larger group rather than trying to operate as an individual in competition with others. Norms are not questioned, just accepted.

Ability for learning: They are still unable to accept feedback and will see feedback as a sign of disapproval from others or a reinforcement of what they should be doing to fit the norms.

Motivation: At this level the motivation is acceptance by the groups that the individual deems to be important or valuable. There is a large focus on fitting in and conforming, even if that means fitting into a group that is "non-conformist".

Emotional Intelligence: Their self-awareness may seem genuine to them at this stage, however the individual is getting their idea of who they are from external sources and norms. Therefore they are cultivating an ego image rather than getting a sense of their true self. In terms of "other awareness", understanding is only limited to the "in-groups" or those who follow a given norm. They will understand that others can be different to them but may be unaware that others may actually perceive them differently to how they perceive themselves. Much of what they imagine others think of them has more to do with their own hopes and fears than with actual reality. Relating to others may seem to be functional with the chosen groups, however there will be disdain or intolerance towards those who are in the "out-groups".

Level of Personal Identity

General Description of the Level of Personal Identity

Adults who function at this level begin to have some idea of what they are actually like as a person and will attempt to find their niche or cultivate relationships that are more in tune with who they are. They become capable of some degree of self-reflection and they have the ability to step back and see themselves fairly objectively. The individual at this level will start to express their own opinions and views and take their own direction, no longer needing to fit in as they did at the previous level – the focus is on standing out; they may assert their identity with such vigour that they can actually alienate themselves from others to some extent. As they now focus on what they, as an individual, believe to be right, they may criticise others' opinions and views and discredit anything that does not fit their viewpoint. Feeling as if they now know the "right answers", individuals at this level will enjoy getting into debates with others or imposing their opinions on others. They can also display perfectionistic tendencies or high standards at this level.

The positive aspects of those operating at this level are that they will be trying to do things to the best of their ability and will be focused on the completion of short-term goals. In their work they are likely to enjoy changing or initiating things. However they often assume that they are correct and are therefore unlikely to test their views against other perspectives or objective data. Generally they can function fairly well at this stage when working in their comfort zone, however they will have difficulty with difference. Frequently individuals who function well at this level in their own area of expertise can be promoted to management positions in which they often struggle. This "technical expert but ineffective manager" pattern is often encountered by coaches. The main defences used by people at this level are intellectualisation and rationalisation.

Individuals usually capable of operating at higher levels of development may revert to this level when they are trying to assert their individuality, when they are in a conflict of opinions, or when they are generally under pressure.

Type-Related Aspects

The individual may have some idea of what their preferences are but use these in a one-sided way with little allowance for their non-preferred styles. This can be where individuals find themselves following a poor or quick experience with the MBTI®. Many of the characteristics that will be seen at this level are "typical" of their given MBTI® type. In Jungian terms this is the beginning of differentiation.

Dynamics of the Psyche

There is an increase in the field of awareness at this stage; however it will be limited to aspects of the conscious ego. The use of Will is a fairly good balance of strong and skilful as the individual is now consciously directing some of their functions but may push them too strongly at times. As individuals at this level are fairly entrenched in behaving according to their type/ego image, they may not use their outward facing sub-personalities or persona with much skill to adapt to different situations as they will be fairly committed to "being themselves". However, if "putting on a face" is seen as a means to an end, they are likely to be more content to use sub-personalities as necessary. There may be some awareness of the "voices" of the inner sub-personalities, particular the inner critic.

Leadership Capabilities

Cognitive capacity: At this level they can see that there are actually "shades of grey" rather than just black and white, however they will believe that their own particular shade of grey is the right one. They will only be capable of seeing a small part of the context in which the tasks or problems they are working on are set, and will tend to see each of these in isolation. Their perspective will be fairly short term and they may find it difficult to prioritise as they will be largely unaware of the connections between different tasks.

Ability for learning: They are likely to take feedback personally and their immediate response will be to defend their position. Feedback will be only be accepted from those whose opinions they respect.

Motivation: Individuals at this level are concerned with standing out and being noticed, usually for their expertise or authority. They tend to focus mainly on either the completion of tasks or the building of good relationships depending on their type. Their motivation is to be seen as useful and skilled.

Emotional Intelligence: Self-awareness and other awareness may be developing, however the scope of the awareness is limited to the conscious or obvious aspects (i.e. the conscious aspects of the ego). There will be awareness that others are different, however these differences are not often appreciated or valued, and the individual may be critical towards those with other views and see them as being wrong.

Level of Determined Action

General Description of the Level of Determined Action

This level is a marked difference from the previous level and is where effective functioning begins to take place. Adults who function at this level are concerned with achieving longer term goals and maximising their strengths. They are likely to have a good sense of who they are and how they differ from others, and will have some appreciation of the value of these differences. Therefore individuals at this level have the ability to be part of different groups, or associate with people who are different to them without feeling torn or confused. They become interested in what makes other people tick and are also capable of self-awareness and of accepting feedback about themselves. It is at this stage that individuals can be truly introspective and concerned with

The Shadows of Type

whether they live up to their beliefs, however this can lead to severe self-criticism.

They are keen to take actions that have some benefit to others, however they believe that there are answers to everything and take a "scientific" view of the world. They will have an understanding of individual differences and may even seek out the views of others who may have alternative opinions, yet these views will only be accepted if they do not encroach on their fundamental beliefs. Rather than shun, coerce or belittle others, individuals at this level will use their skills of persuasion to influence others. The level of Determined Action is so named because individuals at this level often have a need to accomplish something meaningful and can become preoccupied with getting things done and taking responsibility. Unfortunately this means that they are often distracted from the present moment and, in addition, they can become overworked.

People at this level have usually had some form of self-development or learning experience. The defences most often employed at the level of Determined Action are intellectualisation, rationalisation and suppression of negative aspects.

Individuals usually capable of operating at higher levels of development may revert to this level when they are focusing on goals or under pressure to deliver results, or when they are experiencing impatience with a situation.

Type-Related Aspects

Individuals at this level will be aware of their type, either explicitly through having some active development or implicitly as a result of self-reflection. They are likely to use their preferences with some degree of balance, unlike the one-sidedness of the previous levels and, in spite of whether they have a preference for Thinking or Feeling, they will be able to use both assertive and accommodating styles fairly appropriately. They will be aware of their blind spots and a few of their negative points, but are unlikely to have any awareness of their shadow sides. If an individual at the previous level is beginning to move into this level, a good, balanced Myers-Briggs feedback will be very beneficial in making their type-awareness more explicit and increasing their capacity for more skilful direction of the Will via the functions. In addition to this, the individual may begin to understand the value of the opposites. At this stage, in Jungian terms, the individual will be healthily differentiated.

Dynamics of the Psyche

The field of awareness will encompass much of the ego and be drawing in new learning from the middle unconscious, however individuals at this level are likely to be unaware of their shadow aspects. The use of Will is strong as they are determined to achieve their goals, and skilful as they consciously direct their energies and strengths into their work. Persona and sub-personalities are likely to be used fairly appropriately to respond to different people and situations, however there may still be some interference from certain unconscious sub-personalities.

Leadership Capabilities

Cognitive capacity: At this level, they believe that there are answers to most things and often take a rather "scientific" approach to seeing the world and solving problems – "The Truth Is Out There". They are capable of objectivity regarding problem-solving and interpersonal behaviour. They will have a greater perspective on the wider context within which they are operating and will have a longer-term view than that of the previous level. Generally they are able to make fairly effective leaders and managers.

Ability for learning: Individuals functioning at this level will seek and accept feedback with little defence, particularly if they see it as helping them to achieve their goals. However they may reject feedback that is contradictory to their fundamental ideas. They are capable of reflecting back on previous events and objectively evaluating themselves. Additionally they will not always assume that they are right and will often check their views out with others or against objective data.

Motivation: At this level the motivation is to attain goals or positions that will be considered to be excellent personal achievements.

Emotional Intelligence: Individuals at this level will have a good sense of who they are and demonstrate a good level of empathy towards others. They will be interested in what makes people tick and appreciate the difference in others provided that it doesn't affect their goals or challenge their "truths". They will be able to hypothetically consider how others may be thinking or feeling about a given situation. Individuals at this level can belong to different groups of different people without feeling conflicted. Rather than force or coerce others, they will use persuasion and influence to try and win others over. At this level they will appreciate team-work and working with others.

Level of Considerate Individualism

General Description of the Level of Considerate Individualism

Adults who function at this level have a very good sense of self-awareness and a genuine appreciation of the differences that others bring. They become aware that reality is actually subject to perception; that is, people interpret the world according to their own beliefs, preferences, frameworks and perceptions. Thus the scientific approach of the level of Determined Action is no longer valid, and the individual takes a more holistic and fluid approach to seeing the world.

They no longer have the need to try to explain everything and realise that the truth can never be found; paradoxes and contradictions can be intriguing. They are able to take multiple perspectives on matters and recognise there is not always a clear answer to everything. They can become concerned with the wish to accomplish something personally meaningful, independent of any socially approved task. Individuals at this level become very psychologically minded and have the ability to observe their own process; process becomes more interesting to them than the results. They are also more oriented to the present than at the previous level, as well as being able to take a past and a future perspective. Considerate Individualists can be more aware of their physical feelings and develop more of a body-mind connection than they were able to at previous levels.

Considerate Individualists do not merely pay lip service to understanding and appreciating the views of others who are different to themselves; they really do appreciate different perspectives and will search for different viewpoints within themselves too. The downsides of this level is that the person can be so concerned with allowing everybody to air their views etc, that they can be frustratingly slow to make decisions. For the individuals themselves, a downside of their level is the sense of internal confusion and conflict that can result from attempting to hold various viewpoints and from knowing that there may be no truths; as well as shades of grey there is the entire spectrum to deal with. This can sometimes cause them to feel conflicted and have doubt regarding their own inner beliefs and integrity.

Individuals usually capable of operating at higher levels of development may revert to this level during times of self-doubt, confusion or general stress.

Type-Related Aspects

At this level, individuals will have a real awareness of their type either implicitly or explicitly, and some awareness of the tensions of their

The Levels of Ego Development

non-preferred styles and their shadow sides, both light and dark. They will use their type with a considerable degree of flexibility and awareness. They will also realise that their perceptions are filtered through their preferences and that this may distort the truth. At this stage, bringing the other aspects of the psyche (e.g. shadow, persona, sub-personalities) into coaching with the Myers-Briggs can be beneficial. In Jungian terms, this is the beginning of individuation.

Dynamics of the Psyche

The field of awareness will now include the shadow aspects of the ego and may be starting to reach into the higher and lower unconscious. Skilful use of the Will combined with the use of the good Will and a balanced strong Will at this level will help to make actions considered, appropriate and beneficial to others. The persona will be mainly congruent with the personality (i.e. not a mask hiding a completely different person, but an adaptation suited to the situation) and the individual will be aware of most of their sub-personalities.

Leadership Capabilities

Cognitive capacity: There is no longer the need to find answers or outcomes as there is a realisation that not everything is logical or scientific and that the absolute truth cannot always be found or even exist. When considering a given situation they will be aware of an even wider contextual setting than at the previous level and will continuously question the assumptions they may be making when doing this. Individuals at this level enjoy the idea of paradoxes although they can become confused by the different perspectives they hold.

Ability for learning: Feedback is considered to be necessary for self-development by individuals at this stage and it is therefore requested and welcomed. At the level of Considerate Individualism, there is the ability to reflect on one's actions and feelings as they are occurring rather than retrospectively after the event. This self-monitoring allows the individual to adapt their approach as they are interacting in response to the immediate feedback they are giving themselves.

Motivation: Individuals at this level are concerned with doing something that has a sense of purpose for them or is self-fulfilling, irrespective of whether others would consider it a particularly impressive achievement.

Emotional Intelligence: At this level, emotional intelligence is well developed in all areas; self-awareness and other awareness. They are also likely to have a good sense of the mind-body connection. They will be truly tolerant and accepting of individual differences and aim to do the best by others. At the previous level they were able to hypothetically consider the feelings and perspectives of another; at this level that ability extends to being able to see their whole frame of reference (i.e. the context within which the other is operating), rather than it being hypothetical and restricted to what the other's viewpoint is. As leaders or managers they will want to get all perspectives and find consensus, however this may be frustrating to those who like more direction.

Level of Integration and Authenticity

General Description of the Level of Integration and Authenticity

At this level, the confusion and conflict experienced at the previous level is resolved as the individual is able to take a systems view of the world. They have the ability to perceive patterns and trends and to synthesise apparently conflicting information, and they have an understanding of complex interconnected systems. They have a well-integrated sense of identity, including the integration of sub-personalities and many of the previously "cut off" parts of the personality. This is due to their ability for self-reflection and non-judgemental awareness of their thoughts, feelings and processes. At this level they will be capable of demonstrating authenticity.

They are actively concerned with self-actualisation and appreciate the learning they can get from interacting with others. Although they will experience paradoxes and contradictions, they will accept these as part of life rather than getting frustrated by them. They may get angry about injustices and other issues of importance to them, however they will not seek to blame others or punish. When taking action or interacting with others they will feel like they are "in flow"; that is attuned to what they are doing with a good level of awareness but not the inner dialogue experienced at the previous level. Most individuals at this level will also have glimpses of the transpersonal and have occasional peak experiences and moments of clarity. Their defences are used maturely and often include suppression, altruism and humour.

Type-Related Aspects

The individual will have a very well-integrated personality type, with awareness and integration of the shadow aspects of their type. They will use their type with flexibility and appropriateness, and will also be able to make good use of their non-preferred functions. As well as the "gifts" of their type being present, the positive qualities of the type will be manifest. At this stage, the work with type can begin to move into the transpersonal levels and include aspects such as the "light shadow" and the exploration of the true self. This is the stage that Jung would describe as individuation.

Dynamics of the Psyche

A good balance of all aspects of the Will with the beginnings of the Transpersonal Will may be being experienced. The individual at this level is functioning authentically so the natural flexibility and empathy they demonstrate at this level will be genuine aspects of their true selves. They will have a strong connection with the I and a developing connection to the Self.

Leadership Capabilities

Cognitive capacity: At this level everything is seen as part of a system. Individuals are able to take an objective view of themselves and of a given situation at the same time. They can see the connections and inter-relationships between most things. They will enjoy paradoxes and contradictions and will be able to integrate different perspectives rather than becoming conflicted by them.

Ability for learning: Individuals at this level will be seeking self-actualisation and will actively look for opportunities for feedback to help this process. Another feature of this level is that the individual will be comfortable making mistakes and learning from them, and to tolerate others making mistakes as learning experiences.

Motivation: The individual will not only seek purpose for themselves in what they do but will be interested in having purpose for others and making a real difference.

Emotional Intelligence: Individuals at this level demonstrate high levels of empathy and can really get into the shoes of others. They have the ability to view situations from multiple frames of reference and see the points of conflict and similarity, thus being able to create win-win solutions. They will also know themselves extremely well. These individuals will make truly inspirational leaders and their acceptance and tolerance of others will make them excellent role models for others. One possible downside of this level is that they may become tempted by the "dark side" of power.

Magician Level

General Description of the Magician Level

Few people will ever reach the Magician Level as this is where the transpersonal realms really begin. At this level, individuals are no longer subject to the ego and can observe it objectively, recognising how it directs their actions and thoughts and limits their potential. Magicians have an awareness of the ego and its methods of self-preservation. The realisation of this permits the Magician to see how constraining the ego can be to self-realisation. As well as understanding that the absolute truth can never be found, individuals at the Magician level will also see thought and cognition as illusive and constructed. They no longer see opposites (e.g. good/evil, life/death, love/hate, etc) but view these constructs as necessary to define each other, or as "two sides of the same coin". Individuals at this level become true, disidentified observers of their processes, and they are also likely to have frequent transpersonal "peak experiences". Their view of the world is across all time frames, plus they have vision prior to and beyond their own lives. They make use of mature defences such as sublimation and non-hostile humour. The risk at this stage is falling victim to hubris – feeling superior to others.

Type-Related Aspects

At this level the individual will recognise that there is no duality in the preference pairs and that they are co-dependent and part of each other. This will allow greater and more natural access to the non-preferred functions. As they are developing more genuine spirituality, they may have easier access to and appreciation of the inferior function. The transcendent function, providing a third option from what are seemingly dualities, will also frequently come into play as the unconscious is allowed to access the present.

Dynamics of the Psyche

The Will is very well-balanced with the Strong Will being attenuated. The Transpersonal Will is also present here. There will be a strong sense of connection to the true Self.

The Levels of Ego Development

Leadership Capabilities

Cognitive capacity: The individual at Magician level is able to objectively view the ego and the inter-relationships between dualities, opposites, and dichotomies. By managing to be present and aware they are no longer selective in their attention, as driven by the ego. That is to say that they will be non-judgementally aware of their feelings and reactions and be able to adapt as appropriate, and that this will happen "in the moment" with no delay for active reflection or interference from inner dialogue.

Ability for learning: Despite their advanced stages of development, Magicians know that learning is eternal and will gain new insight from the smallest of events or observations.

Motivation: Magicians are motivated to make a difference and be of use without personal gain or the desire for recognition.

Emotional Intelligence: Although spiritual intelligence may have always been present, this may become more prominent yet well-balanced with emotional intelligence and rational intelligence. In relating to others, Magicians will respond to non-tangible energetic fluctuations (vibrations) and intuitive sensations.

The Levels of Development, Psychological Type and Psychosynthesis

Considering what has been discussed in previous chapters regarding the Myers-Briggs typology, the psyche, the psychosynthesis model, the field of awareness, and the use and functions of the Will, the connections between these and vertical levels of development can be conceptualised as follows:

o As the individual progresses through the levels of development the use of the Will moves from using mainly Strong Will, to include the balanced use of Skilful Will.

o If Good Will is also present the individual is likely to attempt to direct their actions for the benefit of others and for personal meaning. Eventually, at the higher levels, the Transpersonal Will can also become influential.

o The field of awareness expands with each level, the connection to the self becomes stronger and the personality generally becomes more integrated. *(See Fig.6)*.

The Shadows of Type

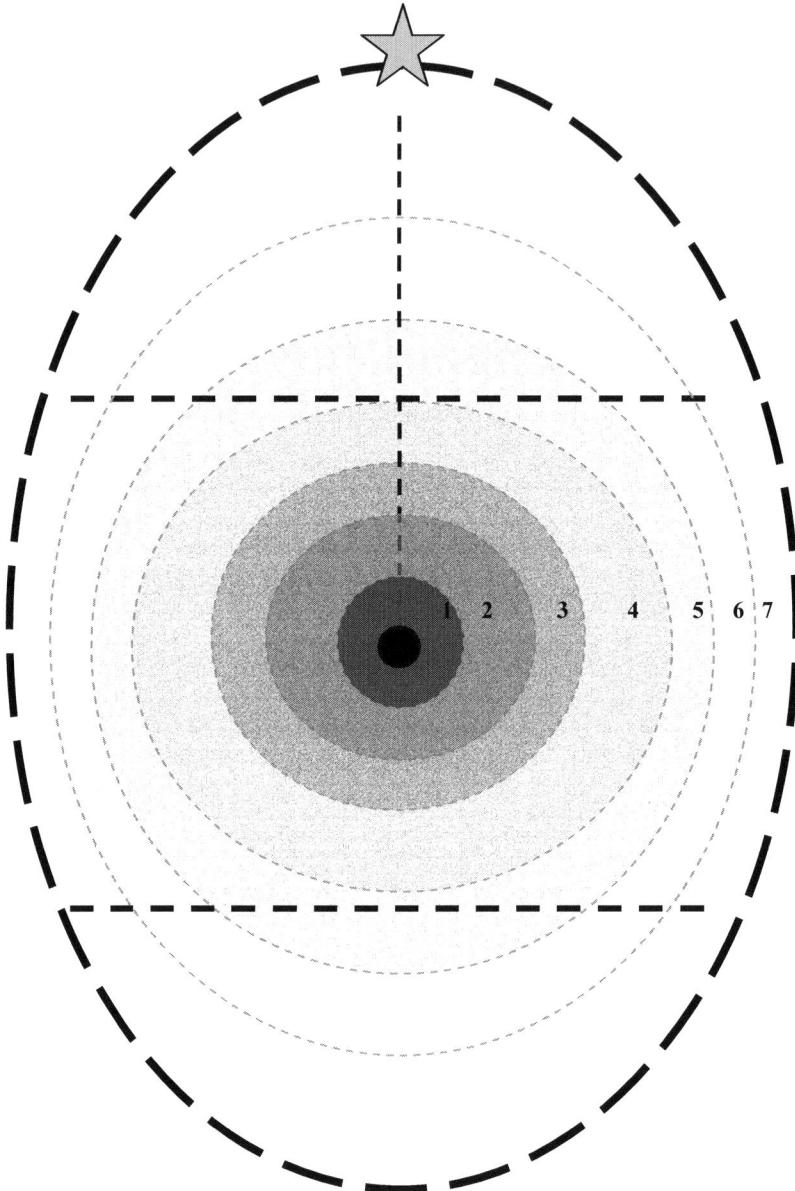

1. Power and Control   2. Social Identification   3. Personal Identity
4. Determined Action   5. Considerate Individualism
6. Integration and Authenticity   7. Magician

Fig.6: Mapping the levels of development onto the psychosynthesis model: increases in the field of awareness

The Levels of Ego Development

- o The I/personal self will become an observer of the personality and increasingly move towards being an integrated part of the personality.
- o In Jungian terms there is a gradual movement through differentiation towards individuation.

Summary of the Seven Levels

Magician Level: This rare level of insight enables individuals to take multiple perspectives on complex issues and generate seemingly impossible solutions. Individuals at this level have incredible self-awareness and operate in a state of "flow".

Level of Integration and Authenticity: Individuals at this level demonstrate authenticity and will respond to challenge without defensiveness. They have the ability to see everything as part of a wider system and can adapt and respond appropriately to complex situations.

Level of Considerate Individualism: Individuals who function at this level have a very good sense of self-awareness and a genuine appreciation for the differences in others. They are able to take multiple perspectives on matters and recognise there is not always one clear answer or way.

Level of Determined Action: Individuals operating at this level are concerned with achieving goals and maximising personal strengths. They are likely to have a good sense of who they are and how they differ from others, and will have some appreciation of the value of these differences.

Level of Personal Identity: Individuals who function at this level have some idea of what they are actually like as a person and attempt to find their niche or cultivate relationships that are more in tune with who they are. Generally they can function fairly well at this stage when working in their comfort zone, however they will have difficulty with difference.

Level of Social Identification: Individuals who function at this level may have fairly smooth social relationships with the people and groups that they choose to associate with, however they may not be in touch with their real selves and will be intolerant of those who are different. The primary concern is being seen to fit in.

Level of Power and Control: Individuals at this level are largely ineffective and are likely to have disrupted or dysfunctional relationships. They are operating from the point of view of survival of the fittest and see every situation or interaction as something they need to win. They have little to no awareness of the needs or motives of others and will not understand compromise or consultation.

Chapter Summary

- ❖ Ego development levels describe how an individual's ability for making meaning of the world changes as they grow and develop.
- ❖ When developing from childhood to adulthood individuals must pass through the levels in sequence. It is not believed to be possible to skip a level.
- ❖ Individuals often experience a period of fluctuation and confusion when in transition from one stage to another.
- ❖ Individuals may not constantly operate out of the level that they have developed to. Once at higher levels they may employ the styles of lower levels as necessary, determined by the situation, or may revert to lower levels when under pressure.
- ❖ Some adults get stuck at certain lower levels of development for various reasons, mainly environmental.
- ❖ Most people are at the Expert and Achiever levels (Personal Identity and Determined Action levels respectively).
- ❖ Jane Loevinger's original model of ego development has been developed and adapted by several other researchers for application to adult functioning and leadership development.
- ❖ Most of these descriptions use language that can sound like expressions of different types. Therefore, the descriptions have been re-written and re-named to be "type-neutral".
- ❖ As people develop through the levels, their field of awareness expands, they use more Skilful Will, they are increasingly able to self-monitor, and they become more connected to their true Self.

Chapter Six

The Developmentally Levelled Type Descriptions

Bringing together the various models – psychological type, psychosynthesis and ego development – descriptions of each of the 16 Myers-Briggs® types have been developed. These descriptions detail how adults of each type will *typically* operate at each of the levels of development.

Each type description includes the hierarchy of the functions, the main characteristics of the type when functioning well, the overall expression of the type when distorted, and the core values that each type is likely to aspire to. Taking the eight-function models of type into account, the "conflicting functions" for each type have also been included in the descriptions. These are the non-preferred functions that individuals of the given type are likely to have most difficulty interacting with, understanding the positives of, or integrating into their own personalities. These functions may also produce negative emotional reactions in us. The function that is in contrast to the dominant, however, can sometimes act as an accessible alternative to using the dominant, according to Lenore Thomson. Aspects of Eve Delunas' "Survival Games" theory are included in the level of Power and Control descriptions and Naomi Quenk's "Grip" theory is included in the descriptions of the Introverted Feeling types.

The following descriptions should be used in conjunction with the descriptions of the ego development levels.

ENFJ

Hierarchy of Functions:

Dominant: Extraverted Feeling

Auxiliary: Introverted Intuition

Tertiary: Sensing

Inferior: Introverted Thinking

Features and Distortions of the ENFJ Type:

ENFJs put plans and actions in place to help others develop, to make a difference and to create harmony.

They can become overbearing and intrusive towards others and oversensitive to the comments and opinions of others. They can also be forceful in trying to persuade others to get on board with their ideas.

Conflicting Functions:

Introverted Feeling, as the opposite orientation to the dominant, is likely to be perceived as idealistic, "do-gooding", and not putting any actual effort into getting others involved or taking any real action.

Introverted Thinking, as their inferior function, is likely to be perceived as cold, detached, selfish, of no use to other people.

Extraverted Thinking, as the contrast to the dominant function, is likely to be perceived as overbearing and cold, detached and uncaring.

Core Values: Mutual support, harmony and compassion.

Power and Control

ENFJs operating at this developmental level are likely to respond to most situations using a distortion of their dominant Extraverted Feeling preference and will often be seen as over involved, hypersensitive, overbearing, and needy. With Introverted Intuition as their Be ENFJs can be keen to consider alternatives and possibilities for others, interested in being involved in initiatives that they consider to be helpful to others, and want to be seen as helpful and useful. However this can lead to them being over dependent on involvement with others, opinionated, manipulative, insistent, controlling, bossy and, at times, self-righteous.

As Extraverted Feelers, they tend to avoid getting into direct conflict with others, but will tend to deal with their enemies by gossiping about them and being judgemental about them, rarely expressing their true feelings to the individual concerned in a direct manner. In the workplace they like to be part of a mutually supportive group and are likely to try to be influential in the group, sometimes seeking to be the "unofficial" group leader. As subordinates, they will be dedicated if they find their boss inspirational and if the boss relates to them well on a personal level; if not they are likely to criticise the boss indirectly by expressing their disdain to others and trying to win support for their views.

ENFJs at this level are usually fairly pleasant towards others provided that they are getting their own way. With people who they do not have a good rapport with they may always be on guard and looking to be offended; for this reason they often misinterpret what others say and selectively attend to the parts that could be potentially offensive. At other times, they may go to the opposite extreme and be blindly optimistic, denying any obvious negatives in a situation. If they are feeling threatened or insecure, particularly in situations where they are lacking self-confidence or where they feel personally affronted, they may play ego-defensive survival games that involve repressing their feelings and attempting to be logical about everything; they will delude themselves that they are coping well and having no negative feelings. They may also become critical, negative, inflexible, blunt, dogmatic, and pressuring towards others, and make hurtful personal comments. They are likely to be unaware of how others may be different to them and merely see difference as being wrong or selfish in some way.

Social Identification

ENFJs will usually attempt to be influential within a group and often take on the role of the organiser, carer and "agony aunt/uncle". They will use their natural preferences to support other group members and will be very sensitive to the degree of harmony within the group. However they may also be indirectly critical about or dismissive towards those whom they see as being not good team players or a threat to the group cohesiveness. In general, they will be desperate never to be seen as selfish or uncaring.

If ENFJs end up being in groups that do not support their preferences, they may suppress their natural styles and make clumsy use of their underdeveloped non-preferred functions, often channelling them through their Fe and Ni preferences, such as trying to resolve what they perceive to be a conflict situation by telling those involved to simply stop arguing and make up. They may also employ their defensive games, blocking out their true feelings and deluding themselves that everything is OK, or avoiding subjects that they are sensitive about. They may also imagine that others are thinking badly of them by misinterpreting comments or body language. ENFJs at this level can be very critical of "out-groups" and, if defending against them is necessary, they will try to rally support and can create "us and them" situations.

Personal Identification

At this level of development ENFJs can begin to use their preferences fairly effectively in their lives and work. They are likely to be organised, expressive, gregarious, enthusiastic, and helpful to others, and will enjoy generating or working with new ideas. They will prefer to work in environments where there is a good sense of team spirit and harmony. However they may push their type preferences too strongly at times and become judgemental of others, inflexible, bossy, controlling, intense, overwhelming and forceful. They will often take on others' problems or take responsibility for others inappropriately and, therefore, find themselves over burdened, however they may not be direct in expressing how they feel about this. Their focus is likely to be fixed on organising others and maintaining a level of harmony and, as such, they may become sensitive to any disharmony between others and try to get everyone on-board with the same shared vision.

At this level, ENFJs can be impulsive, hasty, impatient, oversensitive, imagine others are criticising them, deny negative realities, overlook facts that contradict with their ideals, and unwilling to accept other people's value systems. They will have a generally good idea about the kind of person they are and will notice the differences between themselves and others; however they are likely to regard the different styles of others as undesirable or dull and un-inspirational. For example they will not understand how people with T preferences can make decisions that are not acceptable to everybody and will see their logical detachment as uncaring, harsh or selfish; or they will regard people with S preferences as lacking vision and obsessive about unimportant things.

In dealing with others they will be quick to give advice and sympathy but shy away from delivering feedback that they perceive to be negative. They will want overt appreciation and approval from others and may feel offended if this is not forthcoming.

Determined Action

ENFJs really begin to use the strengths of their preferences at this level and will be enthusiastic, methodical, appreciative, empathic, inclusive, concerned and co-operative. In dealing with others they will be approachable, supportive, caring and encouraging. They are often seen as the maternal or paternal figure in a group or team as they will usually be actively concerned with each individual, however at times they may become competitive.

Although ENFJs operating at this level are generally effective in the workplace, they will still have a tendency to get over involved with personal issues and put their personal convictions above objective logic. They are also likely to be too hasty in attempting to get plans in place, spend a considerable amount of time trying to get consensus decisions, and be easily bored with details and practicalities. They will realise that they have some blind spots in terms of their awareness of the finer points of implementing their actions and their discomfort with objective decision making, and they are likely to begin to realise that there is some value to be gained from S and T ways of thinking. Therefore, they may seek viewpoints from those they see as different to themselves; however they will only incorporate these ideas if they do not go too strongly against their own preferences.

ENFJs at this stage will also still struggle to understand their conflicting functions – Introverted Feeling, Extraverted Thinking and Introverted Thinking. There is an interest in self-improvement at this level, and the ENFJ will seek feedback from others; needing a balance of positives and negatives to feel motivated to try to learn from the feedback and accept it non-defensively.

Considerate Individualism

ENFJs at this level of development will move away from using the strengths of their type to co-ordinate and help others, and move towards using these strengths to support, guide and facilitate the activities of others. They will be warm, curious, creative, fun, enthusiastic, responsive, positive, engaging and affiliative in their approach, beginning to enjoy the journey of their auxiliary Introverted Intuition; taking time to reflect on other options and possibilities rather than rushing towards organising others. They will start to allow more flexibility in their way of operating and may let others take on the co-ordinating or mediating role, rather than attempting to be the centre point of everything. They no longer thrive on appreciation and gratitude from others, but enjoy being helpful to others without payback. They may become concerned with whether or not their actions really make a difference to others and begin to seek a greater purpose from their work.

Interpersonally, they will coach and support others, encouraging others to find their own direction, rather than feeling like they have to protect or nurture them. Others are likely to describe them as warm, supportive, friendly, trustworthy, sociable and devoted to their values or causes.

As their self-awareness develops, they will become aware of the shadow sides of their preferences (the characteristics of the lower levels) and become mindful observers of their processes. Toning down their Fe and Ni preferences allows more access to their non-preferred sides, however their use of these is likely to be channelled via their Fe and Ni preferences. For example, when making an objective majority decision they may conceptualise it as "this time there are some losers, but they will get their way another time". Nevertheless, they will see the real value inherent in the S and T approach.

The ENFJ may sometimes feel as if they are losing their sense of interpersonal connectedness as, where they previously thought that they knew what the right way to act was, they will now often encounter situations where they can see other options for action and be prepared to take tough, non-consensual decisions.

Integration and Authenticity

At this level, the qualities of the ENFJ preferences can shine through –, inspiration, supportiveness, insightfulness, imaginativeness, and confidence about their values. ENFJs can appear to be facilitative, genuine, socially adept, authentic, and content with themselves, having the ability to self-validate rather than be dependent on the responses of others. They will lead by example, delegate effectively, enjoy discussing others' views and opinions and be able to create a spirit of genuine team cohesiveness, and also be able to deal tactfully with difficult interpersonal issues and differences. Although they recognise that not everybody can like everybody else, they may still find those who do not attempt to create harmony frustrating.

At this level, they become comfortable with the fact that they do not have to be the "social glue" in a group, and they can be more content with disharmony than they had previously been. They are no longer concerned with defending their image of being caring, nurturing and helpful and will enjoy simply being with other people. They will seek to understand others and value the diversity that others can bring. Through increased mindfulness, they will often be able to access their S and T preferences and adapt their actions appropriately. By not investing so much energy in being concerned with the affairs of others, they can begin to pay attention to the present and enjoy the moment.

Magician

At this level ENFJs realise that their drive to create harmony, organise others and be seen as helpful and caring is ego-driven and a distraction from their true self. They will also be more accepting of how people are and appreciate the different values others have, realising that being concerned with trying to make others maintain harmony and work together cohesively, is also a function of their own ego.

Being able to let go of dualities, they will see that Thinking is part of the same concept as Feeling, and that Sensing is part of the same concept as Intuition, seeing the similarities in the functions rather than the differences and therefore being able to gain easy and natural access to S and T. At this stage, they may also frequently experience the transcendent function – where from two apparent opposites a third way emerges, often in a form that is symbolic or intuitive.

ENFP

Hierarchy of Functions:

Dominant: Extraverted Intuition

Auxiliary: Introverted Feeling

Tertiary: Thinking

Inferior: Introverted Sensing

Main Features and Distortions of the ENFP Type:

ENFPs look to the outer environment to inspire new ideas and possibilities for making a difference or realising their ideals.

They can become novelty-seeking, scattered, easily distracted and slow to take purposeful action.

The Shadows of Type

Conflicting Functions:

Introverted Intuition, as the opposite orientation to the dominant, is likely to be perceived as limiting, lacking in novelty, isolative and inflexible.

Introverted Sensing, as their inferior function, is likely to be perceived as slow, lacking in excitement or inspiration, pointless, overly perfectionistic, and generally dull.

Extraverted Sensing, as the contrast to the dominant function, may be seen as reckless and focused on immediate gratification.

Core Values: Imagination, variety and good-will.

Power and Control

ENFPs functioning at this level will often appear to be impulsive, lacking self-control, hyperactive, hasty, noisy and rebellious as they tend to react to most situations using a distortion of their dominant Extraverted Intuition. They will use their auxiliary Introverted Feeling to consider their actions in the light of their inner values and how others will be affected, however this can often lead to them making ill-considered suggestions to others about what they believe is the right thing to do – at times being quite forceful with their opinions. As Extraverted types, they will be persistent when they are trying to persuade others, often talking over others and not listening to others.

As they do not like direct conflict ENFPs will rarely be explicit about wanting to get their own way, but will instead be overwhelmingly relentless in trying to encourage others to their way of thinking, sometimes becoming repetitive and dogmatic. ENFPs enjoy novelty, trying something different and acting on an inspirational whim; however this can lead to them obsessively pursuing new, often unrealistic, ideas and aspirations. In the workplace they like to be part of a supportive team but, as relationships are important to them, they can often become overly dependent on others or possessive over certain individuals. As subordinates they will look up to a boss who they see as inspirational and who encourages their ideas, however they may react rebelliously if they do not have a good rapport with their boss or colleagues, sometimes sabotaging the ideas of others if they do not agree with them.

If they are feeling defensive, particularly in cases where their ideals are being threatened, they may deny/repress their true feelings and delude themselves that everything is OK as an ego-defensive survival tactic. They are also likely to hop from one subject to another to avoid talking about anything that they find anxiety provoking. They may get into a trap of hastily embarking on new ideas without due consideration and jumping from one thing to another without completion or any feeling of satisfaction. Although they consider themselves to be sensitive to other people, they are likely to be unaware of how others really may be as their perceptions of other people will be distorted by their own preferences. When faced with differences that they cannot understand, ENFPs can be intensely judgemental about other people.

Social Identification

ENFPs are often naturally concerned with how others perceive them and are keen to give the impression of being competent yet personable, and knowledgeable yet spontaneous. Therefore, ENFPs will frequently employ sub-personalities and personas both consciously and unconsciously in order to manage the impression they give to others. They can also be fairly guarded in how much they want others know about them and can frequently repress their feelings or aspects of their personality when they are around others who they do not know intimately or feel comfortable with.

ENFPs will often seek a position of influence within a group but not necessarily want to be in the main leadership position, whether they find themselves in type-supportive or non-supportive groups. If they are not the group leader, they are likely to only want to follow a leader they consider to be original or fashionable in some way. In general, ENFPs enjoy being part of a group and working with others, and can be excellent team players. However they can be bitterly judgemental about people who are very different to themselves (or the norms that they may be upholding at this stage) or who they do not understand. As they tend to be naturally optimistic and like to look on the bright side, they can be repelled by people who are "pessimistic" (realistic), sarcastic or detached, or, if they care about them, they may try to change their view to "optimism".

Personal Identification

ENFPs at this level begin to channel their dominant Extraverted Intuition into their lives and work; looking for new ideas, scanning the environment for inspiration and looking for ways to realise their values and aspirations with an optimistic and "anything is possible" attitude. In working with others they often bring energy and enthusiasm to a situation and can encourage others to consider things from a completely different perspective.

They are often keen to work with others and promote a sense of team spirit, but can become frustrated with people who they do not consider to be enthusiastic enough about the team's activities. These tendencies can make them eager to get involved in too many initiatives and with too many people, resulting in them overextending themselves and finding it difficult to say "no" to others. At times they may still push their type preferences too strongly and become hypersensitive, novelty seeking, impulsive, unfocused and easily distracted.

At this level ENFPs often take an instruction and then decide to re-interpret it and do something completely different; this can be frustrating if others are depending on predictable output from them. They may also find themselves starting new initiatives with enthusiasm and energy, and then getting quickly bored and lacking motivation to complete the project. If they have an inspirational idea they can often be selective in their attention to reality and ignore process, detail or limitations that may prevent their idea coming to fruition.

ENFPs at this level will have a generally good idea about the kind of person they are and will notice the differences between themselves and others; however they are likely to regard the different styles of others as undesirable or dull and un-inspirational. For example they will not understand how people with T preferences can make decisions that are not acceptable to everybody and will see their logical detachment as uncaring, harsh or selfish; or they will regard people with Sensing preferences as lacking vision and being obsessive about unimportant things.

Determined Action

ENFPs at this level really begin to use the strengths of their preferences and will be flexible, optimistic, spontaneous, lively, empathic and innovative. They will be change-oriented, aware of future possibilities and comfortable with taking appropriate risks. With others they will come across as team-focused, supportive, personable, friendly and caring. They can also make fairly effective mediators, not dismissing or ignoring conflict, but trying to find points of consensus. If they have positions of leadership or influence they will be enthusiastic, co-operative and inclusive in their approach.

They will realise that they have some blind spots in terms of their attention to detail, their motivation to stick with a task to completion and their motivation to evaluate their ideas with realism and practicality, and they are likely to begin to realise the value that can be gained from S and T ways of working. Therefore, they may seek viewpoints from those they see as different to themselves, however they will only incorporate these ideas if they do not go against their own values and ideas too strongly. For example, a person with an Introverted Sensing preference may suggest investing some time carrying out research prior to a change initiative, and the ENFP may rationalise that, whilst this information may have some use, creativity and inspiration would be more conducive to bringing about the change because, in truth, they find the idea de-energising and damaging to the momentum of the change initiative. At this stage the ENFP will also still struggle to understand their conflicting functions – Introverted Intuition, Introverted Sensing and Extraverted Sensing.

ENFPs at this level can be fairly psychologically curious and they will have an interest in increasing their self-awareness. Therefore ENFPs will seek feedback from others, needing encouragement from the positive aspects of the feedback balanced with developmental suggestions to inspire them to learn and grow. ENFPs operating at this level will be effective in the workplace provided they have a degree of freedom, flexibility and support; however they will still feel confined by schedules and procedures and demotivated by harsh reality checks.

Considerate Individualism

At this level of development ENFPs will move away from using their preferences to initiate new ideas and projects, and move towards using these strengths to be innovative, creative and inspirational. They will be adaptable, curious and perceptive, using their auxiliary Introverted Feeling to evaluate their ideas and set a direction that they consider to be congruent with what is really important to them. Instead of switching their energy from one idea to the other, they will begin to be more focused and evaluative about their ideas, and take care in implementing those ideas that are important to them. They no longer thrive on recognition for their originality and spontaneity, and are likely to feel more comfortable with "what is" instead of constantly seeking "what could be".

As their self-awareness develops, they will become aware of the shadow sides of their preferences (the characteristics of the lower levels) and become mindful observers of their processes. As a type that is typically "not present" and easily distracted, this ability to self-monitor will have a quieting effect on their outward appearance. This will enable them to become better mentors and coaches to any individuals they may be leading or working with. Toning down their

The Shadows of Type

Ne and Fi preferences allows more access to their non-preferred sides, however their use of these are still likely to be channelled via their Ne and Fi preferences. For example, when considering how to get the best results, they will view this result as being the one that everybody can get on board with. Nevertheless, they will see the real value inherent in the S and T approach.

As they become more aware of the present and more grounded they will be more responsive to the realities of situations rather than taking an abstract or extrapolation from reality, yet they will deal with these realities creatively and by envisioning a range of possible options and perspectives. At this level, ENFPs will begin to feel comfortable dropping their optimistic mask from time to time and allowing others to see their true feelings.

Integration and Authenticity

At this level, the qualities of the ENFP preferences can shine through – they will be seen as insightful, inspiring, versatile, imaginative and confident. The ENFP can appear to be visionary; seeing patterns and connections that may not be obvious, creating developmental cultures and climates, and enthusing others with their optimism. They often take the role of catalysts for change because of their visionary approach. They will be very aware of the emotions of themselves and others and will therefore be good at developing and inspiring others.

At this level, they become comfortable with the fact that they do not have to try to be different or original and can be comfortable with and appreciative of stability. They are no longer concerned with defending their image of originality and idealism and enjoy the learning they get from being with a variety of other people, including those who they previously had little appreciation for. Through increased mindfulness, they will often be able to access their S and T preferences and adapt their actions appropriately; paying attention to the present, being more in touch with their physical bodies, truly empathising with others, and calming their urge for novelty in order to just "be" with people.

Magician

ENFPs realise that their drive for inspiration and their unwavering optimism is ego-driven and a distraction from their true self. They will also be more accepting of others being who and what they are, realising that encouraging others to develop, not understanding why people would not want to develop new ideas, is also a function of their

> own ego.
>
> Being able to let go of dualities, they will see that Intuition is part of the same concept as Sensing, and that Feeling is part of the same concept as Thinking, seeing the similarities in the functions rather than the differences and therefore being able to gain easy and natural access to S and T. At this stage, they may also frequently experience the transcendent function – where from two apparent opposites a third way emerges, often in a form that is symbolic or intuitive.

ENTJ

Hierarchy of Functions:

Dominant: Extraverted Thinking

Auxiliary: Introverted Intuition

Tertiary: Sensing

Inferior: Introverted Feeling

Main Features and Distortions of the ENTJ Type:

ENTJs see logical systems, enjoy achieving outcomes and getting things done.

They can worry about their own competence and have an intolerance of others' perceived incompetence, becoming judgemental, dismissive and domineering.

Conflicting Functions:

Introverted Thinking, as the opposite orientation to the dominant, is likely to be perceived as slow, unproductive, procrastinating, avoiding making decisions, overly perfectionistic, and generally dull.

Introverted Feeling, as their inferior function, is likely to be perceived as pointless, oversensitive, sentimental, time-wasting, unproductive, weak and submissive.

Extraverted Feeling, as the contrast to the dominant function, is likely to be perceived as overly emotional and controlling.

The Shadows of Type

Core Values: Competence, resilience and achievement

Power and Control

ENTJs who are operating at this level of development are likely to respond to most situations using a distortion of their dominant Extraverted Thinking preference and will often be seen as arrogant, aggressive, detached and confrontational. They will use their auxiliary Introverted Intuition to look for potential improvements and have a keen critical eye, however this can lead to opinionated criticism about what is wrong with everything and how it could be better. As Extraverted types, they will argue and challenge relentlessly in an attempt to shout down those who they are in conflict with and can appear overpowering, unwilling to listen and condescending.

In the workplace they like to be in charge and, if they are not in a position of power, they may attempt to undermine the decisions or ideas of others. As subordinates they can be difficult to manage as they will focus in on any fault they perceive in their boss and make judgements on the boss's competence. If they are feeling threatened, particularly in terms of their authority or competence, they may play ego-defensive survival games that involve criticising the logic of others, even countering with an illogical viewpoint just to be adversarial, using unemotional logical rationalisations or avoidance of showing others anything that they consider to be imperfect for fear of judgements of incompetence.

At this level, they easily fall into bullying behaviours, may enjoy belittling those who they perceive as weak, or can deliberately try to make others feel incompetent. It is essential for them, at this level, to maintain an image of being strong and independent so they will often suppress or hide any signs of vulnerability or inability. They may be unaware of how others may be different to them and merely see them as being wrong or ineffective in some way.

Social Identification

Whether ENTJs find themselves in type-supportive or non-supportive groups, they will often try to get into a position of leadership or at least influence within the group. If they are not the group leader, they are likely to only want to follow a leader they look up to and respect. They will use their natural preferences to defend other group members and fight for their "team" as required, however they may also be condescending and belittling towards those that they see as weak or as

The Developmentally Levelled Type Descriptions

a threat to them. In general, they will be desperate never to lose face or be seen as incompetent or weak in front of others.

If their ENTJ characteristics do not "fit" they may suppress their natural styles and make clumsy use of their underdeveloped non-preferred functions, often channelling them through their Te and Ni preferences. For example, trying to do something nice and kind for somebody by giving them a gift that will help them to improve themselves.

Personal Identification

ENTJs at this level begin to channel their dominant Extraverted Thinking into their lives and work; seeking challenges, noticing opportunities to make improvements and generally "getting things done" in an action-oriented, decisive and logical manner. Whatever they do, they will want to be better than everybody else and can be fairly competitive. They will prefer to work in environments that allow a degree of independence and power, and will often look for positions of leadership or responsibility.

However they may push their type preferences too strongly at times and become demanding, impatient, domineering, insensitive, bitterly sarcastic, bossy, controlling and forceful. They will want everybody to work in the same way that they do and to the same standards, so may also find it difficult to trust others enough to delegate and have trouble letting go of their tasks and assignments.

They will have a generally good idea about the kind of person they are and will notice the differences between themselves and others, however they are likely to regard the different styles of others as failings and weaknesses. For example they will not understand why people with Feeling preferences get so personally involved, and will see their subjectivity as weakness and as a flaw in their functioning; or they will regard people with Perceiving preferences as frustratingly indecisive and even lazy.

In dealing with others they will be quick to give remedial feedback but overlook opportunities for praise and appreciation. They may also deliver harsh truths in the spirit of helping the other person to improve, but not realise the impact of the blunt delivery of the message. A common phrase used by ENTJs at this level is "I don't suffer fools".

Determined Action

At this level, ENTJs really begin to use the strengths of their preferences and will be analytical, systematic, and forward-thinking. They will have high aspirations and strive for improved efficiency and the implementation of plans and initiatives. In dealing with others they will be fair, appropriately challenging, directive, and encouraging.

They will realise that they have some blind spots in terms of their attention to detail, ability to stick with routine tasks and interpersonal sensitivity, and they are likely to begin to realise that there is some value to be gained from S and F ways of thinking. Therefore, they may seek viewpoints from those they see as different to themselves, however they will only incorporate these ideas if they do not go against their preferences too strongly. For example, a person with an Introverted Sensing preference may suggest investing some time carrying out research prior to a change initiative, and the ENTJ may rationalise that, whilst this information may have some use, forward-thinking and working toward a vision would be more effective because, in truth, they find the idea de-energising and damaging to the momentum of the change initiative.

At this stage the ENTJ will also still struggle to understand their conflicting functions – Introverted Thinking, Introverted Feeling and Extraverted Feeling. There is an interest in self-improvement at this level, and the ENTJ will seek feedback from others, often focusing more on the "valuable" negative feedback than the positive feedback as it is addressing the negatives that will lead to improvement. ENTJs operating at this level will be effective in the workplace, however they will still overuse rationalisation and logic and overlook personal connectedness.

Considerate Individualism

ENTJs at this level of development will move away from using the strengths of their type to achieve tangible goals, and move towards using these strengths to facilitate progress. They will be conceptual and strategic in their approach, beginning to enjoy the journey of their auxiliary Introverted Intuition rather than rushing towards their destination. They will start to allow perceived imperfections and incompletion to occur and will select the challenges they wish to engage in rather than attempting to take on everything. They no longer thrive on recognition for their achievements, but enjoy being and learning.

As their self-awareness develops, they will become aware of the shadow sides of their preferences (the characteristics of the lower levels) and become mindful observers of their processes. Toning down their Te and Ni preferences allows more access to their non-preferred sides, however their use of these are likely to be channelled via their Te and Ni preferences. For example, when considering the impact of an action on people (F), they will conceptualise it in terms of the logical benefits – contented workers are more productive so it is important to address the people issues. Nevertheless, they will see the real value inherent in the S and F approach.

Interpersonally, they will coach and facilitate others, encouraging others to find their own direction, rather than lead and mentor. ENTJs may feel as if they are becoming incompetent or ineffective at times because, where they previously thought that they knew all the answers, they will now often encounter situations where they can accept a number of different viewpoints and not reach a clear and logical conclusion.

Integration and Authenticity

At this level, the qualities of the ENTJ preferences can shine through – objectivity, focus, vision, synthesis of ideas, enthusiasm and commitment. The ENTJ can appear to be a visionary thinker, able to see the potential in others, even those who are different to themselves, and nurture and guide them. Although they recognise that people are responsible for their own development, they can still become impatient with people who do not seem to be striving towards this.

At this level, they become comfortable with the fact that they do not have to try to reach conclusions and can be content with ambiguity and open-endedness. They are no longer concerned with defending their image of competence and independence and enjoy the learning they get from being with a variety of other people. Through increased mindfulness, they will often be able to access their S and F preferences and adapt their actions appropriately; paying attention to the present, being more in touch with their physical bodies, truly empathising with others, and stopping their drive to action in order to just "be" with people.

Magician

ENTJs realise that their drive for continuous improvement towards becoming the best that they can be via their achievements and visionary thinking is ego-driven and a distraction from their true self.

The Shadows of Type

> They will also be more accepting of others being who and what they are, realising that encouraging others to develop, not understanding why people would not want to strive to be their best, is also a function of their own ego. Being able to let go of dualities, they will see that Feeling is part of the same concept as Thinking, and that Sensing is part of the same concept as Intuition, seeing the similarities in the functions rather than the differences and therefore being able to gain easy and natural access to S and F. At this stage, they may also frequently experience the transcendent function – where from two apparent opposites a third way emerges, often in a form that is symbolic or intuitive.

ENTP

Hierarchy of Functions:

Dominant: Extraverted Intuition

Auxiliary: Introverted Thinking

Tertiary: Feeling

Inferior: Introverted Sensing

Main Features and Distortions of the ENTP Type:

ENTPs look to the outer environment to inspire new ideas and possibilities for solving problems or making improvements.

They can become novelty-seeking, scattered, condescending, easily bored and slow to take purposeful action.

Conflicting Functions:

Introverted Intuition, as the opposite orientation to the dominant, is likely to be perceived as limiting, lacking in novelty, isolative and inflexible.

Introverted Sensing, as their inferior function, is likely to be perceived as slow, lacking in excitement or inspiration, pointless, overly perfectionistic, and generally dull.

The Developmentally Levelled Type Descriptions

Extraverted Sensing, as the contrast to the dominant function, may be seen as reckless and focused on immediate gratification.

Core Values: Innovation, competence and efficiency

Power and Control

At this level ENTPs are likely to react to most situations using a distortion of their dominant Extraverted Intuition preference and will often be seen as brash, rebellious, hasty and novelty-seeking. They will use their auxiliary Introverted Thinking to look for flaws and imperfections, however this can lead to blunt and often inappropriately positioned suggestions as to how things should be changed to make them better. As Extraverted types, they will argue and challenge relentlessly in an attempt to shout down those who they are in conflict with and can appear confrontational, unwilling to listen, abrasive and condescending.

ENTPs enjoy challenging the status quo and playing devil's advocate, however, when operating at this level, they can become relentlessly adversarial and unwilling to drop an argument, often using distorted logic to try and push their viewpoint. At times they may initiate a debate by spontaneously saying something controversial just to get a reaction or push others' buttons. In the workplace they like to be independent and work in their own, unrestricted manner, and, as subordinates they can be difficult to manage as they will focus in on any fault they perceive in their boss and make judgements on the boss's competence.

If they are feeling threatened, particularly in terms of their ability to pursue novelty and stimulation, they may play ego-defensive survival games that involve criticising the logic of others, using unemotional logical rationalisations or avoidance of showing others anything that they consider to be imperfect for fear of judgements of incompetence. They may also get into a trap of hastily embarking on new ideas without due consideration and jumping from one thing to another without completion. They may be unaware of how others may be different to them and merely see them as being wrong or misguided in some way, and they can be somewhat more likely than other types at this level to be unaware of or inconsiderate of their impact on others.

Social Identification

Whether ENTPs find themselves in type-supportive or non-supportive groups, they will often try to get into a position of influence within the group but not necessarily want to be in the main leadership position. If they are not the group leader, they are likely to only want to follow a leader they look up to and respect. They will often take the role of leading others in the group to have fun or even get up to mischief. It will be important for them not to appear conformist or dull so they will often "conform" to groups and ideals that are seen as new, exciting, interesting and not mainstream; however they are likely to have a condescending attitude to anybody they perceive as ordinary or conformist.

Often, ENTPs consider their "group" as being superior to others. If their ENTP characteristics do not "fit" they may suppress their natural styles and make clumsy use of their underdeveloped non-preferred functions, often channelling them through their Ne and Ti preferences. For example, trying to do something nice and kind for somebody by giving them a gift that is intended to be fun and humorous but is actually somewhat offensive or misplaced.

Personal Identification

ENTPs at this level begin to channel their dominant Extraverted Intuition into their lives and work; looking for new initiatives, generating new ideas, scanning the environment for inspiration and seeking improvements in an energetic and often light-hearted/humorous manner. Whatever they do, they will want to be seen as original and innovative and can be fairly competitive with others in this arena. They will prefer to work in environments that allow a high degree of independence and will often look for positions that challenge their intellect, but without being so laden with responsibility or structure that they cannot enjoy themselves.

However they may push their type preferences too strongly at times and become novelty-seeking, easily bored, interrogative, opinionated, impatient, uninhibited, abrupt and impulsive. They may also become scattered in their approach to work and lack completion, implementation or follow through on their actions. In their interactions with others they may be outspoken, flippant, glib, overly competitive and seek to be centre of attention.

They will have a generally good idea about the kind of person they are and will notice the differences between themselves and others, however they are likely to regard the different styles of others as failings and weaknesses. For example, they will not understand why people with Sensing preferences feel the need to check out information and require a degree of surety about their actions, seeing this as an inability to be flexible or independent-minded; or they will regard people with Judging preferences as somewhat uptight. In dealing with others they will be quick to give critical advice but overlook opportunities for praise and appreciation. They may also deliver harsh truths in the spirit of helping the other person to improve, but not realise the impact of the blunt delivery of the message.

Determined Action

ENTPs at this level really begin to use the strengths of their preferences and will be versatile, questioning, energetic, rational, objective and curious. They will be change-oriented, aware of future possibilities, analytical and comfortable with taking appropriate risks. They will realise that they have some blind spots in terms of their attention to detail, their motivation to stick with a task to completion and their interpersonal sensitivity, and they are likely to begin to realise that there is some value to be gained from S and F ways of thinking. Therefore, they may seek viewpoints from those they see as different to themselves, however they will only incorporate these ideas if they do not go against their own preferences too strongly. For example, a person with an Introverted Sensing preference may suggest investing some time carrying out research prior to a change initiative, and the ENTP may rationalise that, whilst this information may have some use, forward-thinking, inspiration and innovation would be more effective because, in truth, they find the idea de-energising and damaging to the momentum of the change initiative.

At this stage the ENTP will also still struggle to understand their conflicting functions – Introverted Intuition, Introverted Sensing and Extraverted Sensing. There is an interest in self-improvement at this level, and the ENTP will seek feedback from others, often focusing more on the "valuable" negative feedback than the positive feedback as it is addressing the negatives that will lead to improvement.

ENTPs operating at this level will be effective in the workplace provided they have a degree of freedom and flexibility; however they will still feel confined by schedules and procedures and not always consider emotional implications or details. It is not unusual for ENTPs at this level to consider working for themselves in some capacity.

Considerate Individualism

At this level of development ENTPs will move away from using the strengths of their type to look for new or different ideas, and move towards using these strengths to be innovative, creative and entrepreneurial. They will be conceptual and strategic in their approach, making good use of their auxiliary Introverted Thinking and critically evaluating their ideas; implementing them only when they have been carefully considered. In dealing with other people their enthusiasm and positive energy can be infectious and inspiring to others. They will be constructively challenging rather than just being critical, and they will seek opportunities rather than novelty. They no longer thrive on recognition for their originality and spontaneity, and are likely to feel more content with "what is" instead of constantly seeking "what could be".

As their self-awareness develops, they will become aware of the shadow sides of their preferences (the characteristics of the lower levels) and become mindful observers of their processes. Toning down their Ne and Ti preferences allows more access to their non-preferred sides, however their use of these are still likely to be channelled via their Ne and Ti preferences. For example, when considering the impact of an action on people (F), they will conceptualise it in terms of the logical benefits – contented workers are more productive so it is important to address the people issues. Nevertheless, they will see the real value inherent in the S and F approach.

Interpersonally, they will coach and facilitate others, encouraging others to find their own direction, rather than wanting everybody to follow their way of thinking. They may enjoy positions of non-bureaucratic leadership and, in general, they will enjoy being challenged.

Integration and Authenticity

At this level, the qualities of the ENTP preferences can shine through – they will be seen as innovative, resourceful, imaginative, enterprising, ingenious, adaptable and insightful. The ENTP can appear to be a visionary thinker; seeing patterns that may not be obvious to others, creating global solutions and being quick to respond to changes in the environment. They often take the role of catalysts for change because of their visionary approach. They are likely to be able to see the potential in others, even those who are different to themselves, and often be skilled at motivating others, as many ENTPs at this level are good at reading people.

At this level, they become comfortable with the fact that they do not have to try to be different or original and can be comfortable with and appreciative of stability. They are no longer concerned with defending their image of originality and independence and enjoy the learning they get from being with a variety of other people. Through increased mindfulness, they will often be able to access their S and F preferences and adapt their actions appropriately; paying attention to the present, being more in touch with their physical bodies, truly empathising with others, and calming their urge for novelty in order to just "be" with people.

Magician

ENTPs realise that their drive for originality, innovation and improvement is ego-driven and a distraction from their true self. They will also be more accepting of others being who and what they are, realising that encouraging others to develop, not understanding why people would not want to strive to be original, is also a function of their own ego.

Being able to let go of dualities, they will see that Feeling is part of the same concept as Thinking, and that Sensing is part of the same concept as Intuition, seeing the similarities in the functions rather than the differences and therefore being able to gain easy and natural access to S and F. At this stage, they may also frequently experience the transcendent function – where from two apparent opposites a third way emerges, often in a form that is symbolic or intuitive.

ESFJ

Hierarchy of Functions:

Dominant: Extraverted Feeling

Auxiliary: Introverted Sensing

Tertiary: Intuition

Inferior: Introverted Thinking

Main Features and Distortions of the ESFJ Type:

ESFJs put plans and actions in place that involve helping others or bringing others together.

They can become overbearing and intrusive towards others and oversensitive to the comments and opinions of others. They may put others before themselves or become "martyrs" to others.

Conflicting Functions:

Introverted Feeling, as the opposite orientation to the dominant, is likely to be perceived as idealistic, "do-gooding", and not actually taking any useful or practical action to help others.

Introverted Thinking, as their inferior function, is likely to be perceived as cold, detached, selfish, of no use to other people.

Extraverted Thinking, as the contrast to the dominant function, is likely to be perceived as overbearing and cold, detached and uncaring.

Core Values: Generosity, secure relationships and harmony

Power and Control

At this level of development ESFJs are likely to respond to most situations using a distortion of their dominant Extraverted Feeling preference and will often be seen as interfering, hypersensitive, meddling, and needy. In combination with their auxiliary Introverted Sensing, ESFJs can be protective of traditions, particularly those involving family or friends, keen to maintain high standards, be seen to do the right thing, and try to help and protect those who are important to them, however this can lead to them being pernickety, overly conventional, obsessive, change-resistant, intrusive, and gossipy about others who do not uphold the same standards as they do.

As Extraverted Feelers, they tend to shy away from direct conflict with others, but will tend to deal with their enemies by viciously gossiping about them and being judgemental about them, rarely expressing their true feelings to the individual concerned in a direct manner. In the workplace they like to be part of a cohesive group and are likely to try to be influential in the group, although not an obvious out-front leader. As subordinates, they will be relatively diligent provided that they agree with the way in which the boss operates on an interpersonal level; if not they are likely to criticise the boss indirectly by expressing their disdain to others, usually trying to win support for their views.

ESFJs at this level are usually fairly pleasant towards others provided that they are getting their own way. With people who they are wary of they may always be on guard and looking to be offended or find opportunities to be judgemental; for this reason they often misinterpret what others may say and selectively attend to the parts that could be potentially offensive. At other times, they may go to the opposite extreme and be blindly optimistic, denying any obvious negatives in a situation.

If they are feeling threatened or insecure, particularly in situations where they are not getting support for their plans or when they are feeling personally affronted, they may play ego-defensive survival games that involve criticising others, nagging, complaining, self-pitying or becoming overprotective towards others. These survival games are attempts at manipulating others to get their own way, trying to get people involved with them, or trying to shed some of their responsibilities. They are usually played out at an unconscious level. They are likely to be unaware of how others may be different to them and merely see difference as being wrong or selfish in some way, taking what they see of others at a surface level.

Social Identification

Part of the SJ temperament is a concern for belonging and being seen to do the right (i.e. socially acceptable) thing. Therefore, at this level SJs will naturally gravitate to the idea of upholding norms, traditions and belonging to groups. ESFJs will usually attempt to be influential within a group and often take on the role of the co-ordinator of activities, the mediator of disagreements and the "agony aunt/uncle". They will use their natural preferences to support other group members and will be very sensitive to the degree of harmony within the group. However they may also be indirectly critical about or dismissive towards those that they see as anti-social, non-conformist or not fully committed. In general, they will be desperate never to lose face in front of others or be seen to have let others down.

If ESFJs end up being in groups that do not support their natural styles, they may desperately try to fit in by creating new rules or norms in their minds. They may suppress their natural styles and make clumsy use of their underdeveloped non-preferred functions, often channelling them through their Fe and Si preferences, such as trying to resolve what they perceive to be a conflict situation by telling those involved to simply stop arguing and make up. However, in general, they are more likely to avoid getting involved with people they consider to be different to the norm and will seek out type-alike or type-supportive groups.

As their preferences often fit with widely accepted social norms, ESFJs rarely feel like or appear to be misfits. ESFJs at this level can be very critical of "out-groups" and see them as subversive or as simply just "wrong".

Personal Identification

ESFJs operating at this level begin to use their preferences fairly effectively in their lives and work. They are likely to be hard-working, precise, diligent, enjoy pleasing others, thorough, structured, helpful and loyal. Whatever they do, they will want to do right by others and may get obsessive about the finer details. They will prefer to work in environments that have some degree of structure and clear role definitions, and where there is a good sense of team spirit and harmony. However they may push their type preferences too strongly at times and become judgemental of others, moralistic, inflexible, pernickety, bossy, controlling and forceful. They will want everybody to work in the same way that they do and to the same standards, so may also find it difficult to trust others enough to delegate without subsequent interference. Their focus is likely to be fixed on organising others and maintaining a level of harmony and, as such, they may become overly concerned with people pleasing, easily hurt or offended, conflict avoidant, have loss of boundaries, be too accepting, and inappropriately put others first.

They will have a generally good idea about the kind of person they are and will notice the differences between themselves and others; however they are likely to regard the different styles of others as undesirable or "weird". For example they will not understand how people with Thinking preferences can make decisions that are not acceptable to everybody and will see their logical detachment as uncaring, harsh or selfish; or they will regard people with Perceiving preferences as lacking in effort and commitment. In dealing with others they will be quick to give advice and sympathy but will shy away from delivering feedback that they perceive to be negative. They will want overt appreciation from others for their actions and may feel easily offended if this is not forthcoming.

Determined Action

ESFJs really begin to use the strengths of their preferences at this level and will be enthusiastic, orderly, appreciative, empathic, inclusive, concerned and co-operative. They will have high standards and often go the extra mile to ensure things are "just so". In dealing with others they will be empathic, supportive, caring and encouraging. They are often seen as the "social glue" in a group or team, however at times they may become competitive. Although ESFJs operating at this level are generally effective in the workplace, they will still have a tendency to get over involved with personal issues and put their personal convictions above objective logic. They are also likely to be too hasty in attempting to get plans in place, spend a considerable amount of time trying to get consensus decisions, and have a dislike for ambiguity or lack of clarity.

They will realise that they have some blind spots in terms of their awareness of the wider or future implications of their actions, their ability to quickly adapt to change and their discomfort with objective decision making, and they are likely to begin to realise that there is some value to be gained from N and T ways of thinking. Therefore, they may seek viewpoints from those they see as different to themselves; however they will only incorporate these ideas if they do not go too strongly against their own preferences.

At this stage the ESFJ will also still struggle to understand their conflicting functions – Introverted Feeling, Introverted Thinking and Extraverted Thinking. There is an interest in self-improvement at this level, and the ESFJ will seek feedback from others; needing a balance of positives and negatives to feel motivated to try to learn from the feedback.

Considerate Individualism

ESFJs at this level of development will move away from using the strengths of their type to orchestrate the activities of others, and move towards using these strengths to support, guide and facilitate the activities of others. They will be caring, energetic, reasonable, responsible, dedicated, organised and procedural in their approach, beginning to enjoy the journey of their auxiliary Introverted Sensing, taking time to reflect on realistic information and experience rather than rushing towards getting plans in place. They will start to allow more flexibility and variety to be part of their way of operating and may let others take on the co-ordinating or mediating role, rather than attempting to take responsibility for everything.

They no longer thrive on appreciation and gratitude from others, but enjoy being helpful to others with little payback. They may become concerned with whether or not their actions really make a difference to others and begin to seek a greater purpose from their work. Interpersonally, they will coach and support others, encouraging others to find their own direction, rather than feeling like they have to protect or nurture them. Others are likely to describe them as tactful, realistic, reliable and consistent.

As their self-awareness develops, they will become aware of the shadow sides of their preferences (the characteristics of the lower levels) and become mindful observers of their processes. Toning down their Fe and Si preferences allows more access to their non-preferred sides, however their use of these is likely to be channelled via their Fe and Si preferences. For example, when making an objective majority decision they may conceptualise it as "this time there are some losers, but they will get their way another time".

Nevertheless, they will see the real value inherent in the N and T approach. The ESFJ may feel as if they are losing their sense of values or surety at times because, where they previously thought that they knew what the right way was, they will now often encounter situations where they can accept a number of different viewpoints and not reach a clear and acceptable conclusion.

Integration and Authenticity

At this level, the qualities of the ESFJ preferences can shine through – loyalty, generosity, consistency, warmth, decisiveness, clarity and confidence about their values. The ESFJ at this level will be seen by others as sociable, outgoing, caring, genuine in their interactions and content with themselves. They will lead by example, delegate effectively, enjoy discussing others' views and opinions and be able to create a spirit of genuine team cohesiveness, as well as dealing with difficult interpersonal issues and differences. Although they recognise that not everybody can like everybody else, they may still find those who do not attempt to create harmony frustrating.

At this level, they become comfortable with the fact that they do not have to be the "social glue" in a group, and they can be more content with spontaneity and disharmony than they had previously been. They are no longer concerned with defending their image of being caring, nurturing and helpful and enjoy the learning they get from being with a variety of other people. Through increased mindfulness, they will often be able to access their N and T preferences and adapt their actions appropriately. By not investing so much energy in being concerned with the affairs of others, they can pay real attention to the present and enjoy the moment without always trying to organise and perfect it.

Magician

ESFJs realise that their drive to organise, to do the right thing by others and to be seen as helpful and caring is ego-driven and a distraction from their true self. They will also be more accepting of others being who and what they are, realising that being concerned with trying to make others maintain harmony and work together cohesively, is also a function of their own ego. Being able to let go of dualities, they will see that Thinking is part of the same concept as Feeling, and that Intuition is part of the same concept as Sensing, seeing the similarities in the functions rather than the differences and therefore being able to gain easy and natural access to N and T. At this stage, they may also frequently experience the transcendent function – where from two apparent opposites a third way emerges, often in a form that is symbolic or intuitive.

ESFP

Hierarchy of Functions:

Dominant: Extraverted Sensing

Auxiliary: Introverted Feeling

Tertiary: Thinking

Inferior: Introverted Intuition

Main Features and Distortions of the ESFP Type:

ESFPs live for the moment, are fun loving and enjoy being with others.

They can become thrill seeking, scattered and create small crises in order to stimulate excitement.

Conflicting Functions:

Introverted Sensing, as the opposite orientation to the dominant, is likely to be perceived as dull, pointless and a distraction from appreciating the here and now.

Introverted Intuition, as their inferior function, is likely to be perceived as spending time being concerned about things that are not important and looking for patterns that are of little practical use compared to living in the moment.

Extraverted Intuition, as the contrast to the dominant function, is likely to be seen as impractical, ungrounded and intangible.

Core Values: Freedom, optimism and experiencing life

Power and Control

ESFPs functioning at this level will often appear to be brash, hyperactive, reckless and hedonistic as they tend to react to most situations using a distortion of their dominant Extraverted Sensing. They will use their auxiliary Introverted Feeling to consider their actions in the light of their inner values and how others will be affected; however this can often lead to them taking impulsive actions that aim to lighten the mood or create fun for themselves and others, ignoring or disregarding any serious aspects to the situation – often being somewhat overwhelming and taking no notice of others' objections. As Extraverted types, they will be persistent when they are trying to persuade others, often talking over others, becoming loud and not listening to others. As they do not like direct conflict ESFPs will rarely be explicit about wanting to get their own way, but will instead be overwhelmingly relentless in trying to encourage others to their way of thinking, sometimes becoming repetitive and dogmatic.

ESFPs enjoy action, fun, stimulation and dealing with sudden crises, however when they are under-stimulated they may create crisis situations or over dramatise a problem just to get a buzz. In the workplace they like to be part of a friendly team and will often be the entertainer in a group ("class clown" when at school), but they can be vicious in their mocking of people who they consider to be "nerdy" or uptight. They may also get pleasure from making others feel embarrassed. As subordinates they will need the freedom to work in their own way and can be deliberately disruptive if they are in structured or rule-bound settings.

If they are feeling defensive, particularly in cases where their freedom or enjoyment are being threatened, they may play ego-defensive survival games such as throwing tantrums, becoming violent or undertaking risky/thrill-seeking behaviours in order to create excitement for themselves and make those around them feel uncomfortable. They may also get into a trap of impulsively taking actions based on immediate needs, getting bored before completing tasks, and lacking the motivation to commit to anything or anybody. They can be overindulgent in activities, food, drink, etc and be reluctant to admit when they are feeling like they are spinning out of control. Although they consider themselves to be sensitive to other people, they are likely to be unaware of how others really may be as their perceptions of other people will be distorted by their own preferences.

Social Identification

ESFPs are often naturally sensitive to being in friendly and supportive atmospheres, but are also aware that they do not always fit into groups or cultures; for example schools and offices can often feel too restrictive and "serious". For this reason, they will tend to take the role of the entertainer and creator of fun and, sometimes, mischief in a group. Despite this tendency to stand out from the crowd, they will still be intensely concerned with what others may be thinking of them and if they are liked.

In general, ESFPs enjoy being part of a group and working with others, and can be excellent team players. However they can be bitterly judgemental about people who they see as being different to themselves and harshly mocking of others without necessarily meaning to cause any offence. As they tend to be naturally optimistic and like to look on the bright side, they can be repelled by people who are "pessimistic" (realistic), sarcastic or detached.

Personal Identification

ESFPs at this level begin to channel their dominant Extraverted Sensing into their lives and work; being spontaneously responsive to problems and observant about the realities or a situation with an optimistic and "anything is possible" attitude. In working with others they often bring energy and enthusiasm to a situation and can point out details and observations that others may miss or be unaware of. They will usually be seen as friendly, appreciative, concerned for others, inclusive and fun-loving. They are often keen to work with others and promote a sense of team spirit, but can become frustrated with people who they do not consider to be enthusiastic enough about the team's activities.

At times they may still push their type preferences too strongly and become hypersensitive, impulsive, excitement-seeking and easily distracted. They may also find themselves starting new initiatives with enthusiasm and energy, and then getting quickly bored and lacking motivation to complete the project. If they have an exciting idea they can often be selective in their attention to any downsides and ignore process, detail or limitations that may prevent them from taking action. They may also attempt to manipulate rules to suit their needs, or oversimplify things to justify their actions or intentions.

ESFPs at this level will have a generally good idea about the kind of person they are and will notice the differences between themselves and others; however they are likely to regard the different styles of others as undesirable or dull and un-exciting. For example they will not understand how people with T preferences can make decisions that are not acceptable to everybody and will see their logical detachment as uncaring, harsh or selfish; or they will regard people with N preferences as being out of touch with reality.

Determined Action

ESFPs at this level really begin to use the strengths of their preferences and will be observant, practical, realistic, active and enthusiastic. With others they will come across as empathic, warm, sympathetic, supportive and fun. They can also make fairly effective mediators, not dismissing or ignoring conflict, but trying to find points of consensus. If they have positions of leadership or influence they will be co-operative and inclusive in their approach, attempting to bring about consensus and harmony. They will realise that they have some blind spots in terms of their awareness of longer-term implications and their motivation to look for connections and patterns. They may also experience demotivation and frustration when having to work alone or on repetitive tasks.

At this level they are likely to begin to realise the value that can be gained from N and T ways of working. Therefore, they may seek viewpoints from those they see as different to themselves, however they will only incorporate these ideas if they do not go against their own preferences too strongly. At this stage the ESFP will also still struggle to understand their conflicting functions – Introverted Sensing, Introverted Intuition and Extraverted Intuition.

ESFPs at this level will begin to take an interest in what makes them and others tick and will seek feedback from others, needing encouragement from the positive aspects of the feedback balanced with developmental suggestions to inspire them to learn and grow. ESFPs operating at this level will be effective in the workplace provided they have a degree of freedom and flexibility; however they will still feel confined by schedules and procedures and de-motivated by having to consider potential negatives or downsides.

Considerate Individualism

At this level of development ESFPs will move away from using their preferences to fire-fight and respond to immediate crises, and move towards using these strengths for troubleshooting, resolving conflict, mediating and taking considered risks. They will be adaptable, easygoing and perceptive, using their auxiliary Introverted Feeling to evaluate their ideas and initiate actions that they consider to be congruent with what is really important to them. Instead of switching their energy from one activity to the next, they will begin to be more focused and considered about what they are doing, taking action only when the purpose has been carefully considered. In their interactions with others they will be tactful, considerate, generous and playful.

They no longer thrive on recognition for their liveliness and entertainment value, and are likely to feel more comfortable with stillness and contemplation than they had previously been. As their self-awareness develops, they will become aware of the shadow sides of their preferences (the characteristics of the lower levels) and become mindful observers of their processes. As a type that is typically easily distracted and externally focused, this ability to self-monitor will have a quieting effect on their outward appearance. This will enable them to become better mentors and coaches to any individuals they may be leading or working with.

Toning down their Se and Fi preferences allows more access to their non-preferred sides, however their use of these are still likely to be channelled via their Se and Fi preferences. For example, when considering how to get the best results they will view this result as being the one that everybody can get on board with. Nevertheless, they will see the real value inherent in the N and T approach. They will have a real appreciation for being in the moment and living for today but without a disregard for consequences or the impact on others. At this level, ESFPs will begin to feel comfortable dropping their optimistic mask from time to time and allowing others to see their true feelings.

Integration and Authenticity

At this level, the qualities of the ESFP preferences can shine through – they will be seen as expedient, resourceful, secure and exuberant. The ESFP can appear to be free and easygoing; loving life, enjoying the world and radiating a sense of freedom. They will be very aware of interpersonal dynamics and will be effective at motivating others through their optimism, enthusiasm and encouragement. They will also be genuinely accepting and tolerant of the imperfections and flaws in others; being empathic and considerate in how they approach them.

At this level, they become comfortable with the fact that they do not have to try to be lively and entertaining and can be comfortable with and appreciative of being a quiet observer or participant. They are no longer concerned with defending their image of carefree spontaneity and enjoy the learning they get from being with a variety of other people, including those who they previously had little appreciation for. Through increased mindfulness, they will often be able to access their N and T preferences and adapt their actions appropriately; giving consideration to future possibilities, truly empathising with others, and calming their urge for excitement in order to just "be" with people.

Magician

ESFPs realise that their drive for excitement and their unwavering optimism is ego-driven and a distraction from their true self. They will also be more accepting of others being who and what they are, realising that encouraging others to live for the day, and not

> understanding why people would be concerned with "what might be" is also a function of their own ego.
>
> Being able to let go of dualities, they will see that Sensing is part of the same concept as Intuition, and that Feeling is part of the same concept as Thinking, seeing the similarities in the functions rather than the differences and therefore being able to gain easy and natural access to their N and T sides. At this stage, they may also frequently experience the transcendent function – where from two apparent opposites a third way emerges, often in a form that is symbolic or intuitive.

ESTJ

Hierarchy of Functions:

Dominant: Extraverted Thinking

Auxiliary: Introverted Sensing

Tertiary: Intuition

Inferior: Introverted Feeling

Main Features and Distortions of the ESTJ Type:

ESTJs are action-oriented, seek efficiency in carrying out tasks, and are pragmatic.

They can become impatient to take action and inflexible once they have made up their minds.

Conflicting Functions:

Introverted Thinking, as the opposite orientation to the dominant, is likely to be perceived as slow, unproductive, procrastinating, avoiding making decisions, overly perfectionistic, and generally dull.

Introverted Feeling, as their inferior function, is likely to be perceived as pointless, oversensitive, sentimental, time-wasting, unproductive, weak and submissive.

Extraverted Feeling, as the contrast to the dominant function, is likely to be perceived as overly emotional and controlling.

Core Values: Results, pragmatism and efficiency

Power and Control

ESTJs who are operating at this level of development are likely to respond to most situations using a distortion of their dominant Extraverted Thinking preference and will often be seen as arrogant, aggressive, dogmatic and confrontational. They will use their auxiliary Introverted Sensing to look for inefficiencies and to notice impracticalities, however this can lead to opinionated criticism, inadaptability and stubborn rejection of any new ideas or changes ("this is the way it has to be"). As Extraverted types, they will argue relentlessly, often repeating themselves or going into excessive detail, in an attempt to shout down those who they are in conflict with and can appear overpowering, unwilling to listen and condescending.

In the workplace they like to be in charge and, at this level, may micro-manage or be overly directive, now allowing others to try new approaches or adaptations. As subordinates, they will be relatively diligent provided that they agree with the direction the boss is setting; if not they are likely to criticise the boss and try to do things their own way which, of course, they perceive as being the right and only way. ESTJs at this level are often insensitive towards others, and will usually just "say it as it is" with no consideration or care about how others may be affected.

If they are feeling threatened or insecure, particularly in situations where there is uncertainty, inefficiency or ambiguity, they may play ego-defensive survival games that involve criticising, nagging, complaining, self-pitying or being victim to physical ailments. These survival games are attempts at manipulating others to get their own way, trying to get people involved with them, or trying to shed some of their responsibilities. They are usually played out at an unconscious level. At this level, they easily fall into bullying behaviours, may enjoy belittling those who they perceive as weak, or can deliberately try to make others feel incompetent. It is essential for them, at this level, to maintain an image of being strong so they will often suppress or hide any signs of vulnerability or inability. They are likely to be unaware of how others may be different to them and merely see difference as being wrong or ineffective in some way, taking what they see of others at a surface level.

Social Identification

Part of the SJ temperament is a concern for belonging and being seen to do the right (i.e. socially acceptable) thing. Therefore, at this level SJs will naturally gravitate to the idea of upholding norms, traditions and belonging to groups. However, ESTJs will often try to get into a position of leadership or control within a group. They will use their natural preferences to support other group members and often try to co-ordinate the activities of the group members, however they may also be condescending and belittling towards those that they see as weak, non-conformist or incompetent. In general, they will be desperate never to lose face or be seen to have made a mistake or be weak in front of others.

If ESTJs end up being in groups that do not support their natural styles, they may desperately try to fit in by creating new rules or norms in their minds. They may suppress their natural styles and make clumsy use of their underdeveloped non-preferred functions, often channelling them through their Te and Si preferences, such as trying to help somebody by telling them exactly what they need to do, usually based on a single example of their own or other person's experience. However, in general, they are more likely to avoid getting involved with people they consider to be different to the norm and will seek out type-alike or type-supportive groups.

As their preferences often fit with widely accepted social norms, ESTJs rarely feel like or appear to be misfits and generally have little trouble fitting in. ESTJs at this level can be very critical of "out-groups" and see them as subversive or as simply just "wrong".

Personal Identification

ESTJs at this level begin to use their preferences fairly effectively in their lives and work. They are likely to be hard-working, procedural, meticulous, straightforward, directive and critically logical; generally "getting things done" in an action-oriented, decisive and efficient manner. Whatever they do, they will want to do it to a high standard and can often be overly perfectionistic. They will prefer to work in environments that have some degree of structure and clear role definitions and will often look for positions of leadership or responsibility. However they may push their type preferences too strongly at times and become demanding, impatient, domineering, insensitive, inflexible, pernickety, bossy, controlling and forceful. They will want everybody to work in the same way that they do and to the same standards, so may also find it difficult to trust others enough to delegate and have trouble letting go of their tasks and assignments.

Their focus is likely to be fixed on outputs and goals and, as such, they may make hasty decisions and refuse to listen to alternatives or options. At times they may have a "know-all" attitude and may appear outwardly overconfident. They will have a generally good idea about the kind of person they are and will notice the differences between themselves and others, however they are likely to regard the different styles of others as failings and weaknesses. For example they will not understand why people with Feeling preferences get so personally involved and will see their subjectivity as weakness and as a flaw in their functioning; or they will regard people with Perceiving preferences as frustratingly indecisive and even lazy.

In dealing with others they will be quick to give remedial feedback or advice but overlook opportunities for praise and appreciation. They may also deliver harsh truths in the spirit of helping the other person to learn, but not realise the impact of the blunt delivery of the message.

Determined Action

At this level, ESTJs really begin to use the strengths of their preferences and will be logically analytical, systematic, action-oriented, conscientious, structured, methodical, consistent, stable, driven, realistic and pragmatic. They will have high standards and strive for efficiency and results, typically going the extra mile to deliver. In dealing with others they will be fair, appropriately challenging, directive, and encouraging, and at times they may be competitive.

ESTJs operating at this level will be generally effective in the workplace, however they will still often overuse rationalisation and logic and overlook personal connectedness. They are also likely to be too quick to seek closure, put output above personal contributions, have a dislike for ambiguity and expect high standards from others. They will realise that they have some blind spots in terms of their awareness of the wider or future implications of their actions, their ability to quickly adapt to change and their interpersonal sensitivity, and they are likely to begin to realise that there is some value to be gained from N and F ways of thinking. Therefore, they may seek viewpoints from those they see as different to themselves; however they will only incorporate these ideas if they have clear benefits and do not slow down the process significantly.

At this stage the ESTJ will also still struggle to understand their conflicting functions – Introverted Thinking, Introverted Feeling and Extraverted Feeling. There is an interest in self-improvement at this level, and the ESTJ will seek feedback from others, often focusing more on the "valuable" negative feedback than the positive feedback as, in their view, it is addressing the negatives that will lead to improvement.

Considerate Individualism

ESTJs at this level of development will move away from using the strengths of their type to achieve tangible goals, and move towards using these strengths to anticipate problems, identify flaws and make practical improvements. They will be resourceful, objective, responsible, dedicated, organised and procedural in their approach, beginning to enjoy the journey of their auxiliary Introverted Sensing, taking time to reflect on knowledge and experience rather than rushing towards the destination. They will start to allow perceived imperfections and incompletion to occur and will select the challenges they wish to engage in rather than attempting to take on everything.

They no longer thrive on recognition for their achievements, but enjoy being and learning. Interpersonally, they will coach and facilitate others, encouraging others to find their own direction, rather than lead and mentor. Others are likely to describe them as firm yet fair leaders. As their self-awareness develops, they will become aware of the shadow sides of their preferences (the characteristics of the lower levels) and become mindful observers of their processes.

Toning down their Te and Si preferences allows more access to their non-preferred sides, however their use of these is likely to be channelled via their Te and Si preferences. For example, when considering the impact of an action on people (F), they will evaluate it in terms of the logical benefits – contented workers are more productive so it is important to address the people issues. Nevertheless, they will see the real value inherent in the N and F approach.

ESTJs may feel as if they are becoming incompetent or ineffective at times because, where they previously thought that they knew all the answers, they will now often encounter situations where they can accept a number of different viewpoints and not reach a clear and logical conclusion.

Integration and Authenticity

At this level, the qualities of the ESTJ preferences can shine through –

objectivity, focus, expedience, clarity of vision, enthusiasm and commitment. The ESTJ can appear to be a realistic and clear thinker, able to see the talent in others, even those who are different to themselves, and nurture and guide them. They will lead by example, delegate effectively, enjoy discussing others' views and opinions and be able to create cohesive teams with shared principles. Although they recognise that people are responsible for their own self-improvement, they can still become impatient with people who do not seem to be striving towards this.

At this level, they become comfortable with the fact that they do not have to try to reach conclusions and can be more content with ambiguity and open-endedness than they had previously been. They are no longer concerned with defending their image of competence and decisiveness and enjoy the learning they get from being with a variety of other people. Through increased mindfulness, they will often be able to access their N and F preferences and adapt their actions appropriately. By not seeing everything as a task to be completed and stopping their drive to action, they can pay real attention to the present and enjoy the moment without always trying to "do something" with it.

Magician

ESTJs at this level realise that their drive for efficiency and results and towards becoming the best that they can be via their achievements and clear thinking is ego-driven and a distraction from their true self. They will also be more accepting of others being who and what they are, realising that encouraging others to develop, not understanding why people would not want to strive for improvement, is also a function of their own ego.

Being able to let go of dualities, they will see that Feeling is part of the same concept as Thinking, and that Intuition is part of the same concept as Sensing, seeing the similarities in the functions rather than the differences and therefore being able to gain easy and natural access to N and F. At this stage, they may also frequently experience the transcendent function – where from two apparent opposites a third way emerges, often in a form that is symbolic or intuitive.

ESTP

Hierarchy of Functions:

Dominant: Extraverted Sensing

Auxiliary: Introverted Thinking

Tertiary: Feeling

Inferior: Introverted Intuition

Main Features and Distortions of the ESTP Type:

ESTPs enjoy living for the moment, and being action-oriented, adaptable and responsive.

They can become easily bored, restless and disruptive, instigating mischief to excite themselves.

Conflicting Functions:

Introverted Sensing, as the opposite orientation to the dominant, is likely to be perceived as dull, pointless and a distraction from appreciating the here and now.

Introverted Intuition, as their inferior function, is likely to be perceived as spending time being concerned about things that are not important and looking for patterns that are of little practical use compared to living in the moment.

Extraverted Intuition, as the contrast to the dominant function, is likely to be seen as impractical, ungrounded and intangible.

Core Values: Autonomy, pragmatism and action

Power and Control

ESTPs functioning at this level will often appear to be chaotic, abrasive, opportunistic and hedonistic as they tend to react to most situations using a distortion of their dominant Extraverted Sensing. They will use their auxiliary Introverted Thinking to rationalise and justify their actions; however this can often lead to them taking impulsive actions with little thought for consequences, and they will attempt to justify this using whatever logic they can find to fit; even if their justifications are, in fact, illogical. As Extraverted types, they will be persistent when they are trying to persuade others, often talking over others, becoming loud and not listening to others. ESTPs at this level may enjoy getting into debates and arguments, however they may become unintentionally forceful, blunt and sometimes offensive as they will be caught up in the moment and, as auxiliary Introverted Thinking types, will be oblivious to the feelings and reactions of others.

ESTPs enjoy action, excitement, stimulation and dealing with sudden crises, however when they are under-stimulated they may create crisis situations or over dramatise a problem just to get a buzz. In the workplace they like to be part of a team and will often be the entertainer in a group ("class daredevil" when at school), however if things do not go their way or the team has too much structure they can become rejecting of teamwork and collaboration and determinedly strive for their need for freedom. Generally they are exciting and entertaining company, but they can be vicious in their mocking of people who they consider to be dull or uptight. They may also get pleasure from making others feel embarrassed. As subordinates they will need the freedom to work in their own way and can be deliberately disruptive if they are in structured or rule-bound settings.

If they are feeling defensive, particularly in cases where their freedom or enjoyment are being threatened, they may play ego-defensive survival games such as throwing tantrums, becoming violent or undertaking risky/thrill-seeking behaviours in order to create excitement for themselves and make those around them feel uncomfortable. Some ESTPs can even indulge in delinquent behaviours just to see what they can get away with or to perpetuate their daredevil image. They may also get into a trap of impulsively taking actions based on immediate needs, getting bored before completing tasks, and lacking the motivation to commit to anything or anybody. They can be overindulgent in activities, food, drink, etc and be reluctant to admit when they are feeling like they are spinning out of control.

Social Identification

ESTPs are often drawn to being in teams and interacting with others, but are also aware that they do not always fit easily into the norms of groups or cultures; for example schools and offices can often feel too restrictive and "serious". For this reason, they will tend to take the role of the entertainer and creator of fun and mischief in a group, often taking pleasure in the reactions of others to their daredevil tendencies.

Whether ESTPs find themselves in type-supportive or non-supportive groups, they will often try to get into a position of influence within the group or be the centre of attention, but not necessarily want to be in the main leadership position. In general they are fun to be around; however they can be bitterly judgemental about people who they see as being different to themselves and harshly mocking of others without necessarily meaning to cause any offence.

If their ESTP characteristics do not "fit" they may suppress their natural styles and make clumsy use of their underdeveloped non-preferred functions, often channelling them through their Se and Ti preferences. For example, trying to do something nice and kind for somebody by giving them a gift that is intended to be fun and humorous but is actually somewhat offensive or misplaced. As auxiliary Introverted Thinkers, they are often unaware at this level of the actual feelings, motivations or reactions of others as they will take everything "as seen" and attempt to interpret other people using logic rather than empathy or sensitivity.

Personal Identification

At this level, ESTPs will channel their dominant Extraverted Sensing into their lives and work; being spontaneously responsive to problems and observant regarding the realities of their circumstances, with a "can do" attitude to most situations. In working with others they often bring energy and enthusiasm to a situation and can point out details and observations that others may miss or be unaware of. They will usually be seen as gregarious, straightforward, logical and practical. In working with others they will be action-oriented and enthusiastic, however they can also be competitive and sometimes become overwhelmed by the urge to "show off".

At times they may still push their type preferences too strongly and be impatient, restless, unappreciative, impulsive, excitement-seeking and easily distracted. They can also become arrogant and insistent that their own logic is correct and be selective in their attention to personal issues or consequences. They frequently find themselves starting new initiatives with enthusiasm and energy, and then getting quickly bored and lacking motivation to complete the project. If they have an exciting idea they can often ignore any downsides and be dismissive of process, detail or limitations that may prevent them from taking action. They may also attempt to manipulate rules to suit their needs, or oversimplify things to justify their actions or intentions.

ESTPs at this level may have a generally good idea about the kind of person they are and will notice the differences between themselves and others; however they are likely to regard the different styles of others as undesirable or dull and un-exciting. For example they will not understand how people with Feeling preferences get so personally involved and see their subjectivity as weakness and as a flaw in their functioning; or they will regard people with Intuition preferences as being out of touch with reality.

Determined Action

ESTPs at this level really begin to use the strengths of their preferences and will be observant, practical, realistic, specific, active and analytical. They will demonstrate strengths in being able to assess immediate needs take measured risks. With others they will come across as rational, enthusiastic, inclusive and fun. They will be able to take tough decisions when necessary and will enjoy helping others out of tricky situations and solving problems for them. If they have positions of leadership or influence they will encourage others towards spontaneity and creative, yet pragmatic, solution-focused actions.

They will realise that they have some blind spots in terms of their awareness of longer-term implications and their motivation to look for connections and patterns. They may also experience demotivation and frustration when having to work alone or on repetitive tasks. At this level they are likely to begin to realise the value that can be gained from N and F ways of working. Therefore, they may seek viewpoints from those they see as different to themselves, however they will only incorporate these ideas if they do not go against their own preferences too strongly.

At this stage the ESTP will still struggle to understand their conflicting functions – Introverted Sensing, Introverted Intuition and Extraverted Intuition. ESTPs at this level will begin to take an interest in what makes them and others tick and will seek feedback from others, often focusing more on the "valuable" negative feedback than the positive feedback, as it is addressing the negatives that will lead to improvement.

ESTPs operating at this level will be effective in the workplace provided they have a degree of freedom and flexibility; however they will still feel confined by schedules and procedures and can be resentful towards any "shoulds", "musts" and "oughts" that may be present in their environment.

Considerate Individualism

At this level of development ESTPs will move away from using their preferences to fire-fight and respond to immediate crises, and move towards using these strengths for troubleshooting, resolving conflict, seeking compromise and taking considered risks. They will be adaptable, easygoing and perceptive, using their auxiliary Introverted Thinking to carefully consider the outcomes and consequences of their intended actions. Instead of switching their energy from one activity to the next, they will begin to be more focused and considered about what they are doing, taking action only when the purpose has been carefully considered. In their interactions with others they will be tactful, fair, energetic and playful.

They no longer thrive on recognition for their liveliness and entertainment value, and are likely to feel more comfortable with stillness and contemplation than they had previously been. As their self-awareness develops, they will become aware of the shadow sides of their preferences (the characteristics of the lower levels) and become mindful observers of their processes. As a type that is typically easily distracted and externally focused, this ability to self-monitor will have a quieting effect on their outward appearance. This will enable them to become better mentors and coaches to any individuals they may be leading or working with.

Toning down their Se and Ti preferences allows more access to their non-preferred sides, however their use of these are still likely to be channelled via their Se and Ti preferences. For example, when considering the impact of an action on people (F), they will conceptualise it in terms of the logical benefits – contented workers are more productive so it is important to address the people issues. Nevertheless, they will see the real value inherent in the N and F approach. They will have a real appreciation for being in the moment and living for today but without a disregard for consequences or the impact on others.

Integration and Authenticity

At this level, the qualities of the ESTP preferences can shine through – they will be seen as expedient, resourceful, autonomous, adaptable and inventive. They will often demonstrate strengths in being able to create simplicity from complexity, identifying ways to improve existing systems and bringing fun to the workplace. ESTPs can appear to be free, fun loving and easygoing; enjoying the world and radiating a sense of freedom. They will be aware of interpersonal dynamics and will be effective at motivating others through their realistic optimism, enthusiasm and encouragement. They will also be genuinely accepting and tolerant of the imperfections and flaws in others; being empathic

The Shadows of Type

and considerate in how they approach them.

At this level, they become comfortable with the fact that they do not always have to try to be a focus of attention with others and can be comfortable with and appreciative of being a quiet observer or participant. They are no longer concerned with defending their image of carefree spontaneity and enjoy the learning they get from being with a variety of other people, including those who they previously had little appreciation for. Through increased mindfulness, they will often be able to access their N and F preferences and adapt their actions appropriately; giving consideration to future possibilities, truly empathising with others, and calming their urge for excitement in order to just "be" with people.

Magician

ESTPs at this level realise that their drive for excitement and action is ego driven and a distraction from their true self. They will also be more accepting of others being who and what they are, realising that encouraging others to live for the day, and not understanding why people would be concerned with "what might be" is also a function of their own ego.

Being able to let go of dualities, they will see that Sensing is part of the same concept as Intuition, and that Thinking is part of the same concept as Feeling, seeing the similarities in the functions rather than the differences and therefore being able to gain easy and natural access to their N and F sides. At this stage, they may also frequently experience the transcendent function – where from two apparent opposites a third way emerges, often in a form that is symbolic or intuitive.

The Developmentally Levelled Type Descriptions

INFJ

Hierarchy of Functions:

Dominant: Introverted Intuition

Auxiliary: Extraverted Feeling

Tertiary: Thinking

Inferior: Extraverted Sensing

Main Features and Distortions of the INFJ Type:

INFJs quickly see the connections between things and use these to generate creative ideas, often with a view to helping others.

They can be unrealistically idealistic and overly concerned with the opinions of others.

Conflicting Functions:

Extraverted Intuition, as the opposite orientation to the dominant, can be seen as an overwhelming and emotionally draining barrage of ill-considered and illogical ideas that cause confusion.

Extraverted Sensing, as their inferior function, can be seen as meaningless and purposeless thrill-seeking and acting irresponsibly without consideration of consequences.

Introverted Sensing, as the contrast to the dominant function, can be seen as narrowly focused, pernickety, and self-limiting.

Core Values: Vision, insight and harmony

Power and Control

INFJs who are operating at this level of development are likely to respond to most situations using a distortion of their dominant Introverted Intuition preference and often be seen as single-minded, intolerant, impractical and unrealistic. They will use their auxiliary Extraverted Feeling to consider how their ideas will work in relation to others and to put their ideas into action; however they may be selective in the information they choose to include in their planning and end up taking actions that are somewhat detached from reality or, with great but unspoken resentment, take actions that are more focused on keeping others happy rather than doing what they would like to. They can also become easily overwhelmed and pessimistic about their abilities, relationships and their general place in the world.

INFJs will usually feel uncomfortable with conflict and be hesitant to get involved. They are likely to withdraw from conflict situations and will either let others take charge or make a dramatic exit and take stubbornly independent action. With people they feel comfortable with they can get into arguments where they stubbornly insist on the correctness of their own vision and refuse to listen to any other views. In the workplace they like to be part of small, cohesive teams but are likely to be hypersensitive at this level to any disharmony in the team.

Many INFJs may be secretive about their ideas and plans in order to prevent others from trying to change them or from judging them. They can often be seen by others as intense, eccentric, guarded, self-pitying and resentful. In addition to this, as with most other Introverted types with Feeling preferences operating at this level, they can be seen as aloof, oversensitive, and self-absorbed. As subordinates they can be difficult to manage as they will focus intently on what their boss is like as a person and be resentful of them if they do not support their values.

If they are feeling threatened, particularly in terms of their feelings of individuality, their perceived uniqueness or their ideals, they may play ego-defensive survival games that involve shutting out emotions and deluding themselves that they are coping. They may also imagine that others are thinking badly of them by misinterpreting comments or body language. They may be unaware of how others may be different to them and merely see them as being wrong, amoral or unpleasant in some way; or they will often turn this in on themselves and feel like misfits in the world. They can be quick to judge others and will be very sensitive to what they think the other person's opinion of them is.

Social Identification

INFJs often find themselves being part of groups that do not support their preferences and having to "make do" with joining in with others' plans, interests or activities. Nevertheless, they will often come across as personable, friendly, caring and accommodating due to their Extraverted Feeling preference.

If their INFJ characteristics do not "fit" they may sometimes suppress their natural styles and make clumsy use of their underdeveloped non-preferred functions, often channelling them through their Ni and Fe preferences. For example, trying to take charge of a situation where they perceive conflict by telling the people concerned to simply stop and make up.

Depending on the situation, sometimes INFJs will stubbornly cling onto trying to be "themselves" when in a group, as they are often ego-identified with being individualistic. However, the INFJ will indulge their need for belonging at this level by pursuing interests and hobbies that are congruent with their preferences; this can serve the dual purpose of making them feel less of a misfit, but also making them feel as if they have a private or secret other life. If they manage to get into type supportive-groups they will be unlikely to want a position of leadership or influence, but will feel content being part of a supportive and like-minded team.

As with most introverted types they will value being part of a group that has a "turn-taking" communication pattern and with people who are good listeners. With regard to those perceived as being "out-groups", INFJs can be very quick to make judgements and particularly harsh in their criticisms. Their loyalty to their friends and ideals can make them very defensive in the face of threats.

Personal Identification

At this level, INFJs begin to channel their dominant Introverted Intuition into their lives and work; generating ideas, seeing connections and possibilities that may not be obvious to others, and trying to find ways to make the world a better place. They will usually be imaginative, helpful and caring, however this may not come across to others clearly if their dominant Introverted Intuition is excessively overriding their auxiliary Extraverted Feeling.

They will prefer to work in environments that allow time for people to get to know each other as individuals and will function best in small groups or when working alone. However, they may push their type preferences too strongly at times and become hypersensitive, moody, dramatic, and start telling others what is best for them. They may become frustrated about wanting to bring the world in line with their ideals and suffer disappointment due to having unrealistic expectations. They often find it difficult to allow others to see their visions and ideas, and, as with many Introverted types, find it difficult to verbalise their insights and ideas. Therefore they can find it difficult to delegate and have trouble handing over their ideas and plans. If they find themselves in situations that do not allow them to present ideas or be imaginative they may quietly and secretively get on with initiatives on their own without consultation.

They will generally have a good idea about the kind of person they are and will notice the differences between themselves and others, however they are likely to regard the different styles of others as harsh, pushy or insensitive. For example they will not understand why people with Thinking preferences can take a detached viewpoint and see their objectivity as a lack of care or empathy; or they will regard people with perceiving Preferences as frustratingly indecisive and even lazy.

Others may experience INFJs at this level as being hard to get to know, hypersensitive, idealistic, unassertive, conflict-avoidant and prone to outbursts of "artistic temperament". If they find like-minded people, INFJs can become over dependent on them or obsessive about their connectedness to them. In dealing with others they will be quick to give advice and sympathy but shy away from delivering feedback that they perceive to be negative. They will want encouragement, appreciation and approval from others and may feel offended if this is not forthcoming.

Determined Action

INFJs at this level really begin to use the strengths of their preferences and will be creative, conceptual, idealistic, complex, deep, organised and driven. In their work and lives they will be interested in finding meaning in what they do and want to be making a difference. They will demonstrate long-range vision, often use models to make sense of things, and will be sensitive to interpersonal dynamics. In dealing with others they will be attentive, caring, collaborative and empathic.

They will realise that they have some blind spots in terms of their attention to detail, ability to stick with routine tasks and comfort with making tough decisions, and they are likely to begin to realise that there is some value to be gained from S and T ways of thinking. Therefore, they may seek viewpoints from those they see as different to themselves, however they will only incorporate these ideas if they do not go against their preferences too strongly, although they will make every effort to accommodate others. As Introverted types, they may tend to overuse their auxiliary function (Extraverted Feeling), particularly at this stage; this can often manifest as being people pleasing, unassertive and reliant on others.

At this stage INFJs will still struggle to understand their conflicting functions – Extraverted Intuition, Extraverted Sensing and Introverted Sensing. There is an interest in self-improvement at this level, and the INFJ will seek feedback from others, needing a balance of positives and negatives to feel motivated to try to learn from the feedback and accept it non-defensively.

INFJs operating at this level will be effective in the workplace, however they will still be prone to thinking through ideas alone, overlooking details, avoiding truths if they go against their vision, and being easily bored with routine or precision work.

Considerate Individualism

INFJs at this level of development will move away from using the strengths of their type to produce imaginative ideas, and move towards using these strengths to demonstrate global vision, realise insightful initiatives and suggest creative solutions. They will be conceptual and insightful in their approach, and begin to refine their auxiliary Extraverted Feeling; becoming less concerned with pleasing and appeasing others, and more genuine and committed in their actions. In general they will be more trusting of their own insights and less reliant on confirmation from others. In dealing with others they will be compassionate, gentle, loyal and humanistic.

INFJs at this level can often be visionary in their thinking and have the ability to demonstrate new ways of seeing and conceptualising things. At this stage they will allow themselves to recognise that their ideals can not always be realised and generally take a more realistic view of what they can and cannot influence. They no longer thrive on wanting to be recognised for their individuality and imaginativeness, but enjoy taking time to enjoy the simple pleasures in life.

As their self-awareness develops, they will become aware of the shadow sides of their preferences (the characteristics of the lower levels) and become mindful observers of their processes. Toning down their Ni and Fe preferences allows more access to their non-preferred sides, however their use of these are likely to be channelled via their Ni and Fe preferences. Nevertheless, they will see the real value inherent in the S and T approach.

If managing or working with people, they will coach and facilitate, using a supportive style and being accepting of and understanding towards others' differences. As they have a natural interest in the achievement and development of others they will find great satisfaction from helping others in these ways. The INFJ may feel as if they are becoming cynical or losing touch with their values at times because, where they previously thought that they knew their own mind, they will now often encounter situations where they can accept imperfection and harsh realities.

The Shadows of Type

Integration and Authenticity

At this level, the qualities of the INFJ preferences can shine through. They will be strongly intuitive, uncannily empathic, inspiring, wise and visionary. The INFJ can appear to be spiritual or mystical to others and be able to clearly understand how people and systems inter-relate. Although they recognise that people are responsible for their own development, they can still become frustrated with people who do not seem to be striving towards this.

At this level, they become comfortable with the fact that they can resist the drive to relentlessly pursue creativity and uniqueness and can enjoy activities that are purely for enjoyment or that have no meaningful outcome. They are no longer concerned with defending their image of being intelligently insightful and imaginative and enjoy the learning they get from being with a variety of other people, even those who they previously found abrasive or superficial.

Through increased mindfulness, they will often be able to access their S and T preferences and adapt their actions appropriately; paying attention to the present, being more in touch with their physical bodies, and stopping the drive to please and gain approval from others in order to just "be" with people or enjoy their time alone.

Magician

INFJs realise that their concern with inspirational vision and imaginativeness is ego-driven and a distraction from their true self. They will become more accepting of others being who and what they are, realising that trying to encourage others to be creative and values-oriented is also a function of their own ego.

Being able to let go of dualities, they will see that Thinking is part of the same concept as Feeling, and that Sensing is part of the same concept as Intuition, seeing the similarities in the functions rather than the differences and therefore being able to gain easy and natural access to S and T. At this stage, they may also frequently experience the transcendent function – where from two apparent opposites a third way emerges, often in a form that is symbolic or intuitive.

INFP

Hierarchy of Functions:

Dominant: Introverted Feeling

Auxiliary: Extraverted Intuition

Tertiary: Sensing

Inferior: Extraverted Thinking

Main Features and Distortions of the INFP Type:

INFPs live life guided by their personal values and are often concerned with making a difference to people thorough working to realise their ideals.

They can become self-righteous, self-absorbed and harshly judgemental of anyone or anything that is not congruent with their values. The values system itself can become distorted.

Conflicting Functions:

Extraverted Feeling, as the opposite orientation to the dominant, is usually seen as intrusive, interfering, meddling in other peoples' business and a desperation to be liked by others.

Extraverted Thinking, as their inferior function, can be seen as taking hasty, ill-considered action and as overwhelming and domineering.

Introverted Thinking, as the contrast to the dominant function, can be perceived as detached, overly formulaic and lacking the human touch.

Core Values: Integrity, individuality and congruence

Power and Control

INFPs at this level of development are likely to respond to most situations using a distortion of their dominant Introverted Feeling preference and will often be seen as isolative, resentful, petty, eccentric, and melancholic. Others may feel that they are "walking on eggshells" with them. They will use their auxiliary Extraverted Intuition to look for inspirational ideas to inform their ideals about how life and the world should be, however, at this level, this can often manifest itself as unrealistic idealism, impracticality, eccentricity and, sometimes, rebelliousness.

As Introverted types, INFPs will often deal with conflict by stating their viewpoint concisely, then withdrawing from any further discussion and either taking stubbornly independent action or going off in a huff. If they choose to enter into a debate they can become dogmatically insistent that only their views and values are valid. As INFPs often take the position of going with the flow until there is an important issue at stake, they tend to fall into their "grip" response of Extraverted Thinking in a "straw that broke the camel's back" manner; suddenly, and as a surprise to those present, launching into a blunt and sometimes vicious tirade.

In the workplace they like to be able to work independently and will often take unusual and unconventional courses of action. They can often be seen by others as distant, defensive, impulsive, guarded, quick to take offence and sometimes forceful in expressing their opinions. In their interactions with others, INFPs at this level can be fairly harsh in their criticism of people who they consider to be living immorally or without values. As subordinates they will look up to a boss who they see as inspirational and who supports their views on life, however they may react rebelliously if they do not have a good rapport with the boss or colleagues, sometimes quietly sabotaging the ideas of others if they do not agree with them.

If they are feeling defensive, particularly in cases where their ideals being threatened, they may deny/repress their true feelings and delude themselves that everything is OK as an ego-defensive survival tactic. They may also imagine that others are thinking badly of them by misinterpreting comments or body language. Although they are typically interpersonally sensitive, at this level they will only have a selective and biased view of how others may be different to them. If the INFP feels like the only person who is "seeing the truth" or "making a difference", they will become very frustrated with and intolerant of those around them and can fall into the "martyr" role. They can also turn this in on themselves and feel like misfits in the world.

Social Identification

INFPs often find themselves being part of groups that do not support their preferences and having to "make do" with joining in with others' plans, interests or activities. However, INFPs are usually happy to go with the flow of the group and often take the role of the quiet but supportive group member.

If their INFP characteristics do not "fit" they may sometimes suppress their natural styles and make clumsy use of their underdeveloped non-preferred functions, often channelling them through their Fi and Ne preferences. For example, trying to take charge of a situation where they perceive conflict by telling the people concerned to simply stop and make up.

Depending on the situation, sometimes INFPs will stubbornly cling onto trying to be "themselves" when in a group, fully aware that they are taking a nonconformist attitude. Some INFPs will be deliberately rebellious or "nonconformist" at this level, instead conforming to the "rebel" stereotype. Nevertheless, the INFP will indulge the need for belonging characterised by this level by pursuing interests and hobbies that are congruent with their preferences; this can serve the dual purpose of making them feel less of a misfit, but also making them feel as if they have a private or secret other life. They may also look for opportunities to be part of groups, either physically or, more often, virtually, who support the causes or values that they believe in; for example helping at a homeless shelter, or taking membership of an organisation such as Amnesty or Friends of the Earth.

If they manage to get into type-supportive groups they are unlikely to seek a position of leadership or influence but will have a key role as a harmoniser, mediator and supporter. They may find it difficult to assert themselves in a group as they will be concerned with maintaining harmony, however this can often lead to them getting into situations they do not want to be in and quietly harbouring feelings of resentment. As with most Introverted types they will value being part of a group that has a "turn taking" communication pattern and with people who are good listeners.

Personal Identification

At this level INFPs begin to channel their dominant Introverted Feeling into their lives and work; they will be values-driven, committed, determined and looking to take purposeful action. They will usually be creative and insightful, however this may not come across to others clearly if their dominant Introverted Feeling is excessively overriding their auxiliary Extraverted Intuition. They will prefer to work in environments that have a harmonious atmosphere, and will function best in small groups or when working alone. However they may push their type preferences too strongly at times and become oversensitive, idealistic, opinionated, dogmatic, impatient, perfectionistic and judgemental.

Others may experience INFPs at this level as being hard to get to know, unrealistic, distractible, easily discouraged and self-effacing. INFPs at this level frequently have difficulty in verbally expressing what is important to them and in translating their values into actions. In communicating they may overuse their Extraverted Intuition, going off on many tangents and giving long explanations, but neglecting to clearly convey their conclusions or decisions. They can also become argumentative and avoid taking advice from others or reject logic-based opinions.

In dealing with others they will be quick to give advice and sympathy but shy away from delivering feedback that they perceive to be negative. They will want encouragement, appreciation and approval from others and may feel offended if this is not forthcoming. If they find themselves in situations that do not allow them to present ideas and opinions they may quietly and secretively get on with initiatives on their own without consultation. They will have a generally good idea about the kind of person they are and will notice the differences between themselves and others, however they will still tend to be harsh in their judgement of those who they perceive as living with no or with the "wrong" values.

INFPs operating at this level frequently "get on their high horse" about certain subjects when they are with people who they feel comfortable with. They will also still have difficulty in understanding people with different type preferences. For example they will not understand how people with Thinking preferences can make decisions that are not acceptable to everybody and will see their logical detachment as uncaring, harsh or selfish; or they will regard people with Sensing preferences as lacking vision and being obsessive about unimportant things.

Determined Action

INFPs at this level really begin to use the strengths of their preferences and will be empathic, sensitive, dependable and caring. They will enjoy working with complexity and finding the connections between things, and will often be pioneers for new initiatives. They will be reserved, modest, non-domineering and psychologically curious. In dealing with others they will be attentive, supportive, collaborative and empathic.

They will realise that they have some blind spots in terms of their attention to detail, ability to stick with routine tasks and comfort with making tough decisions, and they are likely to begin to realise that there is some value to be gained from S and T ways of thinking. Therefore, they may seek viewpoints from those they see as different to themselves, however they will only incorporate these ideas if they do not go against their preferences too strongly, although they will make every effort to accommodate others. As Introverted types, they may tend to overuse their auxiliary function (Extraverted Intuition), particularly at this stage; this can often give the impression of eccentricity or novelty seeking.

At this stage INFPs will still struggle to understand their conflicting functions – Extraverted Feeling, Extraverted Thinking and Introverted Thinking. There is an interest in self-improvement and introspection at this level, and the INFP will seek feedback from others, needing a balance of positives and negatives to feel motivated to try to learn from the feedback and accept it non-defensively. When giving feedback to others, however, they may play down any negatives for fear of de-motivating or offending the other person.

INFPs operating at this level will be effective in the workplace, however they will still be prone to thinking through ideas alone, overlooking details, avoiding truths if they go against their ideals, and being easily bored with routine or precision work.

Considerate Individualism

INFPs at this level of development will move away from using the strengths of their type to try to make the world a better place, and move towards using these strengths to produce creative, long-term initiatives that are often underpinned by a concern for people. They will be open-minded and loyal to their beliefs in their approach to work, and will be seeking purpose in most of the things they engage in. They will begin to refine their auxiliary Extraverted Intuition; becoming less concerned with remaining open to new ideas and reluctant to reach closure, and more focused on implementing timely and practically workable initiatives.

INFPs at this level can often demonstrate long-range vision yet be concise and deliberate in their actions. In themselves they will become more respectful of others' values, views and opinions and show a genuine interest in creating harmony in the face of difference. However the INFP may feel as if they are becoming cynical or losing touch with their values at times because, where they previously thought that they knew their own mind, they will now often encounter situations where they can accept harsh realities and incongruence.

Others are likely to perceive INFPs at this level as gentle, adaptable, modest and true to their beliefs without being forceful. They no longer thrive on recognition for their integrity and idealism, but enjoy taking time to enjoy the simple pleasures in life. As their self-awareness develops, they will become aware of the shadow sides of their preferences (the characteristics of the lower levels) and become mindful observers of their processes.

Toning down their Fi and Ne preferences allows more access to their non-preferred sides, however their use of these are likely to be channelled via their Fi and Ne preferences. For example, when considering how to get the best results, they will view this result as being the one that everybody can get onboard with. Nevertheless, they will see the real value inherent in the S and T approach. Interpersonally, they will support and facilitate others, encouraging others to find their own direction, rather than guide, teach and mentor.

Integration and Authenticity

At this level, the qualities of the INFP preferences can shine through – integrity, congruence, imagination, determination and creativity. The INFP can appear to be an inspirational and visionary thinker, able to see connections and meaning in things that may be masked to others. They will be keen to make a difference to others in a gentle, non-forceful and measured way, promoting harmony rather than forcing it on others. Although they recognise that people are responsible for their own lifestyle choices, they can still become impatient with people who seem to act without care or consideration, or who abuse human rights.

At this level, they become comfortable with the fact that they do not have to relentlessly pursue ideals and righteousness and can enjoy activities that are purely for enjoyment or that do not necessarily have a meaningful outcome. They are no longer concerned with defending their image of being principled and following the "right" path and enjoy the learning they get from being with a variety of other people. Through increased mindfulness, they will often be able to access their S and T preferences and adapt their actions appropriately; paying attention to the present, being more in touch with their physical bodies, truly empathising with others, and stopping their drive for congruence and harmony in order to just "be" with people or enjoy their time alone.

Magician

At this level, INFPs realise that their drive for searching for harmony

The Developmentally Levelled Type Descriptions

> and demonstrating inspirational thinking is ego-driven and a distraction from their true self. They will become more accepting of others being who and what they are, realising that trying to encourage others to be values-based, congruent and peaceful is also a function of their own ego. Being able to let go of dualities, they will see that Thinking is part of the same concept as Feeling, and that Sensing is part of the same concept as Intuition, seeing the similarities in the functions rather than the differences and therefore being able to gain easy and natural access to S and T. At this stage, they may also frequently experience the transcendent function – where from two apparent opposites a third way emerges, often in a form that is symbolic or intuitive.

INTJ

Hierarchy of Functions:

Dominant: Introverted Intuition

Auxiliary: Extraverted Thinking

Tertiary: Feeling

Inferior: Extraverted Sensing

Main Features and Distortions of the INTJ Type:

INTJs quickly see the connections between things and create solutions to complex problems.

They can be stubbornly dismissive of other people's ideas that may disrupt their own ideas and plans.

Conflicting Functions:

Extraverted Intuition, as the opposite orientation to the dominant, can be seen as an overwhelming barrage of ill-considered and illogical ideas that waste time that could have been used more purposefully.

Extraverted Sensing, as their inferior function, can be seen as meaningless and purposeless thrill-seeking and acting irresponsibly without consideration of consequences.

Introverted Sensing, as the contrast to the dominant function, can be seen as narrowly focused, pernickety, and self-limiting

Core Values: Knowledge, truth and independence.

Power and Control

INTJs who are operating at this level of development are likely to respond to most situations using a distortion of their dominant Introverted Intuition preference and will often be seen as single-minded, intolerant, impractical and dogmatic. They will use their auxiliary Extraverted Thinking to look for logical justifications for their ideas and to put their ideas into action; however they may be selective in the information they choose to include in their planning and end up taking actions that are somewhat detached from reality or of little practical benefit. They may find themselves getting into the trap of forcing logic to fit in order to pursue an original or unusual solution.

As Introverted types, INTJs will often deal with conflict by stating their viewpoint concisely, then withdrawing from any further discussion and taking stubbornly independent action. In the workplace they like to be able to work independently and will often take unusual courses of action that others cannot comprehend as they will see it as a bother to try to explain themselves. For this reason, INTJs at this level may be secretive about their ideas and plans in order to prevent others from interfering with them. They can often be seen by others as condescending, isolative, idiosyncratic, pessimistic and dismissive. In addition to this, as with most other Introverted types with Thinking preferences, they can be seen as aloof, detached and impersonal.

They tend to focus in on faults in other people's thinking and can often be heard criticising other people's levels of intelligence before waiting to hear all the facts. They can be easily overwhelmed by situations that they see as chaotic or disorganised and may overcautiously resist taking any action until they are absolutely sure of themselves. As subordinates they can be difficult to manage as they dislike being told what to do, and will focus in on any fault they perceive in their boss and make judgements on the boss's competence.

If they are feeling threatened, particularly in terms of their independence or perceived competence, they may play ego-defensive survival games that involve shutting out emotions, using unemotional logical rationalisations or avoidance of situations where they do not feel competent. They can be impatient and overly task-focused at the expense of listening effectively – others may find them brusque to the point of rudeness. At this level they often lose the ability to be empathic as they are cut off from their own emotional response. They may be unaware of how others may be different to them and merely see them as being wrong or ineffective in some way; or they will often turn this in on themselves and feel like misfits in the world.

Social Identification

INTJs often find themselves being part of groups that do not support their preferences and having to "make do" with joining in with others' plans, interests or activities. If their INTJ characteristics do not "fit" they may sometimes suppress their natural styles and make clumsy use of their underdeveloped non-preferred functions, often channelling them through their Ni and Te preferences. For example, trying to do something nice and kind for somebody by giving them a gift that will help them to improve themselves or think differently in some way.

Depending on the situation, sometimes INTJs will stubbornly cling onto trying to be "themselves" when in a group, fully aware that they are taking a non-conformist attitude. However, the INTJ will indulge the need for acceptance characterised by this level by pursuing interests and hobbies that are congruent with their preferences; this can serve the dual purpose of making them feel less of a misfit, but also making them feel as if they have a private or secret other life. If they manage to get into type-supportive groups they will enjoy being fairly influential but not an out front leader. As with most Introverted types they will value being part of a group that has a "turn taking" communication pattern and with people who are good listeners.

Personal Identification

INTJs at this level begin to channel their dominant Introverted Intuition into their lives and work; generating ideas, looking for ways to improve existing thinking, seeing connections and possibilities that may not be obvious to others, and then converting these into tangible actions. They will usually be logical, organised and decisive, however this may not come across to others clearly if their dominant Introverted Intuition is excessively overriding their auxiliary Extraverted Thinking.

They will prefer to work in environments that allow a degree of independence and will function best in small groups or when working alone. However, they may push their type preferences too strongly at times and become cynical, challenging, intense, impatient, blunt, stubborn and obstinate. They often find it difficult to share their ideas and plans with others, and therefore find it difficult to delegate and have trouble letting go of their plans and tasks. If they find themselves in situations that do not allow them to present ideas and opinions they may quietly and secretively get on with initiatives on their own without consultation.

They will have a generally good idea about the kind of person they are and will notice the differences between themselves and others, however they are likely to regard the different styles of others as illogical or unproductive. For example they will not understand why people with Feeling preferences get so personally involved, and will see their subjectivity as weakness and as a flaw in their functioning; or they will regard people with Perceiving preferences as frustratingly indecisive and even lazy.

Others may experience INTJs at this level as being hard to get to know, always "up to something" and dismissive of their inputs unless they fit in with the INTJs' thinking; then the INTJ can become a bit obsessive about having found a like-minded person. In dealing with others they will be quick to give remedial feedback but overlook opportunities for praise and appreciation. They may also deliver harsh truths in the spirit of helping the other person to improve, but not realise the impact of the blunt delivery of the message. A common phrase used by INTJs at this level is "I don't suffer fools".

Determined Action

At this level, INTJs really begin to use the strengths of their preferences and will be creative, insightful, organised, objective and analytical. They will demonstrate long-range thinking, often use models to make sense of things, and will be confident in trusting their own judgement. In dealing with others they will be fair, appropriately challenging and rational.

They will realise that they have some blind spots in terms of their attention to detail, ability to stick with routine tasks and interpersonal sensitivity, and they are likely to begin to realise that there is some value to be gained from S and F ways of thinking. Therefore, they may seek viewpoints from those they see as different to themselves, however they will only incorporate these ideas if they do not go against their preferences too strongly. As Introverted types, they may tend to overuse their auxiliary function (Extraverted Thinking), particularly at this stage; this can often manifest as critical, impatient and rather to the point.

At this level INTJs will still struggle to understand their conflicting functions – Extraverted Intuition, Extraverted Sensing and Introverted Sensing. There is an interest in self-improvement at this level, and the INTJ will seek feedback from others, often focusing more on the "valuable" negative feedback than the positive feedback, as it is addressing the negatives that will lead to improvement. INTJs operating at this level will be effective in the workplace, however they will still be prone to thinking through ideas alone, overlooking details and paying insufficient attention to personal connectedness.

Considerate Individualism

INTJs at this level of development will move away from using the strengths of their type to produce insightful ideas, and move towards using these strengths to demonstrate global thinking and innovation. They will be conceptual and strategic in their approach, and begin to refine their auxiliary Extraverted Thinking; becoming less critical and impatient, and more tactfully honest and considered in their actions. INTJs at this level can often be revolutionary in their thinking and have the ability to see relationships in things that seem unrelated to most others. In themselves they will become more observant and curious, and in interpersonal settings they will be more tolerant and accepting. They will start to allow perceived imperfections and incompletion to occur and will select the challenges they wish to engage in rather than attempting to take on everything that has captured their interest.

They no longer thrive on recognition for their intellect and insight, but enjoy taking time to enjoy the simple pleasures in life. As their self-awareness develops, they will become aware of the shadow sides of their preferences (the characteristics of the lower levels) and become mindful observers of their processes. Toning down their Ni and Te preferences allows more access to their non-preferred sides, however their use of these are likely to be channelled via their Ni and Te preferences. For example, when considering the impact of an action on people (F), they will conceptualise it in terms of the logical benefits – contented workers are more productive so it is important to address the people issues. Nevertheless, they will see the real value inherent in the S and F approach.

Interpersonally, they will coach and facilitate others, encouraging others to find their own direction, rather than advise, teach and mentor. INTJs may feel as if they are becoming incompetent or ineffective at times because, where they previously thought that they knew their own mind, they will now often encounter situations where they can accept different viewpoints and not reach a clear and logical conclusion.

Integration and Authenticity

At this level, the qualities of the INTJ preferences can shine through – visionary insight, wisdom, originality, broad-mindedness and uncanny awareness. The INTJ can appear to be a visionary thinker, able to synthesise complex issues. At times they can appear spiritual or mystical to others. Although they recognise that people are responsible for their own development, they can still become impatient with people who do not seem to be striving towards this.

At this level, they become comfortable with the fact that they do not have to relentlessly pursue knowledge and can enjoy activities that are purely for enjoyment or that have no meaningful outcome. They are no longer concerned with defending their image of being intelligently insightful and independent and enjoy the learning they get from being with a variety of other people. Through increased mindfulness, they will often be able to access their S and F preferences and adapt their actions appropriately; paying attention to the present, being more in touch with their physical bodies, truly empathising with others, and stopping their drive for knowledge in order to just "be" with people or enjoy their time alone.

Magician

INTJs realise that their drive for accumulating knowledge and visionary thinking is ego-driven and a distraction from their true self. They will become more accepting of others being who and what they are, realising that trying to encourage others to be innovative and acquire knowledge is also a function of their own ego.

Being able to let go of dualities, they will see that Feeling is part of the same concept as Thinking, and that Sensing is part of the same concept as Intuition, seeing the similarities in the functions rather than the differences and therefore being able to gain easy and natural access to S and F. At this stage, they may also experience the transcendent function which will allow new perspectives to emerge, although they are likely to be in a form that is intangible and symbolic or intuitive.

The Developmentally Levelled Type Descriptions

INTP

Hierarchy of Functions:

Dominant: Introverted Thinking

Auxiliary: Extraverted Intuition

Tertiary: Sensing

Inferior: Extraverted Feeling

Main Features and Distortions of the INTP Type:

INTPs can see a problem from many different sides and come up with solutions to complex problems that can often be original or innovative.

They can become very detached and absorbed in their thoughts and can often procrastinate for a long time before taking action as they want their solutions to be perfect.

Conflicting Functions:

Extraverted Thinking, as the opposite orientation to the dominant, can be seen as taking hasty, ill-considered action and as overwhelming and domineering.

Extraverted Feeling, as their inferior function, is usually seen as intrusive, interfering, meddling in other peoples' business and as desperation to be liked by others.

Introverted Feeling, as the contrast to the dominant function, can be perceived as oversensitive, idealistic and avoidant of harsh realities.

Core Values: Intelligence, logic and truth

> **Power and Control**
> INTPs operating at this level of development are likely to respond to most situations using a distortion of their dominant Introverted Thinking preference and will often be seen as isolative, impatient, blunt and uninterested in other people. They will use their auxiliary Extraverted Intuition to look for novel or creative ways to solve problems and find answers, however, at this level, this can often manifest itself as arrogance, impracticality, eccentricity and,

sometimes, rebelliousness. They may find themselves getting into the trap of forcing logic to fit in order to pursue an original or unusual solution. As Introverted types, INTPs will often deal with conflict by stating their viewpoint concisely, then withdrawing from any further discussion and taking stubbornly independent action.

In the workplace they like to be able to work independently and will often take unusual courses of action that others cannot comprehend. For this reason, INTPs at this level may be secretive about whatever they are working on in order to prevent others from interfering with their thought process and approach. They can often be seen by others as distant, undependable, restless, defensive, forgetful, interpersonally oblivious and sometimes forceful in expressing their opinions. In addition to this, as with most other Introverted types with Thinking preferences, they can be seen as aloof, detached and impersonal.

Interpersonally, INTPs can be fairly brutal in their criticism of others as they will see themselves as merely pointing out the truth. They will have little time or value for things that they consider to be illogical or unproductive, such as spending time on a team-bonding exercise. As subordinates they can be difficult to manage as they dislike being told what to do, and will focus in on any fault they perceive in their boss and make judgements on the boss's competence.

If they are feeling threatened, particularly in terms of their independence or perceived competence, they may play ego-defensive survival games that involve shutting out their own emotions – brushing them aside as being irrelevant. Additionally they will use unemotional logical rationalisations or avoid getting involved in situations where they do not feel competent. They may be unaware of how others may be different to them and merely see them as being wrong or ineffective in some way; or they will often turn this in on themselves and feel like misfits in the world. In general, they will see having power and control as being able to shut others out and be left alone rather than engaging in interpersonal power struggles. INTPs at this level can become so pernickety about getting things right and gathering all the necessary information that other people often mistake them for Introverted Sensing types.

Social Identification

INTPs often find themselves being part of groups that do not support their preferences and having to "make do" with joining in with others' plans, interests or activities. If their INTP characteristics do not "fit" they may sometimes suppress their natural styles and make clumsy use of their underdeveloped non-preferred functions, often channelling them through their Ti and Ne preferences. For example, trying to do something nice and kind for somebody by giving them a gift that will help them to improve themselves or think differently in some way.

Depending on the situation, sometimes INTPs will stubbornly cling onto trying to be "themselves" when in a group, fully aware that they are taking a nonconformist attitude. However, the INTP will indulge the need for acceptance characterised by this level by pursuing interests and hobbies that are congruent with their preferences; this can serve the dual purpose of making them feel less of a misfit, but also making them feel as if they have a private or secret other life. They may also look for opportunities to be part of groups, either physically or, more often, virtually, which have an intellectual bias, for example joining a chess club or trying to join MENSA.

If they manage to get into type-supportive groups they will enjoy being fairly influential but not an out front leader. As with most Introverted types they will value being part of a group that has a "turn taking" communication pattern and with people who are good listeners.

Personal Identification

INTPs at this level begin to channel their dominant Introverted Thinking into their lives and work; being creative problem solvers, always looking for ways to improve existing thinking, seeking absolute truths and using their analytical eye to look for optimum solutions. They will usually be conceptual, original and fairly innovative, however this may not come across to others clearly if their dominant Introverted Thinking is excessively overriding their auxiliary Extraverted Intuition.

They will prefer to work in environments that allow a degree of independence and will function best in small groups or when working alone. However they may push their type preferences too strongly at times and become overly complex in their communication, display intellectual snobbery, and be critical, sarcastic and cynical. Others may experience INTPs at this level as being hard to get to know, detached, aloof, insensitive to interpersonal needs and scholarly (or "nerdy").

INTPs at this level are often perceived as procrastinators as they tend to be reluctant to take action unless they believe they have reached the perfect decision or arrived at the absolute truth. In communicating they may overuse their Extraverted Intuition, going off on many tangents and giving long explanations, but neglecting to clearly convey their conclusions or decisions. They can also become argumentative and avoid taking advice or accepting logic from others. In dealing with others they will be quick to give remedial feedback but overlook opportunities for praise and appreciation. They may also deliver harsh truths in the spirit of helping the other person to improve, but not realise the impact of the blunt delivery of the message. They often find it difficult to allow others into their thoughts and ideas, and therefore find it difficult to delegate.

If they find themselves in situations that do not allow them to present ideas and opinions they may quietly and secretively get on with initiatives on their own without consultation. They will have a generally good idea about the kind of person they are and will notice the differences between themselves and others, however they are likely to regard the different styles of others as illogical or unproductive. For example they will not understand why people with Feeling preferences get so personally involved and will see their subjectivity as weakness and as a flaw in their functioning; or they will regard people with Judging preferences as people who rush into things.

Determined Action

At this level, INTPs really begin to use the strengths of their preferences and will be solution-focused, inquisitive, contemplative, precise and calm. They will demonstrate long-range thinking and often create models in their minds to help them find their answers and solutions. They will be autonomous, non-domineering, tolerant and careful. In dealing with others they will be fair, objectively critical, appropriately challenging and rational; however they are likely to maintain an air of interpersonal detachment and can still be oblivious to the implications of their actions on others.

They will realise that they have some blind spots in terms of their attention to detail, their consideration of practicalities and their interpersonal sensitivity. For example, an INTP designing a training course will be focused on getting the teaching across in a way that would result in the students being knowledgeable and competent, but is likely to overlook any element of interactivity, individual learning style, group bonding, etc. Nevertheless, at this stage they will understand that there is some value to be gained from S and F ways of thinking. Therefore, they may seek viewpoints from those they see as different to themselves, however they will only incorporate these ideas if they do not go against their preferences too strongly.

As introverted types, they may tend to overuse their auxiliary function (Extraverted Intuition), particularly at this stage; this can often give the impression of eccentricity or novelty-seeking. At this level, INTPs will still struggle to understand their conflicting functions – Extraverted

Thinking, Extraverted Feeling and Introverted Feeling. There is an interest in self-improvement at this level, and the INTP will seek feedback from others, often focusing more on the "valuable" negative feedback than the positive feedback as it is addressing the negatives that will lead to improvement.

INTPs operating at this level will be effective in the workplace, however they will still be prone to preferring to work on finding solutions alone, being hesitant to take action unless they have complete confidence in their decisions, and paying insufficient attention to personal connectedness.

Considerate Individualism

INTPs at this level of development will move away from using the strengths of their type to solve problems in an original manner, and move towards using these strengths to produce creative, long-term, solutions and demonstrate global thinking. They will be methodical, conceptual and strategic in their approach, and begin to refine their auxiliary Extraverted Intuition; becoming less concerned with remaining open to new ideas and reluctant to reach closure, and more focused on arriving at timely and practically workable solutions. INTPs at this level can often be ingenious in their thinking and have the ability to solve problems that seem impossible to others.

In themselves they will become more observant and curious, and in interpersonal settings they will be more tolerant and accepting, enjoying discussing theories and hearing different viewpoints. Others are likely to perceive them as insightful, principled, unusually quick learners, and relaxed yet measured in their approach to things. They will start to allow perceived imperfections and approximations ("good enoughs") to occur and will be more willing to take decisive action and trust their instincts than at previous levels.

They no longer thrive on recognition for their intellect and originality, but enjoy taking time to enjoy the simple pleasures in life. As their self-awareness develops, they will become aware of the shadow sides of their preferences (the characteristics of the lower levels) and become mindful observers of their processes. Toning down their Ti and Ne preferences allows more access to their non-preferred sides, however their use of these are likely to be channelled via their Ti and Ne preferences. For example, when considering the impact of an action on people (F), they will conceptualise it in terms of the logical benefits – contented workers are more productive so it is important to address the people issues. Nevertheless, they will see the real value inherent in the S and F approach and appreciate being in the moment and spending time relating to others.

Interpersonally, they will coach and facilitate others, encouraging others to find their own direction, rather than advise, teach and mentor. INTPs may feel as if they are becoming incompetent or ineffective at times because, where they previously thought that they could usually find the truth, they will now often encounter situations where they can accept a number of different viewpoints and not reach a clear and logical conclusion.

Integration and Authenticity

At this level, the qualities of the INTP preferences can shine through – mental agility, imagination, decisiveness and creativity. The INTP can appear to be an ingenious thinker, able to see seemingly impossible connections in complex issues. They will be keen to share knowledge generously with others and will usually be able to offer a different and unique perspective on matters. Although they recognise that people are responsible for their own self-improvement, they can still become impatient with people who do not seem to be striving towards this.

At this level, they become comfortable with the fact that they do not have to relentlessly pursue expertise and truth and can enjoy activities that are purely for enjoyment or that do not lead to a logically perfect outcome. They are no longer concerned with defending their image of being intelligently original and independent and enjoy the learning they get from being with a variety of other people. Through increased mindfulness, they will often be able to access their S and F preferences and adapt their actions appropriately; paying attention to the present, being more in touch with their physical bodies, truly empathising with others, and stopping their drive for knowledge and truth in order to just "be" with people or enjoy their time alone.

Magician

At this level, INTPs realise that their drive for searching for the truth and demonstrating original thinking is ego-driven and a distraction from their true self. They will become more accepting of others being who and what they are, realising that trying to encourage others to be inquisitive, logical and questioning is also a function of their own ego.

Being able to let go of dualities, they will see that Feeling is part of the same concept as Thinking, and that Sensing is part of the same concept as Intuition, seeing the similarities in the functions rather than the differences and therefore being able to gain easy and natural access to

The Developmentally Levelled Type Descriptions

> S and F. At this stage, they may also frequently experience the transcendent function – where from two apparent opposites a third way emerges, often in a form that is symbolic or intuitive.

ISFJ

Hierarchy of Functions:

Dominant: Introverted Sensing

Auxiliary: Extraverted Feeling

Tertiary: Thinking

Inferior: Extraverted Intuition

Main Features and Distortions of the ISFJ Type:

ISFJs are reliable, loyal and stable individuals with a strong sense of wanting to do the right thing by others.

They can become obsessive about not being seen in a bad light, not wanting to make a mistake, or not wanting to let others down, leading to paralysis and anxiety.

Conflicting Functions:

Extraverted Sensing, as the opposite orientation to the dominant, can be seen as meaningless and purposeless thrill-seeking and acting irresponsibly without consideration of consequences – deliberately flying in the face of convention and social acceptance.

Extraverted Intuition, as their inferior function, can be seen as novelty-seeking, unnecessary risk-taking, rocking the boat and poorly thought-out ideas aimed at relieving boredom rather than having any practical use.

Introverted Intuition, as the contrast to the dominant function, may be seen as vague, unrealistic and operating on the basis of guess work.

Core Values: Relationships, co-operation and responsibility

Power and Control

ISFJs who are operating at this level of development are likely to respond to most situations using a distortion of their dominant Introverted Sensing preference and will often be seen as rigid, dogmatic, judgemental and inflexible. Even at this level, they are concerned with belonging and acceptance and will use their auxiliary Extraverted Feeling to consider what they can do to connect to others. However as they are concerned with protecting and defending themselves at this level, they may disguise attempts to manipulate others by appearing to be helpful and concerned, or, with great but unspoken resentment, take actions that are more focused on keeping others happy rather than doing what they would like to. They often "get revenge" on people who have offended or upset them by quietly doing something to address the perceived injustice, but that the other person may be completely unaware of. For example, they may deliberately give them a cheaper or less thoughtful birthday present than they would usually have given; the person may not be aware that they have been slighted, but the ISFJ feels satisfaction from their actions.

ISFJs will usually feel uncomfortable with conflict and are likely to withdraw from conflict situations. In differences of opinion they will either let others take charge or, if they feel that something important is at stake, may stage a "one person protest" and opt out; sometimes talking about their position privately with others in order to try to get support for their view. With people they feel comfortable with they can get into arguments where they stubbornly insist on the correctness of their own experience and beliefs and refuse to listen to any other views. In the workplace they like to be part of small, cohesive teams, but are likely to be hypersensitive at this level to any disharmony in the team.

Many ISFJs may be secretive about their thoughts, ideas or interests in order to prevent others from judging them, as it is so important for them to be seen as doing the right thing. They can often be seen by others as short-tempered, self-righteous, guarded, self-pitying and resentful. In addition to this, as with most other Introverted types with Feeling preferences operating at this level, they can be seen as aloof, oversensitive, and self-absorbed. As subordinates they can be difficult to manage as they will focus intently on what their boss is like as a person and have difficulty with feelings of loyalty towards a boss who is not friendly and consistent.

If they are feeling threatened, particularly in terms of their sense of security or their sense of belonging, they may play ego-defensive survival games that involve complaining, nagging, becoming depressed or experiencing physical illnesses. These survival games are attempts at manipulating others to get their own way, trying to get people involved with them, or trying to shed some of their responsibilities. They are usually played out at an unconscious level.

ISFJs at this level are often extremely fearful about getting out of their comfort zone or making mistakes, although they can hide this well and give the outward appearance of graceful perfectionism. They may be unaware of how others may be different to them and merely see them as being wrong, amoral or unpleasant in some way; or they will often turn this in on themselves and feel like they are on a mission to uphold certain standards on behalf of others. They can be quick to judge others and will be very sensitive to what they think the other person's opinion of them is.

Social Identification

Part of the SJ temperament is a concern for belonging and being seen to do the right (i.e. socially acceptable) thing. Therefore, at this level ISFJs will naturally gravitate to the idea of upholding norms, traditions and belonging to groups. If they manage to get into type-supportive groups they will be unlikely to want a position of leadership or influence, but will feel content being part of a supportive and cohesive team. As with most Introverted types they will value being part of a group that has a "turn taking" communication pattern and being with people who are good listeners. They will use their natural preferences to support other group members and will be very sensitive to the degree of harmony within the group. However they may also be indirectly critical about or dismissive towards those that they see as non-conformist, overly independent or not fully committed. In general, they will be desperate never to lose face in front of others or be seen to have let others down.

If ISFJs end up being in groups that do not support their natural styles, they may desperately try to fit in by creating new rules or norms in their minds. As they are people who like to do things to perfection and according to the rules, they will adapt to whatever the new norms and customs of the group are with complete dedication. They may suppress their natural styles and make clumsy use of their underdeveloped non-preferred functions, often channelling them through their Si and Fe preferences, e.g. by trying to resolve what they perceive to be a conflict situation by telling those involved to stop arguing and make up. However, in general, they are more likely to avoid getting involved with people they consider to be different to the norm and will seek out type-alike or type-supportive groups.

As their preferences often fit with widely accepted social norms, ISFJs rarely feel like or appear to be misfits and generally have little trouble fitting in. ISFJs at this level can be very critical of "out-groups" and see them as subversive or as simply just "wrong". Their loyalty to their friends and ideals can make them very defensive in the face of threats.

Personal Identification

At this level, ISFJs begin to channel their dominant Introverted Sensing into their lives and work; being practical, disciplined, dutiful, diligent and committed. They will often demonstrate excellent attention to detail and the ability to remember information about people and take appropriate action; for example remembering a colleague's birthday and ensuring that this is acknowledged, or recalling an earlier conversation with a client and referring to it on their next call, thus building good rapport and making the client feel significant. They will prefer to work in environments that have clear guidelines and structures and where there is time to connect with people on a personal level. However they may push their type preferences too strongly at times and become stubborn, inflexible, authoritarian, over-involved with others, hypersensitive in their relationships with other people and perfectionistic.

At this level they may selectively attend to immediate outcomes and needs, disregarding the bigger picture, and may also selectively attend to information and evidence that fits with their experience or ideas. They will have a generally good idea about the kind of person they are and will notice the differences between themselves and others, however they are likely to regard the different styles of others as irresponsible, "random" or insensitive. For example they will not understand why people with Thinking preferences can take a detached viewpoint and will see their objectivity as a lack of care or empathy; or they will regard people with Perceiving preferences as frustratingly careless and even lazy. They will be distrusting of people who they consider to be disorganised or "big idea" people. Others may experience ISFJs at this level as being hard to get to know well, hypersensitive, serious, conflict-avoidant and reluctant to consider alternatives once their mind has been made up.

In dealing with others they will be quick to give advice and sympathy but shy away from delivering feedback that they perceive to be negative. They will want encouragement, appreciation and approval from others and may feel offended if this is not forthcoming. Overall they can be accommodating and pleasant teamworkers, however they are likely to use suppression and repression where necessary in order to maintain the image of doing the right thing and for fear of making mistakes.

Determined Action

ISFJs at this level really begin to use the strengths of their preferences and will be steady, punctual, procedural, realistic, hardworking, factual, and responsible. In their work they will be interested in achieving goals that will be of benefit to others, and in their home lives they will seek to create a sense of comfort and security. They will attend to information about people or events that have personal significance, and will be sensitive to interpersonal dynamics. In dealing with others they will be attentive, caring, collaborative and empathic.

They will realise that they have some blind spots in terms of their openness to change and ambiguity, and their comfort with making tough decisions, and they are likely to begin to realise that there is some value to be gained from N and T ways of thinking. Therefore, they may seek viewpoints from those they see as different to themselves, however they will only incorporate these ideas if they do not go against their preferences too strongly, although they will make every effort to accommodate others. Many ISFJs, even at this level, can have doubts about their opinions and will often seek the input or approval of others or consider what other people they hold in high regard may advise them to do. As Introverted types, they may tend to overuse their auxiliary function (Extraverted Feeling), particularly at this stage; this can often manifest as being people-pleasing, unassertive and reliant on others.

At this stage ISFJs will still struggle to understand their conflicting functions – Extraverted Sensing, Extraverted Intuition and Introverted Intuition. There is an interest in self-improvement at this level, and the ISFJ will seek feedback from others, needing a balance of positives and negatives to feel motivated to try to learn from the feedback and accept it non-defensively.

ISFJs operating at this level will be effective in the workplace, however they will still be prone to putting the needs of others first (sometimes secretly begrudging this), being impatient or frustrated by ambiguity, and finding it difficult to deviate from a well-crafted plan.

Considerate Individualism

ISFJs at this level of development will move away from using the strengths of their type to be meticulous and practically attentive to others, and move towards using these strengths to be steadfast, trustworthy, effortful, sensitive and kind in their work and lives. They will be thoughtful and focused in their approach, and begin to refine their auxiliary Extraverted Feeling; becoming less concerned with pleasing and serving others, and more genuine and considered in their actions. In general they will be more trusting of their own opinions and less reliant on confirmation from others. In dealing with others they will be compassionate, gentle, loyal and unassuming.

ISFJs at this stage of development will allow themselves to recognise that their ideals and standards can not always be realised and generally take a more realistic view of what they can and cannot influence. They no longer thrive on wanting to be recognised for their "good citizenship" and perfectionism, but enjoy taking time to enjoy the simple pleasures in life and allowing imperfections. As their self-awareness develops, they will become aware of the shadow sides of their preferences (the characteristics of the lower levels) and become mindful observers of their processes. Toning down their Si and Fe preferences allows more access to their non-preferred sides, however their use of these are likely to be channelled via their Si and Fe preferences. For example, they may decide that a change is needed and, taking a deep breath, start by considering what they know has worked for others to inform their course of action. Nevertheless, they will see the real value inherent in the N and T approach.

If managing or working with people, they will coach and guide, using a supportive style and being accepting of and understanding towards others' differences. As they have a natural interest in supporting and helping others they will find great satisfaction from using this type of management style. The ISFJ may feel as if they are becoming disorganised or unclear at times because, where they previously thought that they knew their own mind and how things should be, they will now often encounter situations where they are considering alternatives and unconventional approaches and views.

Integration and Authenticity

At this level, the qualities of the ISFJ preferences can shine through – dependability, decisiveness, loyalty and diplomacy. They will be conscientious and secure in themselves, and affiliative and diplomatic

The Developmentally Levelled Type Descriptions

in their dealings with others. The ISFJ will be truly committed to those around them with a balanced level of responsibility and care. At this level, they can resist the drive to create a favourable outward image by being rule-abiding and perfectionistic, and can instead enjoy activities that are purely for enjoyment and relaxation. They are no longer concerned with defending their image of being responsible and flawless, and enjoy the learning they get from being with a variety of other people, even those who they previously found abrasive or irresponsible.

Through increased mindfulness, they will often be able to access their N and T preferences and adapt their actions appropriately; looking to the bigger picture, able to take an objective standpoint when necessary, open to new experiences, and stopping the drive to please and gain approval from others in order to just "be" with people or enjoy their time alone.

Magician

ISFJs realise that their concern with "doing the right thing and doing it right" is ego driven and a distraction from their true self. They will become more accepting of others being who and what they are, realising that trying to encourage others to be responsible and perfectionistic is also a function of their own ego. Being able to let go of dualities, they will see that Thinking is part of the same concept as Feeling, and that Intuition is part of the same concept as Sensing, seeing the similarities in the functions rather than the differences and therefore being able to gain easy and natural access to N and T. At this stage, they may also frequently experience the transcendent function – where from two apparent opposites a third way emerges, often in a form that is symbolic or intuitive

ISFP

Hierarchy of Functions:

Dominant: Introverted Feeling

Auxiliary: Extraverted Sensing

Tertiary: Intuition

Inferior: Extraverted Thinking

Main Features and Distortions of the ISFP Type:

ISFPs live life guided by their personal values and are often concerned with practically helping people or the causes they believe in.

They can become self-righteous, self-absorbed and harshly judgemental of anyone or anything that is not congruent with their values. The values system itself can become distorted.

Conflicting Functions:

Extraverted Feeling, as the opposite orientation to the dominant, is usually seen as intrusive, interfering, meddling in other people's business and a desperation to be liked by others.

Extraverted Thinking, as their inferior function, can be seen as taking hasty, ill-considered, and impersonal action, and as overwhelming and domineering.

Introverted Thinking, as the contrast to the dominant function, can be perceived as detached, overly formulaic and lacking the human touch.

Core Values: Equality, practical help and freedom

Power and Control

ISFPs at this level of development are likely to respond to most situations using a distortion of their dominant Introverted Feeling preference and may often be seen as isolative, resentful, petty, intolerant and judgemental. Others may feel that they are "walking on eggshells" with them. They will use their auxiliary Extraverted Sensing to look for realistic, immediate and practical ways to make a difference to others according to their ideals about how life should be, however, at this level, this can often manifest itself as inappropriately jumping into take action to create harmony or fun in a situation oblivious to the real needs of the others involved.

As Introverted types, ISFPs will often deal with conflict by stating their viewpoint concisely, then withdrawing from any further discussion and either taking stubbornly independent action or going off in a huff. If they choose to enter into a debate they can become dogmatically insistent that only their views and values are valid. As ISFPs often take the position of going with the flow until there is an important issue at stake, they tend to fall into their "grip" response of Extraverted Thinking in a "straw that broke the camel's back" manner; suddenly, and often as a surprise to those present, launching into a blunt and sometimes vicious tirade.

In the workplace they like to be able to work on their own to some extent, although they will appreciate being part of a supportive and harmonious team. They can often be seen by others as distant, defensive, impatient, guarded, quick to take offence and sometimes forceful in expressing their opinions. ISFPs at this level can be fairly harsh in their criticism of people who they consider to be living immorally or without values. They like the idea of support and, at this level, may be more interested in being supported than giving support to others. Therefore they often become over dependent on selected others and can quickly feel unappreciated and undervalued at the first hint of perceived rejection. ISFPs can also be extremely sensitive to other people's opinions of them. As subordinates they will need the freedom to work in their own way and can be deliberately disruptive if they are in structured or rule-bound settings.

If they are feeling defensive, particularly in cases where their freedom or enjoyment are being threatened, they may play ego-defensive survival games such as throwing tantrums, becoming violent or undertaking risky/thrill-seeking behaviours in order to create excitement for themselves and make those around them feel uncomfortable. They may also get into a trap of impulsively taking actions based on immediate needs, getting bored before completing tasks, and lacking the motivation to commit to anything. If they feel like the only person who is trying to make things "right" or "do what is important", they will become very frustrated with and intolerant of those around them and can fall into the "martyr" role. They can also turn this in on themselves and feel like misfits in the world. Although they consider themselves to be sensitive to other people, they are likely to be unaware of how others really may be as their perceptions of them will be distorted by their own preferences.

Social Identification

ISFPs often find themselves being part of groups that do not support their preferences and having to "make do" with joining in with others' plans, interests or activities. However, ISFPs are usually happy to go with the flow of the group and often take the role of the quiet but supportive group member. If their ISFP characteristics do not "fit" they may sometimes suppress their natural styles and make clumsy use of their underdeveloped non-preferred functions, often channelling them through their Fi and Se preferences. For example, by trying to take charge of a situation where they perceive conflict by telling the people concerned to simply stop and make up.

Some ISFPs will be deliberately rebellious or "nonconformist" at this level, instead conforming to the "rebel" stereotype. Nevertheless, the ISFP will indulge the need for belonging characterised by this level by pursuing interests and hobbies that are congruent with their preferences. If they manage to get into type-supportive groups they are unlikely to seek a position of leadership or influence, but will have a key role as a harmoniser, mediator and supporter. They may find it difficult to assert themselves in a group as they will be concerned with maintaining harmony, however this can often lead to them getting into situations they do not want to be in and quietly harbouring feelings of resentment. As with most Introverted types they will value being part of a group that has a "turn taking" communication pattern and being with people who are good listeners.

Personal Identification

At this level ISFPs begin to channel their dominant Introverted Feeling into their lives and work; they will be values-driven, dedicated, helpful and supportive. They will usually be practical and factual, however this may not come across to others clearly if their dominant Introverted Feeling is excessively overriding their auxiliary Extraverted Sensing. They will prefer to work in environments that have a harmonious atmosphere and will function best in small groups or when working alone. However they may push their type preferences too strongly at times and become oversensitive, opinionated, dogmatic, hasty, perfectionistic and judgemental. Others may experience ISFPs at this level as being hard to get to know, distractible, gullible and self-effacing.

At this level they may overuse their Extraverted Sensing, leaping into action without fully thinking things through. They can also become too laid-back, avoid making decisions or taking responsibility and keen to defend their place in their comfort zone. In dealing with others they will be quick to give advice and sympathy but shy away from delivering feedback that they perceive to be negative. They will want encouragement, appreciation and approval from others and may feel offended or insecure if this is not forthcoming. If they find themselves in situations that do not allow them to present suggestions and opinions they may quietly and secretively get on with initiatives on their own without consultation. They will also resist any attempts by others to control them, but will use a passive-aggressive style rather than be directly confrontational.

They will have a generally good idea about the kind of person they are and will notice the differences between themselves and others, however they will still tend to be harsh in their judgement of those who they perceive as living with no or with the "wrong" values. ISFPs operating at this level frequently "get on their high horse" about certain subjects when they are with people with whom they feel comfortable. They will also still have difficulty in understanding people with different type preferences. For example they will not understand how people with Thinking preferences can make decisions that are not acceptable to everybody and will see their logical detachment as uncaring, harsh or selfish. They will also struggle with seeing the bigger picture and will feel overwhelmed in the face of ambiguity.

Determined Action

At this level ISFPs really begin to use the strengths of their preferences and will be considerate, sensitive, caretaking, gentle and realistic. They will value mutually supportive relationships and will come across to others as adaptable, empathic, playful, unassuming and spontaneous. In their approach to work they will be realistic and aware of the details, and keen to ensure that their undertakings are congruent with their beliefs.

They will realise that they have some blind spots in terms of their consideration of the wider implications of their actions, their ability to stick with routine tasks and their comfort with making tough decisions, and they are likely to begin to realise that there is some value to be gained from N and T ways of thinking. Therefore, they may seek viewpoints from those they see as different to themselves, however they will only incorporate these ideas if they do not go against their preferences too strongly, although they will make every effort to accommodate others.

As Introverted types, they may tend to overuse their auxiliary function

(Extraverted Sensing), particularly at this stage; this can often give the impression of not taking things seriously or thinking things through. At this stage ISFPs will still struggle to understand their conflicting functions – Extraverted Feeling, Extraverted Thinking and Introverted Thinking. There is an interest in self-improvement and introspection at this level, and the ISFP will seek feedback from others, needing a balance of positives and negatives to feel motivated to try to learn from the feedback and accept it non-defensively. When giving feedback to others, however, they may play down any negatives for fear of de-motivating or offending the other person.

ISFPs operating at this level will be effective in the workplace, however they will still be prone to thinking through ideas alone, overlooking future implications, and avoiding truths if they go against their ideals.

Considerate Individualism

ISFPs at this level of development will move away from using the strengths of their type to look for ways to make things better for people, and move towards using these strengths to take practical and timely actions that are often underpinned by a concern for people. They will be open-minded and loyal to their beliefs in their approach to work, and will be seeking purpose in most of the things they engage in. They will begin to refine their auxiliary Extraverted Sensing; becoming less concerned with dealing with immediate needs and reluctant to reach closure, and more focused on taking carefully considered actions that are congruent with what is important to them. Nevertheless, they will still remain present-oriented, observant, playful, responsive and hands-on in their approach.

In themselves they will become more respectful of other people's values, views and opinions and show a genuine interest in creating harmony in the face of difference. However, at times ISFPs may feel as if they are becoming cynical or losing touch with their values because, where they previously thought that they knew what was important to them, they will now often encounter situations where they can accept harsh realities and incongruence, or hold differing views on the same subject. Others are likely to perceive ISFPs at this level as gentle, adaptable, modest and true to their beliefs without being forceful. They will come across as collegiate rather than seeking leadership, and if they are in a lead position they will resist creating hierarchy and consider themselves part of the team.

They no longer thrive on recognition for their integrity and service to others, but enjoy taking time to enjoy the simple pleasures in life. As their self-awareness develops, they will become aware of the shadow sides of their preferences (the characteristics of the lower levels) and become mindful observers of their processes. Toning down their Fi and Se preferences allows more access to their non-preferred sides, however their use of these are likely to be channelled via their Fi and Se preferences. For example, when considering how to get the best results they will view this result as being the one that everybody can get onboard with. Nevertheless, they will see the real value inherent in the N and T approach. Interpersonally, they will support and facilitate others, encouraging others to find their own direction, rather than guide, teach and mentor.

Integration and Authenticity

At this level, the qualities of the ISFP preferences can shine through – compassion, dedication, faithfulness, serenity and liberty. The ISFP can appear to be a true humanitarian who wants to genuinely contribute to others without reward. They will be keen to make a difference to others in a gentle, non-forceful and measured way, promoting harmony rather than forcing it on others. Although they recognise that people are responsible for their own lifestyle choices, they can still become impatient with those who seem to act without care or consideration, or who abuse human rights. At this level they will be uncannily attuned to the needs of others.

ISFPs now become comfortable with the fact that they do not have to relentlessly pursue congruence and righteousness and can enjoy activities that are purely for enjoyment or that do not necessarily have a meaningful outcome. They are no longer concerned with defending their image of being principled and a peacemaker and enjoy the learning they get from being with a variety of other people. Through increased mindfulness, they will often be able to access their N and T preferences and adapt their actions appropriately; paying attention to the present moment with a stillness and wonder instead of taking action, being more in touch with their physical bodies, and stopping their drive for congruence and harmony in order to just "be" with people or enjoy their time alone.

Magician

At this level ISFPs realise that their drive for congruence and peace is ego-driven and a distraction from their true self. They will become more accepting of others being who and what they are, realising that trying to encourage others to be values-based, supportive and

> harmonious is also a function of their own ego.
>
> Being able to let go of dualities, they will see that Thinking is part of the same concept as Feeling, and that Intuition is part of the same concept as Sensing, seeing the similarities in the functions rather than the differences and therefore being able to gain easy and natural access to N and T. At this stage, they may also frequently experience the transcendent function – where from two apparent opposites a third way emerges, often in a form that is symbolic or intuitive.

ISTJ

Hierarchy of Functions:

Dominant: Introverted Sensing

Auxiliary: Extraverted Thinking

Tertiary: Feeling

Inferior: Extraverted Intuition

Main Features and Distortions of the ISTJ Type:

ISTJs are reliable, dependable and stable individuals with a strong sense of wanting to do the right thing in the best manner.

They can become obsessive about not wanting to make a mistake or deviate from the known and secure, leading to paralysis and anxiety.

Conflicting Functions:

Extraverted Sensing, as the opposite orientation to the dominant, can be seen as meaningless and purposeless thrill-seeking and acting irresponsibly without consideration of consequences – deliberately flying in the face of convention and sensible action.

Extraverted Intuition, as their inferior function, can be seen as novelty seeking, unnecessary risk-taking, an inefficient use of time, and poorly thought-out ideas, aimed at relieving boredom rather than have any practical use.

Introverted Intuition, as the contrast to the dominant function, may be seen as vague, unrealistic and operating on the basis of guess work.

The Developmentally Levelled Type Descriptions

Core Values: Competence, consistency and responsibility

Power and Control

ISTJs who are operating at this level of development are likely to respond to most situations using a distortion of their dominant Introverted Sensing preference and will often be seen as dogmatic, impatient, overcautious and inflexible. They will use their auxiliary Extraverted Thinking to look for logical justifications for their ideas and to put their thoughts into action; however they may be selective in the information they choose to include in their planning and only attend to information that is consistent with their own experience, ending up taking actions that feel safe, considered and predictable.

As Introverted types, ISTJs will often deal with conflict by stating their viewpoint concisely, then withdrawing from any further discussion and stubbornly taking action their own way without telling anybody until they have finished. If they continue to argue they may become insistent that only their experience or knowledge is correct and only see negative possibilities in the ideas or opinions of others. They may also make harsh decisions that appear to lack any compassion. In the workplace they prefer to work alone, however if they are working with others they will demand clarity, structure and commitment, therefore they will be very critical and dismissive of people who are spontaneous or laid-back, seeing them as irresponsible and lazy.

They can often be seen by others as blunt, opinionated, isolative, pessimistic and uncompassionate. In addition to this, as with most other Introverted types with Thinking preferences, they can be seen as aloof, detached and impersonal. As subordinates they can be difficult to manage as they consider good management to be directive, consistent and precise. If this is not their boss's style they are likely to make judgements on the boss's competence.

If they are feeling threatened, particularly in terms of their security or perceived competence, they may play ego-defensive survival games that involve complaining, nagging, becoming depressed or experiencing physical illnesses. These survival games are attempts at manipulating others to get their own way, trying to get people involved with them, or trying to shed some of their responsibilities. They are usually played out at an unconscious level. ISTJs at this level are often extremely fearful about getting out of their comfort zone or making mistakes, although they can hide this well and give the outward appearance of arrogant confidence. They may be unaware of how

The Shadows of Type

others may be different to them and merely see them as being wrong or ineffective in some way.

Social Identification

Part of the SJ temperament is a concern for belonging and being seen to do the right (i.e. socially acceptable) thing. Therefore, at this level ISTJs will naturally gravitate to the idea of upholding norms, traditions and belonging. If they manage to get into type-supportive groups they will be unlikely to want a position of leadership or influence, but will feel content being part of a mutually responsible and efficient team. As with most Introverted types they will value being part of a group that has a "turn taking" communication pattern and being with people who are good listeners. However they may also be indirectly critical about or dismissive towards those whom they see as non-conformist, overly independent or not fully committed.

If ISTJs end up being in groups that do not support their natural styles, they may try to fit in by creating new rules or norms in their minds. As they are people who like to do things to perfection and according to the rules, they will adapt to the new norms and customs of the group with complete dedication. They may suppress their natural styles and make clumsy use of their underdeveloped non-preferred functions, often channelling them through their Si and Te preferences, such as trying to help somebody by telling them exactly what they need to do, usually based on a single example of their own or other person's experience.

As their preferences often fit with widely accepted social norms, ISTJs rarely feel like or appear to be misfits, and generally have little trouble fitting in. If they do find themselves spending a lot of time with people or in situations that do not support their preferences, the ISTJ may indulge their need for belonging by pursuing interests and hobbies that are congruent with their preferences; this can serve the dual purpose of making them feel less of a misfit, but also making them feel as if they have a private or secret other life. ISTJs at this level can be very critical of "out-groups" and see them as subversive or as simply just "wrong". Their loyalty to their friends and their sense of what is right can make them very defensive in the face of threats.

Personal Identification

ISTJs at this level channel their dominant Introverted Sensing into their lives and work; being practical, structured, dutiful, diligent and committed. They will approach tasks in a meticulous and detail-conscious way and, in themselves, will be reserved and considered in their actions. They will usually be logical, organised and decisive, however this may not come across to others clearly if their dominant Introverted Sensing is excessively overriding their auxiliary Extraverted Thinking.

They will prefer to work in environments that allow a degree of independence and will function best in small groups or when working alone. Alternatively, if they are working in a large group environment, they will need to have clear guidelines, goals and structures. However they may push their type preferences too strongly at times and become rigid, serious, critical, judgemental, insistent, concrete, and irritatingly predictable. They often find it difficult to trust others to correctly carry out their ideas and plans, and therefore struggle to delegate and let go of their plans and tasks. If they find themselves in situations that do not allow them to present their own views and opinions they may quietly and secretively get on with initiatives on their own without consultation.

They will generally have a good idea about the kind of person they are and will notice the differences between themselves and others, however they are likely to regard the different styles of others as illogical or unproductive. For example, they will not understand why people with Feeling preferences get so personally involved, and will see their subjectivity as weakness and as a flaw in their functioning; or they will regard people with Perceiving preferences as frustratingly indecisive and even lazy. Others may experience ISTJs at this level as inexpressive, controlling, narrow-focused, dismissive of new ideas and tough-minded.

In dealing with others they will be quick to give remedial feedback but overlook opportunities for praise and appreciation. They may also deliver harsh truths in the spirit of helping the other person to improve, but not realise the impact of the blunt delivery of the message. They often use their respect for tradition and experience plus their natural tendency to store and recall information to read others the "rule book". At this level ISTJs can be in serious danger of workaholism.

Determined Action

At this level, ISTJs really begin to use the strengths of their preferences and will be objective, task-focused, analytical, decisive, steadfast, scheduled, reserved, efficient, tenacious, orderly and traditionalistic. They will have high standards and strive for efficiency and results, often going the extra mile. In dealing with others they will be fair, appropriately challenging, directive, and will encourage a rule conscious approach.

ISTJs operating at this level will be generally effective in the workplace, however they will still often overuse rationalisation and logic and overlook personal connectedness as well as having a tendency to get bogged down in data gathering. They are also likely to be very tied to the rule book, put output above personal contributions, have a dislike for ambiguity and expect high standards from others. As introverted types, they may tend to overuse their auxiliary function (Extraverted Thinking), particularly at this stage; this can often manifest as critical, impatient and rather to the point.

They will realise that they have some blind spots in terms of their awareness of the wider or future implications of their actions, their ability to adapt to change and their interpersonal sensitivity, and they are likely to begin to realise that there is some value to be gained from N and F ways of thinking. Therefore, they may seek viewpoints from those whom they see as different to themselves; however they will only incorporate these ideas if they do not go too strongly against their own preferences. At this level, ISTJs will also still struggle to understand their conflicting functions – Extraverted Sensing, Extraverted Intuition and Introverted Intuition. There is an interest in self-improvement at this level, and the ISTJ will seek feedback from others, often focusing more on the "valuable" negative feedback than the positive feedback as, in their view, it is addressing the negatives that will lead to improvement.

Considerate Individualism

ISTJs at this level of development will move away from using the strengths of their type to achieve meticulously executed outcomes, and move towards using these strengths to be realistic, practical, factual, trustworthy and quick-minded. They will be considered and focused in their approach, and will begin to refine their auxiliary Extraverted Thinking; becoming less concerned with consistency and security in their actions and willing to experiment and trust their instincts more. They will also be more open to the information that they can gather from others and open to others' viewpoints. They no longer thrive on recognition for "good citizenship" and efficiency and will begin to relax more and allow things to evolve and contain imperfections rather than trying to perfectly plan them.

Others are likely to describe them as firm yet fair leaders and they are likely to come across as reasonable, clear and concise in communication, witty, steady and helpful. As their self-awareness develops, they will become aware of the shadow sides of their preferences (the characteristics of the lower levels) and become mindful observers of their processes. Toning down their Si and Te preferences allows more access to their non-preferred sides, however their use of these is likely to be channelled via their Si and Te preferences. For example, when considering the impact of an action on people (F), they will evaluate it in terms of the logical benefits – contented workers are more productive so it is important to address the people issues. Nevertheless, they will see the real value inherent in the N and F approach.

Interpersonally, they will coach and facilitate others, encouraging them to find their own direction, rather than advising, teaching and mentoring. The ISTJ may feel as if they are becoming incompetent or ineffective at times because, where they previously thought that they knew what was absolutely right, they will now often encounter situations where they can accept a number of different viewpoints and not reach a clear and logical conclusion.

Integration and Authenticity

At this level, the qualities of the ISTJ preferences can shine through – loyalty, dependability, dedication, independence and fair-mindedness. Although they recognise that people are responsible for themselves, they can still become impatient with people who do not seem to have a strong work ethic. At this level, they become comfortable with the fact that they do not have to relentlessly pursue precision and "rightness" and can enjoy activities that are purely for enjoyment or that have no meaningful outcome. They are no longer concerned with defending their image of being well-informed and consistent and enjoy the learning they get from being with a variety of other people.

In dealing with others they will calmly offer practical help and the gift of their experience without insistence and with open-mindedness. Through increased mindfulness, they will often be able to access their N and F preferences and adapt their actions appropriately; experiencing the present moment, being more in touch with their physical presence, truly empathising with others, and stopping their drive for security in order to just "be" with people or enjoy their time alone.

Magician

ISTJs realise that their drive for reliability, security and accuracy is ego-driven and a distraction from their true self. They will become more accepting of others being who and what they are, realising that

The Shadows of Type

> trying to encourage others to be responsible and meticulous is also a function of their own ego.
>
> Being able to let go of dualities, they will see that Feeling is part of the same concept as Thinking, and that Intuition is part of the same concept as Sensing, seeing the similarities in the functions rather than the differences and therefore being able to gain easy and natural access to N and F. At this stage, they may also frequently experience the transcendent function – where from two apparent opposites a third way emerges, often in a form that is symbolic or intuitive.

ISTP

Hierarchy of Functions:

Dominant: Introverted Thinking

Auxiliary: Extraverted Sensing

Tertiary: Intuition

Inferior: Extraverted Feeling

Main Features and Distortions of the ISTP Type:

ISTPs are responsive problem-solving types, based on their attention to real and detailed information, and have an uncanny ability to see how things work.

They can become very detached and absorbed in their thoughts and can often procrastinate for a long time before taking action, as they will be worried that their solutions may not be perfect.

Conflicting Functions:

Extraverted Thinking, as the opposite orientation to the dominant, can be seen as taking hasty, ill-considered action and as overwhelming and domineering.

Extraverted Feeling, as their inferior function, is usually seen as intrusive, interfering, meddling in other peoples' business, and a desperation to be liked by others.

Introverted Feeling, as the contrast to the dominant function, can be perceived as oversensitive, idealistic and avoidant of harsh realities.

Core Values: Logic, experience and expedience

Power and Control

ISTPs operating at this level of development are likely to respond to most situations using a distortion of their dominant Introverted Thinking preference and will often be seen as isolative, blunt, negative, indecisive and non-empathic. They will use their auxiliary Extraverted Sensing to take in realistic and detailed information to inform their problem-solving and find answers, however, at this level, this can often manifest itself as narrow-mindedness, insistence, obsession and, sometimes, rebelliousness. They may find themselves getting into the trap of forcing logic to fit in order to make their solutions fit with their observations.

As Introverted types, ISTPs will often deal with conflict by stating their viewpoint concisely, then withdrawing from any further discussion and taking stubbornly independent action. In the workplace they like to be able to work with a fair degree of independence, however they can feel unfairly disadvantaged if they find themselves out of their comfort zone with no way of getting the information they need in order to feel competent in their work. They can often be seen by others as withdrawn, detached, guarded, non-committal and sometimes forceful in expressing their opinions. In addition to this, as with most other Introverted types with Thinking preferences, they can be seen as aloof, detached and impersonal.

ISTPs can be fairly brutal in their criticism of others as they will see themselves as merely pointing out the truth. They will have little time or value for things that they consider to be illogical or unproductive, such as spending time on a team-bonding exercise. ISTPs at this level can experience restlessness and disappointment as they often have unrealistic expectations about some of the situations they find themselves in. They may also have hidden feelings of insecurity as they worry about not being right or perfect in their logic. As subordinates they can be difficult to manage because they dislike being told how to do things because they enjoy working at their own pace and in their own style.

If they are feeling threatened, particularly in terms of their freedom or perceived competence, they may play ego-defensive survival games such as throwing tantrums, becoming violent or undertaking risky/thrill-seeking behaviours in order to create excitement for themselves and make those around them feel uncomfortable. They may also withdraw and shy away from situations where they do not feel competent. They may be unaware of how others may be different to them and merely see them as being wrong or strange in some way; or they may turn this in on themselves and feel like misfits in the world, particularly female ISTPs. In general, they will see having power and control as being able to shut others out and be left alone rather than engaging in interpersonal power struggles. ISTPs at this level can become so pernickety about getting things right and gathering all the necessary information that other people often mistake them for Introverted Sensing types.

Social Identification

ISTPs often find themselves being part of groups that do not support their preferences and having to "make do" with joining in with others' plans, interests or activities. If their ISTP characteristics do not "fit" they may sometimes suppress their natural styles and make clumsy use of their underdeveloped non-preferred functions, often channelling them through their Ti and Se preferences. For example, trying to do something nice and kind for somebody by giving them a gift that is intended to be fun and humorous, but which is actually somewhat offensive or misplaced. ISTPs tend to trust and confide in a select few people and it can take time for them to develop this trust. Therefore, in trying to fit in with others they may come across as difficult to get to know or guarded without realising it.

Depending on the situation, sometimes ISTPs will stubbornly cling onto trying to be "themselves" when in a group, fully aware that they are taking a nonconformist attitude. It can be important for them to come across as amusing and light-hearted so they often take the role of the "wit" in the group. However, the ISTP may indulge their dominant function by pursuing solitary interests and hobbies that are congruent with their preferences. If they manage to get into type-supportive groups they will enjoy being a valued group member but not usually be at all interested in taking a lead. As with most Introverted types they will value being part of a group that has a "turn taking" communication pattern and being with people who are good listeners.

Personal Identification

ISTPs at this level begin to channel their dominant Introverted

Thinking into their lives and work and will be analytical, practical, questioning and will look for perfect solutions to problems. They will usually be quick to respond to unexpected events and notice the details of a situation to help them reach a solution, however this may not come across to others clearly if their dominant Introverted Thinking is excessively overriding their auxiliary Extraverted Sensing.

They will prefer to work in environments that allow a degree of freedom provided that the expected outcomes are made clear, and they will function best in small groups or when working alone. However, they may ask others for guidance if they are working in a new field, as they tend to believe that one correct solution exists that will help them. At times they may push their type preferences too strongly and become critical, judgemental, cynical, sceptical and insistent.

Others may experience ISTPs at this level as being hard to get to know, detached, aloof, insensitive to interpersonal needs and scholarly (or "nerdy"). ISTPs at this level are often perceived as procrastinators, as they tend to be reluctant to take action unless they believe they have reached the perfect decision. They may also limit their thinking to immediate results and not consider the long-term aspects. In communicating they may overuse their Extraverted Sensing, going into too much detail and giving long explanations, but neglecting to clearly convey their conclusions or decisions. They can also become argumentative and avoid taking advice or accepting logic from others. In dealing with others they will be quick to give remedial feedback but overlook opportunities for praise and appreciation. They may also deliver harsh truths in the spirit of helping the other person to improve, but not realise the impact of the blunt delivery of the message. They often find it difficult to allow others into their thoughts and actions, and therefore find it difficult to delegate.

They will have a generally good idea about the kind of person they are and will notice the differences between themselves and others, however they are likely to regard the different styles of others as illogical or unproductive. For example they will not understand why people with Feeling preferences get so personally involved and will see their subjectivity as weakness and as a flaw in their functioning; or they will regard people with Judging preferences as people who rush into things.

Determined Action

ISTPs at this level really begin to use the strengths of their preferences and will be objective, analytical, logical, grounded, practical, reactive and spontaneous. They will be results-focused and pragmatic in their problem-solving and often create "blueprints" in their minds to help them find their answers and solutions. They will be reserved, reflective, questioning and non-domineering. In their work they will enjoy taking a hands-on approach and will be willing to take considered risks. In dealing with others they will be fair, objectively critical, appropriately challenging and rational; however they are likely to maintain an element of interpersonal detachment and can still overlook the emotional implications of their actions on others.

They will realise that they have some blind spots in terms of their awareness of the wider consequences of their actions and their interpersonal sensitivity. Nevertheless, at this stage they will understand that there is some value to be gained from N and F ways of thinking. Therefore, they may seek viewpoints from those they see as different to themselves, however they will only incorporate these ideas if they do not go against their preferences too strongly.

As Introverted types, they may tend to overuse their auxiliary function (Extraverted Sensing), particularly at this stage; this can often give the impression that they are fire-fighting or trouble-shooting and the level of consideration that they give to an issue may be masked. At this stage ISTPs will still struggle to understand their conflicting functions – Extraverted Thinking, Extraverted Feeling and Introverted Feeling. There is an interest in self-improvement at this level, and the ISTP will seek feedback from others, often focusing more on the "valuable" negative feedback than the positive feedback as it is addressing the negatives that will lead to improvement.

ISTPs operating at this level will be effective in the workplace, however they will still be prone to preferring to work on finding solutions alone, being hesitant to take action unless they have complete confidence in their decisions, and paying insufficient attention to personal connectedness.

Considerate Individualism

At this level of development ISTPs will move away from using the strengths of their type to solve immediate problems, and move towards using these strengths to be adaptable, informed and quick to assimilate information. They will be methodical, considered, quick on their feet and objective in their approach, and begin to refine their auxiliary Extraverted Sensing; becoming less concerned with dealing with the immediate and stimulating, and more focused on arriving at considered and practically workable solutions that have a strategic element to them. They tend to really enjoy life, create fun and seek variety in a more genuine way at this level than they may have done at previous levels. Others are likely to perceive them as straightforward, principled, fair, tolerant, quick learners, and relaxed yet measured in their approach to things. They will start to allow perceived imperfections and approximations ("good enoughs") to occur and will be more willing to take decisive action and trust their instincts than at previous levels.

They no longer thrive on recognition for their intellect and spontaneity, but enjoy taking time to enjoy the simple pleasures in life. As their self-awareness develops, they will become aware of the shadow sides of their preferences (the characteristics of the lower levels) and become mindful observers of their processes. Toning down their Ti and Se preferences allows more access to their non-preferred sides, however their use of these are likely to be channelled via their Ti and Se preferences. For example, when considering the impact of an action on people (F), they will conceptualise it in terms of the logical benefits – contented workers are more productive so it is important to address the people issues. Nevertheless, they will see the real value inherent in the N and F approach.

Interpersonally, they will coach and facilitate others, encouraging them to find their own direction, rather than advise, teach and mentor. ISTPs may feel as if they are becoming incompetent or ineffective at times because, where they previously thought that they could usually find the truth, they will now often encounter situations where they can accept a number of different viewpoints and not reach a clear and logical conclusion.

Integration and Authenticity

At this level, the qualities of the ISTP preferences can shine through – they will be observant, expedient, resourceful, rational, realistic, egalitarian, independent and confident. The ISTP can appear to be an ingenious thinker, acutely aware of present realities and seemingly able to achieve the impossible. They will be self-determined and sure of themselves and less concerned with having to find perfection.

At this level, they become comfortable with the fact that they do not have to relentlessly pursue perfection and truth and can enjoy activities that are purely for enjoyment or that do not lead to a logically perfect outcome. They are no longer concerned with defending their image of being intelligent and correct and enjoy the learning they get from being with a variety of other people. Through increased mindfulness, they will often be able to access their N and F preferences and adapt their actions appropriately; paying attention to the wider implications and the future, being more in touch with their physical bodies, truly empathising with others, and stopping their drive for truth and exactness in order to just "be" with people or enjoy their time alone.

Magician

At this level ISTPs realise that their drive for searching for the truth and looking for practical solutions is ego-driven and a distraction from their true self. They will become more accepting of others being who and what they are, realising that trying to encourage others to be logical and questioning is also a function of their own ego.

Being able to let go of dualities, they will see that Feeling is part of the same concept as Thinking, and that Intuition is part of the same concept as Sensing, seeing the similarities in the functions rather than the differences and therefore being able to gain easy and natural access to N and F. At this stage, they may also frequently experience the transcendent function – where from two apparent opposites a third way emerges, often in a form that is symbolic or intuitive.

Part Two

Practical Applications

Chapter Seven

Practical Applications of the Shadows of Type Model

The aim of the Shadows of Type approach is to enable individuals and coaches to identify the type-related traps and tensions that can create blocks to effective functioning. The developmentally levelled descriptions also provide a "route map" of the potential developmental path for each type. There are a variety of options for working practically with this model as well as a number of benefits for working with it more implicitly. The following chapters provide suggested applications and techniques for working with the dynamics of psychological type, for addressing different aspects of the psyche, and for working at each particular level of ego development.

Firstly, let us remind ourselves of some key points about working with ego development levels and psychological type.

The Shadows of Type

Working with Ego Development Levels and Psychological Type

Whilst it is perfectly possible to work with the ego development model alone, it is enhanced by the inclusion of psychological type, as type can provide more insight into the tensions and dynamics that may be taking place within a person. The following points should, however, be noted:

- Although individuals may get small glimpses of the higher levels, they are only capable of really understanding the world and acting accordingly within the level they have actually developed to.

- People will frequently operate from lower levels than they are capable of. This happens when they are under pressure, acting defensively, experiencing conflict, lacking energy, or when the situation requires it. It is not uncommon for people to fluctuate through a range of levels in any given day.

- Individuals may experience a period of fluctuation and confusion when in transition from one level to a higher level.

- Individuals need time in any given level to fully develop the cognitive agility, self-awareness and perception of that level.

- Psychological type is a broad system that is concerned with the flow of energy within the psyche. It defines what is more energising, motivating, engaging and natural to us. Each individual's type is overlaid and influenced by personality traits, environmental variables, experience, the influence of those around them (interpersonal dynamics), and psychological maturity.

For these reasons, it is essential that coaches match their interventions to the level of development and depth of type knowledge of their client. Setting goals or challenges that are too far above the client's current level of functioning may well result in disappointment and, in turn, may affect the coaching relationship. It should also be noted that at the various levels of development, clients will respond to feedback, challenge and the coach in different ways. Table 8 summarises, by ego development level, the client's capacity for coaching. Additionally it provides some suggestions regarding the issues that individuals operating at the different levels may be experiencing and approaches to the coaching relationship that the coach may take. Note that this table is not prescriptive; it is intended as a guideline only.

Practical Applications of the Shadows of Type Model

		Capacity for Coaching	Potential Issues	Coaching Style
Power and Control		❖ No conscious awareness of their type preferences. ❖ Feedback is seen as a personal attack to be defended against. ❖ May view the coaching as a confrontation or challenge that they need to win. ❖ Operating on "autopilot" with no self-awareness or reflection. ❖ No awareness of the positives of the difference in others. ❖ Black and white thinking.	❖ Extensive use of unconscious ego defence mechanisms. ❖ Will defend against, justify or blame others for any negatives or issues. ❖ Problems with interpersonal relationships. ❖ Excessively judgemental about others. ❖ Failure in a variety of situations. ❖ Underlying anxiety. ❖ Outward persona of "bravado", arrogant self-confidence or invincibility.	❖ More listening than intervention. ❖ Demonstrate positive regard. ❖ Create a safe environment. ❖ Rapport building is essential. ❖ Challenge very gently. ❖ Get them to identify their problems or issues – do not tell them.
Social Identification		❖ Feedback will be seen as disapproval or as misunderstanding. ❖ Their personal perceptions of the coach will be key to successful working. ❖ May know what they "want to be like". ❖ Consciously directing their outward image – may tell you what they think you want to hear. ❖ Capacity for shame and guilt. ❖ Sensitive to feelings of approval and rejection. ❖ Right or wrong thinking. ❖ Ability to think in the abstract (what if …?).	❖ Repression and suppression of aspects of their personality in order to fit in. ❖ Judgment and rejection of "out groups". ❖ Forming cliques and "us and them" groups at work. ❖ Following norms without question. ❖ Need for acceptance. ❖ Possibly unaware of their own values and aspirations. ❖ Having a sense of being inauthentic. ❖ Alienating self from certain groups.	❖ Rapport building is essential. ❖ Demonstrate positive regard. ❖ Create a safe environment. ❖ Challenge very gently. ❖ Get them to identify their problems or issues – do not tell them. ❖ Work on identifying values. ❖ Work on self-image, ego and aspirations. ❖ Psychological type work looking at self, pressures, archetypal influences and emphasising the positives of the other styles. ❖ Identify the significant relationships for them at the moment.

185

The Shadows of Type

	Capacity for Coaching	Potential Issues	Coaching Style
Personal Identification	❖ Likely to have a sense of ego identity. ❖ Feedback is taken personally so will probably be defended against unless from a respected source. ❖ They are right/know everything. ❖ Little tolerance for interpersonal differences. ❖ Try to find ways to channel their interests or preferences.	❖ Interpersonal insensitivity. ❖ General ego defensiveness. ❖ Forceful or one-sided use of preferences/personality. ❖ Unaware of their blind spots. ❖ Self-awareness is developing but may not be conscious or directed using the Will. ❖ May be trying to find their niche in life and be developing a clear sense of direction.	❖ Challenge using evidence and examples. ❖ Get them to provide realistic examples in order to identify their own issues. ❖ Psychological type work emphasising the positives of their own type, the potential pitfalls (as per type description at this level), and the positives of the other types. Also explore when they may use the opposite style. ❖ Action learning projects
Determined Action	❖ Sense of identity, preferences and differences. ❖ Feedback is welcomed if it helps improvement or achievement. ❖ Suggestions too far removed from ego identity may be rejected. ❖ Understand and have a "logical" appreciation of differences. ❖ "Scientific thinking" – there is an answer or way – anything can be explained. ❖ Very logical and rational. ❖ Concerned with channelling their preferences into achievements. ❖ Will reflect on actions and events and learn from them.	❖ Good understanding of the benefits of difference. ❖ Frustration with those who do not have an achievement drive. ❖ Little or no awareness of the shadow sides of their ego. ❖ In coaching will want to notice improvements and goal attainment. ❖ Will is likely to be skilful but may be too strong.	❖ Can be more direct with feedback and challenge if it is clearly linked to improvement. ❖ Psychological type work to look at the path of further development for their preferences, the potential pitfalls and the shadow sides of their ego (as per descriptions). ❖ Work on accessing their non-preferred sides and what the blockers to this may be. ❖ Encourage reflection and learning from real life examples. ❖ Can use more advanced/creative coaching techniques if objective is clear. ❖ Action learning projects.

Practical Applications of the Shadows of Type Model

	Capacity for Coaching	**Potential Issues**	**Coaching Style**
Considerate Individualism	❖ Good sense of identity and awareness of ego shadow. ❖ Real appreciation for differences. ❖ Feedback is elicited and accepted. ❖ Understand ambiguity and that there are not always absolute truths. ❖ Some understanding that their perception is informed by their preferences. ❖ Include and consult with others. ❖ Likely to really value coaching and accept more creative or abstract techniques. ❖ Able to self-monitor in the present moment and learn/adapt.	❖ Can over-consult with others. ❖ Often feel conflicted or lost by their inability to reach a conclusion or have a clear opinion. ❖ May still be prone to career derailment tendencies. ❖ Seeking sense of purpose and meaning.	❖ Creative coaching techniques can help in exploring the more unconscious aspects. ❖ Work with the discomfort of holding conflicting views. ❖ Interventions that introduce the transcendent function. ❖ Psychosynthesis techniques for working with purpose and meaning. ❖ Allow time for them to discuss their self-reflections and own learning. ❖ Work on prioritising and strategic information gathering. ❖ Psychological type work on shadow of ego and transforming preference strengths into qualities.
Integration and Authenticity	❖ Very good self-awareness, awareness of shadow aspects and willingness to access non-preferred aspects of self. ❖ Take a systems view – understand the connections between things. ❖ Able to take an objective view of themselves and a situation at the same time – witness consciousness.	❖ Some risk of hubris. ❖ Frustration with "the world". ❖ May seek even more sense of purpose and meaning. ❖ May still be prone to career derailment tendencies.	❖ Allow time for them to discuss their self-reflections and own learning. ❖ More facilitative, questioning, and encouraging of self-reflection than action or goal-focused. ❖ Creative techniques and techniques to identify meaning and purpose. ❖ Psychological type work exploring access of non-preferred functions and transcendent function.

The Shadows of Type

	Capacity for Coaching	**Potential Issues**	**Coaching Style**
Magician	❖ Can objectively observe the ego and be aware of the influences of it. ❖ Can learn from the smallest of events or observations. ❖ Understand systems, interdependence, universal viewpoint.	❖ Want to keep learning. ❖ Will learn from abstract ideas and natural events. ❖ May experience frustration with the state of the world.	❖ Allow time for them to discuss their self-reflections and own learning. ❖ More facilitative, questioning, and encouraging of self-reflection than action or goal-focused. ❖ Explore any future aspirations.

Table 8: Coaching capacity, potential issues and suggested approaches by ego development level

Practical Applications of the Shadows of Type Model

Using the levels of ego development to guide coaching work enables coaches to tailor their interventions to the needs of their client. Traditional "horizontal" development techniques, such as training workshops and development centres, tend to have an impact on individuals at lower to medium levels. However at the lower levels, they may selectively attend to the information that suits them. The value of these methods for individuals at the medium to higher levels is limited as they are likely to have already grasped the concepts that they are being presented with. *(See Fig.7)*.

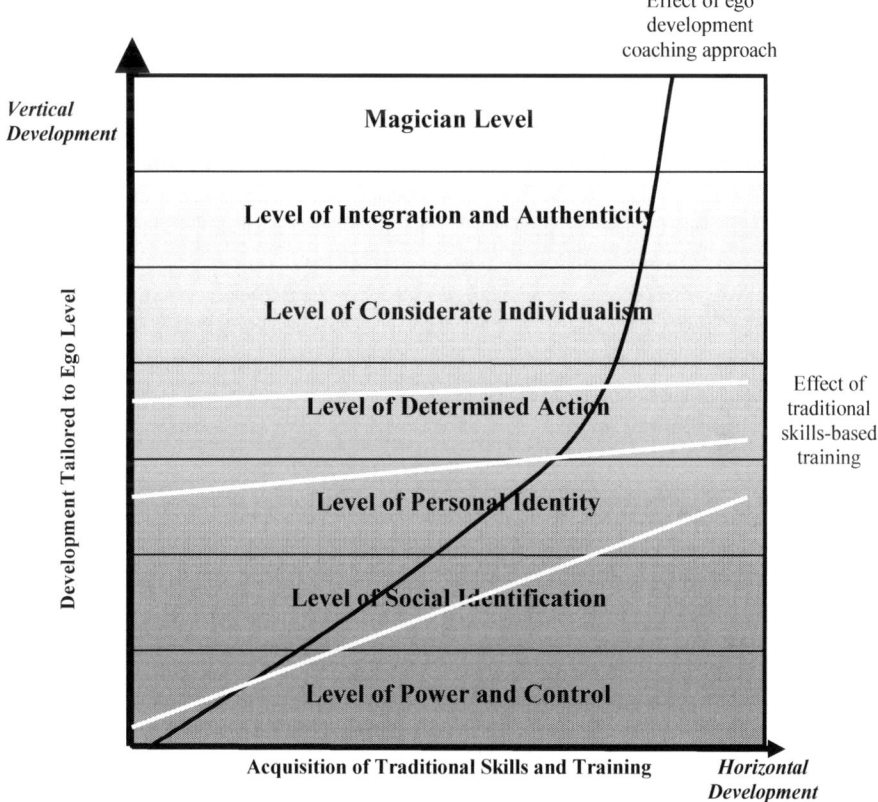

Fig.7: The effectiveness of vertical vs. horizontal development

Goals, action learning projects, challenges and information can be tailored to correspond to further development within a client's given level, or to begin development into the next level.

"Diagnosing" Ego Development Level

The issue of whether or not it is useful, or even possible, to diagnose the ego development level of an individual is not a straight-forward one. As a coach, having an idea of the level that your client is operating at can greatly inform your approach and any intervention design, however it is not necessary to share your "diagnosis" with clients to be able to work effectively with them. Primarily, it is important to note that the information provided in this book can provide a framework to allow coaches to form a hypothesis about their client's level of functioning, but is certainly not a diagnostic tool. As previously mentioned, diagnostic systems for ego development level do exist, for example the Leadership Development Profile (LDP) from Harthill.

Whether or not a coach should share their hypothesis with a client or, alternatively, let them self-assess their level is entirely at the discretion and judgement of the coach. However, this judgement should be exercised with caution. Clients at the lower levels often believe that they are functioning at higher levels of development and may become defensive if faced with a coach's opinion that they may, in fact, be at a low level of ego development. Therefore, if asked to self-assess, they are likely to assess themselves as being at a relatively high level. This is likely to have an impact on both the coaching relationship and the continuation of the coaching work at an appropriate level. Conversely, some clients at the middle to higher levels will be capable of accurately self-assessing their level of development. Therefore, presenting them with summaries of the ego development levels and asking for their thoughts may be useful. However, if they misinterpret the information or make a wrong assessment, this may become an obstacle in the coaching process.

The suggested coaching and development interventions that follow do not require the client to be aware of their ego development level or of the composition of the psyche, however for some of the type specific applications a good knowledge of their psychological type may be necessary or, if this is not the case, adaptations can be made to enable working less explicitly with type. Developmental coaching techniques and psychological type work in general will be useful for helping an individual to develop vertically to some extent, as will action learning projects that have time allocated for reflection. Nevertheless, the next few chapters will look at specific ways to work with the different aspects of the Shadows of Type theory in coaching. Fuller explanations of the coaching techniques in **bold** type can be found in the Glossary of Terms in Appendix One.

Chapter Eight

Techniques for Working With the Dynamics of Psychological Type

In this chapter a range of techniques for exploring and working with the dynamics of psychological type will be presented. Following a reminder of the main points needed for providing a well-balanced and developmentally focused initial feedback session, some techniques for working with the dominant function, with the type dynamics within an individual, including the inferior and contradictory functions, best fit issues, and the transcendent function are suggested.

Providing a Developmentally Focused Feedback Session

Psychological type feedback sessions can often be "hijacked" by the drive to identify the client's type, steering the coach and the client away from exploring type-related opposites and differences. Simply identifying one's type and looking at the type descriptions often leads to the devaluing of psychological type, as the process will merely have confirmed what an individual already knew about themselves; all too often we hear of people commenting that it is no better than reading your horoscope! The true value of working with psychological type comes from identifying your type, but then seeing both the potential gifts and the potential pitfalls that your type may bring you, and exploring how you deal with the opposing preferences within yourself and between yourself and others. This is where the "aha!" moments and valuable insights tend to occur.

Here are some reminders about how to make the most of a feedback session:
- Ensure that the session is introduced thoroughly and that clients understand that –
    - They are the best judge of their type.
    - The questionnaire is a helpful indicator but may not always sort their type accurately.
    - Although the *balance and expression* of their type may change and develop over time, their actual type will remain the same.
    - Type is not about ability or skill.
    - Everybody has all eight preferences within them, but some are more natural and require less energy and effort.
    - We can behave according to or in opposition to our actual type, but behaving in opposition to our type will eventually be de-energising and de-motivating (and may lead to stress).
- Spend an adequate amount of time exploring each dichotomy, even if the client has been quick to identify which side they prefer. Explore:
    - What positives that preference brings to them, and if they see or have experienced any downsides to having that preference.
    - How it feels when they use the opposite style to their preference, and what the benefits or issues are.
    - What their thoughts are about the opposite style? What are their perceived pros and cons of the opposites?
    - Can they identify anybody they work with or are close to who have the opposite preference? How do they interact?
- When using "sorting questions" to help a client to identify their type, remember to fully debrief the question, explaining typically how a person from each side of the dichotomy would respond.

Techniques for Working With the Dynamics of Psychological Type

> Then let the client decide which description is more like them rather than attempting to interpret their responses for them.

o When asking any question, do not take the first response at face value. Probe further into questions, looking for the motivations behind their responses – ask "why?" and "how?"

o Help the client to understand that, no matter how they behave in a given situation, their true preference will usually be the one reacting to or filtering the situation at a deeper level.

o End the exploration of each dichotomy and of the whole type by summarising what their preference or type actually means in practice.

The amount of exploration you can do in a session may be dependent on the developmental level of your client. The higher the level, the more depth you can work at. So, for example, somebody at the level of Power and Control may have little to no psychological mindedness, so a first feedback session may need to be restricted to looking at their type and listening to their opinion of the opposites. The pros and cons of their type, and considering the positives of the opposites may be incomprehensible to them at this stage, but may perhaps be explored after they have had time to assimilate the information and if they show signs that it has made an impression on them. A client at the level of Personal Identification may be getting a sense of who they are, but also have the idea that their type is "best" or "right". They would benefit from considering the pros and cons of their type and the potential benefits of the opposites in a session. Table 8 in the previous chapter and the descriptions of the ego development levels given earlier provide an indication of how to work appropriately with type at each level.

Exploring the Dominant Function

The dominant function represents the core of our identity – how we see ourselves, what most motivates us, and what most concerns us. To explore how the dominant function has been expressed in a client's life, the following types of questions can be explored:

> "What three words would you use to describe yourself?"
>
> "What were your interests or favourite games/pastimes as a child?"
>
> "What aspect of your job do you enjoy most?"

The Shadows of Type

"In an ideal world, what would you want to do and why?"

It is likely that the responses to these types of questions will all have some relationship to the characteristics of the client's dominant function, provided that they have been in environments that have supported the free expression of their type.

To explore the positives and downsides of their dominant function, as well as simply posing the questions, some creative techniques can often be useful. For example, imagery and music that are representative of the dominant functions can be selected by the client and brought to the session (*"What would your theme song be/What song relates most to who you are?"*, or *"What image or object represents your dominant function?"*) and their meaning explored freely with the coach. Table 9 suggests some images and songs that closely connect to the energies and characteristics of the dominant functions.

Exploring the Type Dynamics within an Individual

As noted previously, type theory suggests that we have all eight functions available to us and present in our psyche, although some may be more conscious than others. Sometimes it can be useful to explore the non-preferred functions during coaching, and in particular the contradictory functions that we may struggle with. Exploring the other functions with imagery and music can be interesting. For example, using the images suggested in Table 9, asking the client to describe how they feel about a particular type-related image – its good points and its unappealing points. Their comments will often reflect how they feel about that particular function. For example, they may say a flash of lightning is exciting and impressive, but it leaves nothing and leads to nothing, or, that an oyster and pearl may be perfect and beautiful, but is it really worth investing that much time in something? Clients can also be asked to come up with their own images of the functions as they see them.

Likewise type-relevant songs, like those suggested in Table 9, may be played to the client and then discussed. In one case where I was using music to explore dominant functions with a group, a woman with dominant Extraverted Intuition became irritated by the Introverted Sensing music, saying the beat was too "marchy" and consistent for her. Another group member who had a preference for Introverted Thinking found the Extraverted Feeling music too idealistic and soppy, and commented that the lyrics were about interfering in other people's business.

Techniques for Working With the Dynamics of Psychological Type

Dominant Function	Image	Song
Extraverted Thinking	Fencing sword or épée – swift, efficient, quick.	My Way Frank Sinatra Lyrics by Paul Anka
Extraverted Feeling	Radiant sun – warm, reaches out, positive.	Reach Out And Touch Somebody's Hand Diana Ross By Ashford and Simpson
Extraverted Sensing	Flash of lightning – fast, impressive, energetic.	I'm Free The Who Lyrics by Pete Townsend
Extraverted Intuition	Fireworks – one (idea) after another, energetic, exciting, then on to the next.	All Possibilities Badly Drawn Boy By Badly Drawn Boy
Introverted Thinking	Oyster shell and pearl – working on something until perfect or correct.	My Mind's Eye The Small Faces By Marriott and Lane
Introverted Feeling	Dormant volcano – strong, quiet in appearance, hidden depths.	I Ain't Movin' Desree Lyrics by Desree and Haynes
Introverted Sensing	Oak tree – strong, stable, traditional, grounded.	Senses Working Overtime XTC Lyrics by Andy Partridge
Introverted Intuition	Galaxy – drawing more things in, ever expanding, never ending.	The Windmills of Your Mind The Colourfield By Legrand, Bergaman and Bergman

Table 9: Images and songs that can represent the dominant functions

The Shadows of Type

Free drawing is another useful technique for exploring the preferences; after some discussion about a particular preference, ask the client to draw an image of the preference. This can be a symbol, a shape, a patch of colour or an actual person/object. Using this technique, clients can also be encouraged to draw images of two functions interacting, particularly if they are sensing a conflict between them. These images are then explored with the coach. Free drawing and imagery are particularly good techniques for exploring the contradictory functions. One particularly interesting exercise is getting the client to come up with an image or metaphor, either through drawing or discussion, of the interaction between the dominant and auxiliary functions, or between the dominant and inferior functions.

Constellation techniques can be very useful for exploring type dynamics. When using constellations for type dynamics, ask the client to choose objects (buttons, desk stationery, handbag contents, or whatever comes to hand) to represent the functions that are involved in the client's issue. (It can sometimes be useful to ask the client why they chose a particular object to represent a particular function). Ask the client to position the "functions" in a pattern that represents how they are relating to each other. The reason for the chosen positioning is discussed with the coach. The "functions" can be moved by the client and the new positions discussed, or the coach may choose to rearrange the objects and explore the new positioning with the client, i.e. "what would the impact/effect of this arrangement/relationship be?" Constellation techniques often enable the client to gain a perspective on their situation that they would not otherwise become aware of.

The following case study illustrates this.

Susan, who had a preference for INTJ, was attempting to write an essay but was unable to begin because she kept finding more and more information that she believed may be relevant to the topic. She also explained that she would hate to be unaware of and omit any other theories that may connect to her topic and result in her essay being invalid. This was compelling her to keep researching and reading. Additionally, she felt that she had completely lost touch with the purpose of the work. Susan's coach hypothesised that her dominant Introverted Intuition was being overused and pushing aside her auxiliary Extraverted Thinking which would have moved her ideas into action and kept the objective in mind. This hypothesis was not shared with Susan, however the coach asked her to select and constellate objects to represent her dominant and auxiliary functions.

Susan placed the dominant Ni object at the front of the constellation pattern and the auxiliary Te object well into the background. Instantly she realised for herself that she was overusing her Ni and not allowing any support from her Te function. She moved the two objects closer together, adjusting several times until she came to an arrangement that felt comfortable. In the end, she had the Ni just ahead of the Te, with the Ni "looking" out and forwards, and the Te "looking" at the Ni. She explained that she actually enjoyed the Ni part so much that, despite her frustration at not getting started, she felt uncomfortable letting the Te take the lead. The Ni wanted to "keep an eye" out for things while the Te stepped in to "serve" but not to rush towards getting the essay finished.

Susan reported that she began writing the essay the next day with a feeling of clear objectivity and interest in her work.

Empty Chair techniques are useful for a range of applications of the Shadows of Type model. There are several variations of the empty chair technique, however to use it for exploring type dynamics the coach would usually need to set up two or more chairs, depending on the issue the client is working on, and allocate each one to a particular function. The client can move between the chairs and take on the energy of a particular function, and look at other empty chairs and "view" the energies and characteristics that they represent.

The following case example illustrates how a coach may work with the empty chair technique to explore type dynamics.

Jennifer, an INFJ, had been feeling creatively blocked and unmotivated since her father passed away 18 months earlier. She described this state as not feeling like her usual self and feeling inauthentic. Her coach decided to explore this difference using an empty chair technique.

Two chairs were set up and Jennifer was asked to envisage one as being the chair that contained all the feelings regarding creative flow and authenticity that were more like her usual self, and the other chair as containing the feelings of creative blockage. Jennifer first sat in the "creative blockage" chair and described it as feeling constrained and devoid of feelings. When in the "authenticity" chair, Jennifer's posture and energy changed immediately; she was sitting upright and seemed more alert, yet more relaxed. She described the change in herself as being more aware, physically free, happier, and feeling like many things were possible. Jennifer was asked to look at the empty "creative blockage" chair from her position in the "authenticity" chair and describe what was there. She described it as a weight, a heaviness, and a constraint. The coach asked Jennifer to return to the "creative blockage" chair and immediately her posture and energy changed. She was slumped and still. She stated that, *"It is like being wrapped up. Maybe it's kind of a protective thing but it's gone too far."* She moved back to the "authenticity" chair and, looking back at the "blockage" chair, Jennifer stated that there was an inner judge there, criticising any ideas she had and insisting on things being done "properly and sensibly". As she continued to describe it, it started to sound like a description of distorted ST characteristics. As Jennifer is familiar with type, the coach shared this hypothesis with her.

The coach asked what the possible protective element of this "ST" character was, and Jennifer stated that, following the loss of her father, there was a lot of paperwork and legal work to take care of and that it was easier to handle in "ST" mode. In exploring why the "ST" personality was still clinging on, Jennifer realised that without it she felt vulnerable and exposed, but that she did not want it to be in control. They continued with the chair exercise to facilitate a virtual discussion with the "ST" personality; recognising its qualities and contribution, yet setting it back into a supportive rather than a driving role. Before doing this, the coach asked Jennifer if she sensed any resistance to letting the "ST" personality go. She stated that, *"I don't want it to go, but I want it to leave the good stuff and assist this* (pointing to herself) *to be grounded and practical"*. Jennifer mentally thanked the "ST" personality for its help and repositioned it accordingly in her mind; afterwards stating that she now had a feeling of real gratitude towards that part of herself rather than the resentment she had felt earlier.

Working with Best Fit Issues

Sometimes clients will have difficulty in identifying their preferences, or they will self-assess differently to their questionnaire-based reported type. This can often lead to a very interesting discussion about the use of the different preferences within their type.

These are some of the reasons why individuals may have issues with identifying their best fit type:

- Pressure from society, family or others to fit a certain role.
- Pressure as they grew up to behave a different way.
- Pressure from an organisation to conform to the organisational culture.
- Pressure from themselves to match their own expectations – "shoulds", "musts", "oughts".
- Pressure at work/from work role to behave differently.
- Being unhappy with their own type and valuing other styles more.
- Trying to imitate someone else.
- Feeling like a misfit.

Clients in this situation may make statements like:

"I'm different at work than at home"

"I used to be different/I have changed"

"I do both"

"I should, must, ought to …"

"I have different roles to play"

"It would be better if I was …"

The following questions can be useful in such situations:

"Are there pressures on you, and where do they come from?"

"What expectations do you think others have of you?"

"What is your image of the ideal manager/mother/etc?" (linking to the idea that an archetypal influence may be present).

"What would happen if you showed your true self?"

"How would your natural preferences contribute to a situation where most people were different?"

Some of the techniques in the previous sections for exploring the different preferences and type dynamics can also be useful when working on best fit issues.

The Transcendent Function

The transcendent function is different from the other functions in type theory as it is not a dichotomy of opposites, but a coming together of opposites. It often appears in a symbolic form, the meaning of which needs to be deciphered by the client. The transcendent function offers a third option that unites two apparently opposing choices (e.g. Thinking vs. Feeling). It also unites the conscious and unconscious aspects of the psyche. As Jung says, *"The psychological "transcendent function" arises from the union of conscious and unconscious contents"*. (Jung, from Campbell (ed.), 1976, p.273). For this reason, attempting to evoke the transcendent function is best achieved by using techniques aimed at accessing the unconscious. Talking about it and trying to find an answer (i.e. use of strong and skilful Will) is unlikely to get a result, unless certain verbal techniques such as the repeated question method are used.

The **repeated question** technique requires the coach to ask the same question over and over, each time pausing to allow the client to provide a different response. Eventually, the client may begin to volunteer new responses and ideas that they had not previously considered. This questioning continues until a new perspective has emerged.

Visualisations can also be useful for attempting to access the transcendent function. It is important to get the client into an almost trance-like state or state of deep relaxation before beginning the exercise. The coach can guide the client through any visualisation scenario that they feel is appropriate, however some suggested scenarios are:

- Reaching a crossroads with two options (let the client spend some time looking at the two options), then a third road appears – where does it lead?
- Going along a path and reaching an obstacle – what object/symbol/person magically appears to help you through the obstacle? Explore the meaning of the object.
- Travelling to a comfortable place and meeting a wise being. What does the wise being tell you?

The coach and client should never try to force the transcendent function – strong Will is a block to accessing the transcendent function. The transpersonal Will – where things just come together, or the individual is "in flow" – is usually present when the transcendent function arises. If nothing is forthcoming, take a break, "sleep on it", or accept that accessing the transcendent function is not a straightforward or easy task. Sometimes using the techniques above will not necessarily evoke the transcendent function but will put the

Techniques for Working With the Dynamics of Psychological Type

client in a relaxed state of mind where they may think more clearly and come up with new options.

Of course, there are many other ways to work with the different aspects and dynamics of type in coaching, and many other questions that can be explored in a coaching session. The suggestions above are just a few ideas for techniques that combine coaching with some psychosynthesis approaches.

Chapter Nine

Techniques for Working With Different Parts of the Psyche

Having Assagioli's "egg" diagram in mind when working with a client can sometimes help a coach to notice when the client's issue may be related to a particular aspect of the psyche. This chapter looks at some the exercises and techniques that can be used to explore particular aspects of the psyche. Of course, typological language or the dynamics of the client's type may be combined with these approaches where relevant.

Working with the Ego

Exploring the ego is often necessary before looking at other aspects of the psyche. The ego is our sense of who we are and what we are about. However, as previously noted, there are aspects of our ego that are in shadow. We may be aware of some of these shadow aspects but not particularly happy about them, and other aspects may be completely unknown to us. It can be useful to explain to a client that there known and unknown aspects of the ego prior to beginning any actual exploration or coaching work. A useful tool for this is the Johari Window. The Johari Window was devised by Joseph Luft and Harry Ingham in 1955. It can be used in a variety of ways including group settings, coaching, feedback, and adjective allocation exercises using observations from self and others. A diagram of the Johari Window is presented in Fig.8.

Techniques for Working With Different Parts of the Psyche

	Known to self	Not known to self
Known to others	**Public Self**	**Blind Spots**
Not known to others	**Hidden Self**	**Unconscious Self**

Fig.8: Johari Window

The Public Self is the part of ourselves that we are consciously aware of and that is seen by others. It may also include aspects of the persona or sub-personalities that the client is aware of. The Hidden Self contains aspects of the ego that the client is aware of but that they may not show to others or want others to know about them. The Blind Spots area will contain aspects of the shadow of the ego. Clients will be unaware of this aspect of themselves, but others will be well aware of it. The Unconscious Self not only contains the shadow aspects of the ego but also contains aspects of the middle, lower and higher unconscious. The aim of personal development, in relation to the Johari Window model, is to increase the Public Self area and become more authentic and open. This area is increased by reducing the Hidden Self through building authenticity and trust, and reducing the Blind Spots by learning through feedback and coaching/therapy. The Unconscious Self is not as easy to access, however the aspects of it that relate to the middle unconscious may eventually move into the other areas through coaching or therapy. With more self-development, aspects of the lower and higher unconscious may also be realised.

To work with the known ego (Public Self) that the client is conscious of, you can simply ask them to describe themselves. A psychological type feedback session can also help to explore the conscious ego. To move the client gently into looking at other aspects of their ego (the Hidden Self or Blind Spots), a **Polarities** exercise can be useful. This can be done as a "homework" task or with the coach during the session. The client makes a list of their most obvious characteristics or qualities and fits them into the sentence *"I am ... "*. The next step is to revisit the list and add to each sentence *"... but sometimes I am ... "*. This second step should involve words that are either the opposites of the first set of characteristics or that are variations of them. The idea of this exercise is to start to make the client realise that the ego is not just one-sided and it is not always consistent. It can also be a way of encouraging them to disclose aspects of the Hidden Self, or realise aspects of their Blind Spots. To take this further, the circumstances or feelings that accompany each side of each polarity can be explored, particularly those that have emerged from the Blind Spot area. A variation of this is to take the first list of characteristics and explore what the client sees as the benefits and downsides of each one.

Working with Sub-Personalities

There are many techniques for working with sub-personalities and these are divided into two categories – sub-personalities that the client is aware of, and those that the client is unaware of.

If a client is aware of a sub-personality, the following types of questions can be interesting to explore:

"When does it appear?"

"What does it want/need?"

"What is its contribution?"

"How does it limit you?"

"What emotions are you aware of and where do you feel these emotions in your body?"

"What is it protecting?"

Sub-personalities are not usually entirely unhealthy or unhelpful, they are often either an adaptation of the ego to a particular situation, or a way of protecting some part of the ego. If a client has a problematic sub-personality that they are aware of, it is important to explore the questions above in order to understand its purpose. If it is protective in some way, the sub-personality's function can be preserved once this is made conscious, but its problematic aspects may be adapted.

Another useful way of exploring sub-personalities is the **Empty Chair Technique.** Chairs can be set up to represent the self/I and the sub-personality in question and the client can move between the chairs, and "observe" the sub-personality from the position of the self/ego.

Techniques for Working With Different Parts of the Psyche

An example of this is illustrated in the following case:

> Maria described feeling restricted, tense and somewhat anxious at work, compared to several years earlier when she was usually motivated, creative and energetic. She called this new work persona "Wilma". Two chairs were brought into the session; one to represent the Wilma sub-personality and the other to represent the client's previous self at work. Maria was asked to take the Wilma position first and describe the associated feelings and thoughts there. These were feelings of seriousness, responsibility, fear of failure, being "business-like", etc. In moving to the other chair, Maria immediately became more animated and described feelings of enthusiasm and drive. After more exploration between the two chairs, Maria returned to her original "client" seat to view the two other chairs from a detached perspective. She explained that she realised that Wilma had "appeared" shortly after she had been promoted to a management position that took her from hands-on project work to project team management. The Wilma sub-personality was trying to fit into a "management" archetype in order to provide "good management" to their team. But she, herself, was not in a position that she really enjoyed or that was "authentic" to herself. Maria realised that she, in fact, wanted to be more hands-on again in project work and be part of the team rather than a manager.

When a client is not aware of a sub-personality but has brought an issue to the session about a tension they are experiencing or a feeling of inauthenticity in certain situations, this can be explored by questioning, imagery or metaphor. Some questions that may be useful are:

"What part of you expresses itself in that situation?"

"What is it trying to do for you?"

"What are its positives and its downsides?"

"What qualities is it bringing to you, and can you bring these qualities into your everyday life?"

Asking the client to describe the issue in terms of an image or a metaphor can be useful for opening up a discussion that may help to identify the less conscious aspects of the sub-personality.

The most important aspect of sub-personality work is trying to align the sub-personalities with the sense of the self so that they are not a completely inauthentic expression of the individual; other people can

The Shadows of Type

often see right through a "false face". This can often be related to the "Blind Spots" area of the Johari Window. It is also about bringing sub-personalities into the field of awareness so that the individual has more conscious control over them.

Working with the Middle Unconscious

The main aim of developmental coaching work is to bring more aspects of the individual's personality into the field of awareness. The middle unconscious is the area of "Blind Spots" that we could be made aware of, but habitually are oblivious to. Therefore, *any* coaching work, feedback or psychological type work will begin to bring aspects of the middle unconscious into awareness.

Techniques aimed at raising awareness and getting a client off "autopilot" can also be useful for working in this area. For example, asking the client to take a walk, either as part of the session or as homework, and take notice of everything that touches their senses. Or encouraging a client to look beyond the surface of whatever they are telling you by asking *"can you tell me more about that?"*.

Working with the Higher Unconscious

Working with the higher unconscious is concerned with accessing qualities that the client has, but does not make use of or is unaware of, or about accessing "good" parts of themselves that they have cut off from. Exploring the client's aspirations, hopes and "ideal" self can be useful ways of getting into aspects of the higher unconscious. However most of the effective techniques for working with this area involve using **imagery** or **visualisations.** Some useful scenarios can be:

- o Think of something you have been putting off doing or changing. Visualise yourself going through the rest of your life never having done this. Then visualise yourself after having done it.
- o Imagine you have total freedom to do as you like. What would you be? Look for the qualities in this and explore how they can be brought into current life?
- o What would you want to be like in a few years from now? What qualities would you be expressing? What blocks you from expressing these qualities now? What would be needed to make this a reality?

- What is the most meaningful thing in your life right now? What are the qualities that it brings to you? How can you bring more of this quality into your life?
- Imagine yourself on a journey where you meet a wise being. What one piece of advice do they give you?

It may also be useful to explore what they used to enjoy doing as a child that they no longer do, and try to identify the qualities behind this. When working with psychological type in this area, rather than talking about characteristics or behaviours, try to move into exploration of the qualities of the type. These are described in the higher levels of the developmentally levelled type descriptions.

Working with the Lower Unconscious

Most coaching work does not access the lower unconscious and it is important to be aware of your own limits and boundaries as a coach if you are touching on this area. Likewise, the client should have a good sense of self-awareness in order to work at this level.

To access the shadow areas of the ego, the polarity technique described in the "Working with the Ego" section can be a good start.

Questions that can be useful for exploring the more accessible areas of the lower unconscious can be:

"What are the negative aspects of your type?"

"What are the positive aspects of the opposite types?"

"Have you ever been given any feedback that has been a surprise to you?"

The shadow can have an impact on our everyday behaviour, not just when we are under stress. Some everyday situations that indicate the shadow may be at work are:

- A strong, negative emotional reaction to something/someone.
- A negative, one-sided and harsh judgement of something/someone.
- An absolute lack of understanding of/disdain for other views or motivations.
- Feeling like your "buttons have been pushed".
- The emergence of an instinct that seems "primitive", alien to your sense of self, or wrong.

This is because the ego defence mechanism of projection usually works from the lower unconscious or shadow. If a client reports having an issue with any of the above situations, the following exercise can be useful.

- o Ask about the person or situation that has caused the strong negative reaction.
- o Ask what does the person/situation does to irritate you?
- o Can you think of any positive quality in this behaviour?
- o Is this a quality that you are lacking or that would help you to balance?

Below is a case example in which this series of questions was used:

Mark was having an issue with one of his peers at work, describing him as lazy, irresponsible, too laid-back and more interested in having fun than working. The very sight of this person could send Mark, who was very diligent and hard working, into a silent internal rage. Using the questions suggested above to explore this, it emerged that the peer in question always completed their work and did so to a high standard. The qualities that this person had were a relaxed, collaborative approach to work and a good work-life balance. Mark realised that these were some of the qualities that he desperately needed to bring into his own rather stressful life.

Working with the self/I

A popular psychosynthesis exercise for exploring the self is a **free drawing** exercise where the client is asked to draw whatever comes to mind as the following questions are asked:

"Who am I?"

"Where have I come from?"

"Where am I going?"

The client draws their response to each question on a separate sheet of paper. The images that the client has drawn are discussed and explored with the coach.

Another technique is a relaxation/visualisation technique where the client is asked to relax and then, in turn for about 2 minutes at each stage, observe their physical feelings, then their emotions, then their thoughts. The final question is for the client to try to turn their attention towards *who* has been observing these three areas. This technique aims to separate our "doing" selves from our "being" selves.

Techniques for Working With Different Parts of the Psyche

Other techniques for putting the self/I into the observer position are empty chair techniques or visualisations that ask the client to look in on themselves in a certain situation (for example, visualise that they are in the cinema watching themselves on the screen) and comment on what they see.

One of the developmental models often used in psychosynthesis practice is the Mystic/Pragmatist model *(see Fig.9)*. The horizontal axis has various names – Pragmatist, Immanence, Quantitative – and is concerned with material gains, structure, logic, and achievement. The vertical axis – Mystic, Transcendence, Qualitative – is concerned with spiritual matters, ideals, freedom and anti-materialism. John Whitmore (2009) believes that western culture tends to follow the pragmatist approach, whereas traditionally eastern culture followed the mystic approach.

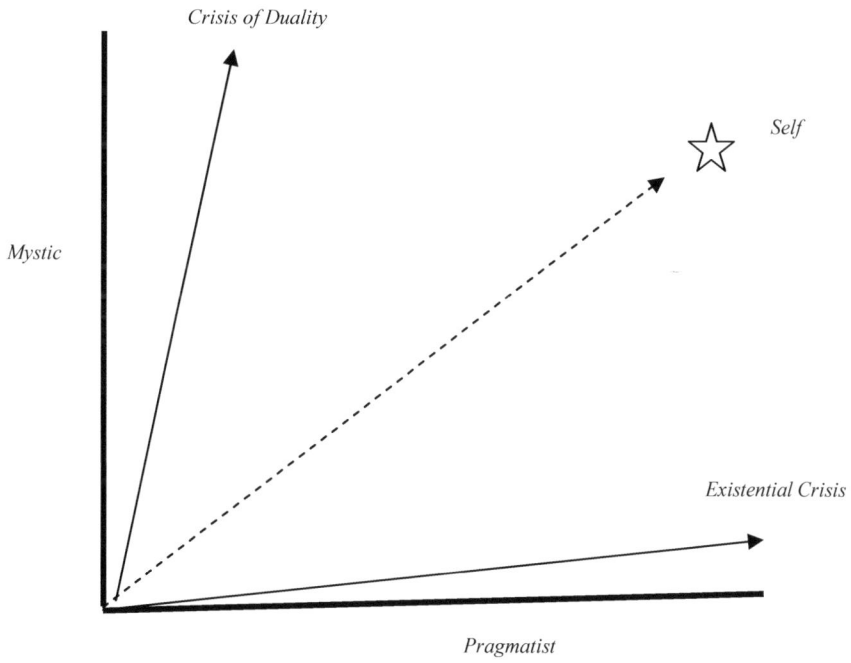

Fig.9: The Mystic/Pragmatist model of development

The ideal path to development and finding one's self is believed to be achieved by finding a balance between the two. There may be times when taking either approach is more appropriate for a given circumstance, however Assagioli believed that the sustained neglect of one approach could lead to crisis. In those that follow the

Mystic path a "crisis of duality" can occur when they experience the tension between their idealistic visions and the harsh realities of life. In those that follow the Pragmatist route an "existential crisis" (also known as "crisis of meaning") can occur when individuals feel a false sense of achievement or lack of purpose in their life, and question the meaning of their life.

Working with this model in coaching simply requires the coach to sketch out and explain the model and, with the client, plot their life journey along the axes. The discussion then turns to how they feel about their life's path and how they can achieve a better balance in their lives. This model can be particularly useful for clients at the levels of Determined Action upwards who are becoming more concerned about purpose and meaning than with achievement, or with people who are going through the stage that Jung called "mid-life".

These are only a selection of techniques for working with the psyche as described by Assagioli's psychosynthesis model. For other psychosynthesis techniques, an excellent resource is *"What We May Be"* by Piero Ferrucci. It is of utmost importance that coaches only explore areas that they feel comfortable working in, and that the client is psychologically ready to address.

Chapter Ten

Techniques for Working at Particular Ego Development Levels

This chapter will consider how to use psychological type with individuals at each level of ego development as well as suggesting other interventions that may be useful to them. The actual approach that a coach may need to take with clients at each level is summarised in Table 8 in chapter seven.

Working with the Level of Power and Control
It is unlikely that a coach will encounter many people who habitually operate at this level, as only a small percentage of the adult population stop developing at this point. However, as employers sometimes refer "problem" employees for coaching, you may find yourself working with individuals who are capable of operating at higher levels, but who frequently regress to this level due to inability to deal with pressure, inadequate coping mechanisms or a general lack of resilience. They will, however, probably be able to look objectively at the behaviours that they display when "visiting" this level.

If an individual is not capable of operating at a higher level, they can be extremely difficult to work with as they will be psychologically unaware, have a low level of self or other awareness (i.e. emotional intelligence), and be defensive in the face of feedback. The best approach to take is to let them talk and do a lot of listening, occasionally asking for clarification or challenging *very* gently.

The Shadows of Type

Individuals at this level may try to either manipulate the coach or sabotage the coaching relationship, so rapport building is essential. When/if there is good rapport between the client and coach, you may be able to ask them to identify any areas of issue for them, focusing on real-life examples. But be aware that you will be getting a one-sided account of events. Attempting psychological type work may be unadvisable as they may selectively attend to the parts they want to and it may re-enforce their ego-image. So if type work is carried out, keep it simple and emphasise that all types are equally valid.

Working at the Level of Social Identification

Individuals at this level are capable of having fairly amicable interpersonal relationships with those they are drawn to and who are considered to be in the "in groups". However they can be bitterly dismissive to those who are in "out-groups". There are two possible overarching issues that can be at play here – the risk of ego entrenchment or the risk of inauthenticity.

If the client is identifying with groups that are similar in some way to their actual self (or ego), the risk is that they will become even more one-sided in their type and judgemental of others. In this case, it is important to build good rapport so that you (as the coach) do not become "out group", but do this without collusion. Working with type here can be very useful for exploring the individual's ego-image, but also for hearing their opinions of the opposites and trying to make them see that all types are equally valid. Different is not wrong or bad.

For clients who are identifying with groups that are very different to themselves, the risk is that they will be repressing and suppressing aspects of their personalities, values and needs in order to fit in. Work that looks at identifying their values, their future goals and their ideal self can be useful, as can the interventions suggested in the "Working with the Ego" section of the previous chapter. Working with type at this level may require some situational exploration as the client is likely to have difficulty identifying their true type. In this case, some of the techniques in the "Working with Best Fit Issues" section may be useful. The aim of working with these clients should be to gently make them see their true selves. Emphasise that differences can complement each other well, so they can interact with and contribute to most groups. If they show negativity towards any particular preferences, it may be important to get them to explore the positives in them.

For either category of client at this level, work looking at the current significant relationships for them can be interesting. The **constellation** technique can be useful for this. Again, any challenge at this level needs to be gentle as the individual is likely to take it as disapproval or misunderstanding.

Working at the Level of Personal Identity

This level, along with the Determined Action level, is where most adults tend to be developed to, so it is likely that you will encounter many clients who operate from this level. At this level, the individual is aware of the conscious aspects of the ego; they will have an idea of who they are, what they like, and what they are about. They will often have found, or be looking for, their niche in life and work. The main issue at this level is one-sidedness, leading to a lack of understanding or insight into the behaviours of others.

The difficulty in coaching somebody at this level is that they often think that they have nothing left to learn or that they know everything. Additionally, they may be defensive about any negative feedback unless it is from a respected source – so it is important to make sure that real examples are used or that examples are elicited from the client.

Working with psychological type at this level can be really useful. For example, in exploring the client's preferences and helping them to find their "niche", and for getting them to start opening their eyes to the opposite types and what they are about. Therefore, it is essential that the coach gives a good, in-depth and balanced feedback, exploring both aspects of each dichotomy. *(See page 191 for a reminder of the key points in a developmentally focused feedback session).*

Other interventions that can be useful at this level are those that explore the ego, described in the "Working with the ego" section, particularly the **polarity** exercises. Setting **action learning projects** followed by reflective practice can also be useful for people at this level.

Working at the Level of Determined Action

As mentioned above, this is one of the levels that most adults will have developed to. Individuals at this level are more accepting of feedback and will have a fairly good sense of who they are. They will also be fairly understanding of others. Psychological type work at this level can look at the opposites of the client's type and start to explore how those opposites work within them. At this level, individuals may find themselves sometimes using or valuing preferences other than their own, so it is useful to build on this. The shadow sides of their ego can also be gently introduced at this stage. Getting the client to talk about what the obstacles and blockers to their effectiveness are and relating these back to their type can be insightful. At this level, but at the judgement of the coach, the levelled type descriptions may be comfortably shared with the client (although the typological "jargon" may need explaining). From this level onwards, the techniques described in the "Exploring the Type Dynamics within an Individual" section can be useful.

Again, **action learning projects** with reflection are very useful at this stage. In particular, getting the client to reflect on things that were not as straightforward as they had expected, or that do not have a clear-cut answer. Other interventions that can be useful from this level onwards are exploring potential career derailers, for example, using the Hogan Development Survey (HDS), assessing their emotional intelligence (EQ) and looking at the client's resilience. Calming physical exercise such as yoga or t'ai-chi can also be useful at this level for temporarily "calming" the client's drive to achieve and encouraging more connectedness to the body in preparation for development to higher levels.

Working at the Level of Considerate Individualism

This is the level that several researchers believe to be the minimum level necessary for leadership in the current complex and challenging business environment. Individuals at this level tend to function well, however they may be prone to over consultation with others and, now they realise that there are often many sides to every issue, they can experience inner conflict resulting from holding various viewpoints. They will also become more concerned with finding purpose and meaning. Working with values and with the Mystic/Pragmatist model (page 209) can often be useful for individuals at this level.

In terms of type work, a more in-depth look at their shadow sides and non-preferred functions can help their development in this level. The coach may also begin to introduce the client to techniques aimed at evoking the transcendent function – or at least allowing a clear mind for problem-solving. Additionally, moving the work with their own type from "characteristics" to "qualities" can begin at this level.

Working at the Level of Integration and Authenticity

The differences between the three highest levels of ego development in this particular model are fairly subtle. The key difference between this level and the previous level is that the individual no longer feels conflicted by their various viewpoints, but accepts them and enjoys the ambiguity. Additionally, they are likely to be able to use "witness consciousness" – being the observer of their own processes. To set this into the psychosynthesis model, it is like the I/self observing the ego but realising that it is ego and not self.

Psychological type becomes less and less pronounced as the individual progresses through these higher levels. However, working on the non-preferred functions and the transcendent function can be useful here. Also, accessing the qualities of the non-preferred preferences can be effective for further development.

Other useful interventions at this stage can be accessing the higher unconscious/light shadow and further acknowledgement and integration of the ego shadow.

Working at the Magician Level

Individuals at this level value feedback, coaching and continued learning, but rather than having obvious development needs, they benefit from having a "sounding board" and someone to share their thoughts with. Therefore the main function of coaching at this level is support and reflection. Of course, each individual may have specific aspects of themselves or qualities that they want to work on and develop.

The individual's level of stress tolerance or resilience will mediate the extent to which they remain "stable" at their maximum level of development, or how much they fluctuate through the levels. However it is believed that the higher the level of functioning is, the higher the level of resilience is likely to be as this is an aspect of emotional intelligence.

It should be noted that these suggested interventions are *typical* of each level but may not necessarily apply to each individual.

The Shadows of Type

Afterword

Bringing together psychological type theory, the dynamics of the psyche, and ego development theory has provided me with the answers to almost all of the questions that I used to ask myself about type. The Shadows of Type theory reinforces the belief that there are no better or worse types – all types are equally valid – but clarifies why some individuals use their preferences more effectively than others.

Creating the developmentally levelled type descriptions has enabled me to create a map of the potential for each type that can act as a guide for further development. This developmental path charts the transformation of our types from instinctive drives that can limit us, to characteristics that can enable us to identify and achieve our goals in life, through to qualities that can help us to realise our potential.

I hope that this theory will make a valuable contribution to the existing body of work of psychological type and personality, as well as being a source of deeper insight for individuals who are exploring their own type, and to coaches and therapists who are using type with their clients.

Thanks to my colleagues, especially Anna, for being there for me when I needed to explore my ideas, to Emma for her amazing attention to detail in checking my draft script, and to Al and Fraser for allowing me the time to write this (even if it was 'P' time!).

Appendix One

Glossary of Terms

Action Learning

Sometimes known as "stretch projects". An individual or a group are asked to work on a project designed to take them out of their usual comfort zone. For maximising the developmental benefits of action learning, formal time for reflection either through coaching or a facilitated group process should be included.

Constellation Technique

Elements of interest are represented by objects or, in a group setting, by other people. These "elements" can be psychological functions, people that we are in relationship with or work with, roles that we undertake, or, in fact, anything that can be involved in a relationship or conflict. The elements are moved into positions relative to each other and discussed, moved into new positions, discussed again, etc. until the client feels comfortable with or gains insight from the constellation pattern.

Conflicting Functions

The functions within our psychological type that we are likely to have most issue with in terms of assimilating them into our personalities or tolerating them in others. These tend to be the opposite preference in the dichotomy to the dominant function, the same preference as the dominant function but in the opposing orientation, and, of course, the inferior function.

Differentiation

The separation of psychological functions into distinct opposites in order for them to be used effectively.

Empty Chair Techniques

These techniques are used to explore different states. A chair is imagined as having the certain qualities, feelings and physical sensations that the client would associate with a particular state that they have experienced or wish to experience. This could be a sub-personality, a different preference, a quality they wish to aspire to, or a state that they have experienced. The client usually feels all of these sensations when they sit in the chair, provided that enough time has been given for them to imagine that the chair has the sensations being ascribed to it. As well as moving into the different chairs, the client can look at the chairs and imagine what the perspective of the "chair" is, however this is best achieved once they have experienced sitting in it. This technique can also be used to attempt to access the perspective of another person. For example, if the client has had a disagreement with someone, they sit in the other person's chair and will often gain insight into the other person's perspective on the situation.

Equivalence and Entropy

The energetic laws of the dynamics of the psyche according to Jung and drawn from the theory of thermodynamics. In Equivalence, preferences that are in opposition are attempting to be equally balanced. Therefore, as energy is directed into a preference, its opposite will be attempting to come to the fore creating a dynamic tension. In Entropy, as energy is directed towards one function, an equal amount of energy is drawn away from the opposite function (i.e. for every action there is an equal and opposite reaction). To illustrate this, imagine that you are pushing a ball down into water. As you push the ball down, the water will resist and attempt to push the ball up again. If you push very hard on the ball, the resistance of the water seems stronger and, if you lose control of the ball, it may jump out of your hands and be out of control, propelled by energy other than your own. This analogy can be used to illustrate the **Grip** model of stress (Quenk) – when conscious energy has been forceful and one sided, it may eventually be expended. This is when the build up of unconscious energy takes charge and the preferences are out of the conscious control of the individual.

Flow State

The term "in flow" is used to describe a state of complete immersion in what one is doing with clarity of mind and immediate self feedback. When in a flow state, the individual may experience a distorted sense of time, but will feel extremely fulfilled and at ease. Flow is sometimes referred to as "being in the zone".

Free Drawing Techniques

These techniques involve asking a client to spontaneously draw whatever is emerging for them. No artistic skill is necessary as the client will know what they are drawing. These techniques are useful for accessing the unconscious or for expressing feelings that are difficult to articulate. Following the drawing, the client and coach discuss what has been drawn and what it means to the client. Clients can be asked to draw actual images, or to represent their instincts using just colours or shapes.

Hubris

The word "hubris" is originally Greek and was used to describe an action that humiliated a person for the gratification of another. Today it is used to describe extreme arrogance, and overestimation of one's importance or abilities, or intoxication with power. There are many cases of leaders who begin their careers successfully and meet their downfall as a result of succumbing to hubris.

Individuation

This is similar to Maslow's idea of self-actualisation. Individuation is the integration and unification of the self through the resolution of psychological conflict. This is related to high levels of ego development.

Mid-life

According to Jung, the first part of life is concerned with differentiation and specialisation of our preferences. By the time most people are in their twenties, their type is well established and they will be fairly identified with it. Mid life is the time when the individual begins to integrate other aspects of their psyche and their non-preferred styles, and "turn down the volume" on their own preferences. Often, it is believed to be the tertiary function that is being accessed more often at this stage. One's actual psychological type does not change at mid life, it merely becomes more balanced. Individuals who resist their natural instinct to develop at mid life, or whose circumstances do not permit development, may become entrenched in their type, displaying one sided characteristics similar to those of the lower levels, or they may have a personal crisis ("mid life crisis") and feel lost and confused.

Neuroticism

This is one of the five factors that are believed to contribute to personality. Neuroticism is a broad term for one's emotional stability/ability to cope with pressure, apprehension/self doubt, level of trust and physical tension. Although some individuals may be prone to high neuroticism, for some it can be a temporary state that they find themselves in when under pressure.

Polarity Technique

This technique is aimed at exploring the ego. The individual is asked to list what they consider to be their main characteristics, illustrating how they see themselves and what their ego image is. They are then asked to add an opposite or vastly different characteristic to each of those listed. So, for example, they may have a statement that says "I am friendly, but sometimes I like to be alone". This exercise helps an individual to begin to disidentify with their ego image and realise they are not one-sided in their personality.

Repeated Question Technique

These exercises are aimed at exhausting the individual's conscious or rational thought patterns to enable alternative or unconscious thoughts to come forward. The same question is asked over and over, each time pausing to allow the client to respond. This is continued until some new options appear or a resolution is emerging. An example would be asking a Thinking type, "What is good about connecting to your emotions".

Transcendent Function

The union of opposites, including the conscious and unconscious, that provides new insights, usually in the form of a symbol.

Transpersonal

The term "transpersonal" is used to describe psychological phenomena that transcend the usual constraints of the ego. It describes states where there are no boundaries and where there is a sense of connectedness to all things.

Visualisation Techniques

There is evidence to show that visualising ones self in a desired state or circumstance is related to achieving that desire. (This is where Assagioli's "Imagination" and "Desire" functions become important). When using visualisation with clients it is important to allow sufficient time for the client to relax and engage in the exercise. A good visualisation attempts to engage all of the client's senses; what they can see in terms of colour, shade light etc, what they can hear, smell, sense on their skin and, if applicable, taste. When a client is relaxed and absorbed in the exercise, time appears to pass quickly, so allow long pauses and silences.

Witness Consciousness

This is also referred to as "mindfulness". It is a state in which the individual can observe their thoughts and mental images without getting caught up in them and allowing the self to become distracted and less "in the moment".

Appendix Two

Ego Defence Mechanisms

Ego defence mechanisms, first postulated by Freud, are instinctive reactions to events that may cause anxiety or tension to the individual's sense of self (i.e. the ego). Defence mechanisms are used universally and can be useful and protective, however they can be potentially harmful when used inappropriately. For example, the initial use of denial as a reaction to bad news can help the news filter in at a manageable rate, however the use of denial to reject truthful feedback can prevent individual development.

Projection:

The attribution of one's own undesirable characteristics onto another person.

These characteristics may be the undesirable aspects of one's own type preferences, their non-preferred functions, or any aspect of their unconscious influences.

Example: A person who pushes himself hard to achieve at work is irritated by a colleague who he describes as lazy and unconscientious, when the colleague is actually achieving all his objectives and has a good work-life balance and a relaxed attitude to work.

Repression

The ego's unconscious attempt to prevent undesirable impulses from reaching consciousness.

Example: A person who is having difficulties at work and feels jealous of his successful colleagues may repress these undesirable feelings of jealousy, however they may eventually break through with force.

Denial

The refusal to perceive or accept a real event that the ego finds unpleasant.

Example: Having clear evidence that there are serious problems in a relationship but refusing to acknowledge this, and carrying on as normal.

Rationalization

The justification of an action through plausible but inaccurate excuses.

Example: An individual who is not successful in his application for a job claims that he did not want the job anyway because it was beneath his capabilities.

Intellectualization

The disassociation of thoughts and feelings by creating logical explanations for painful events.

Example: A person discovers he has a serious illness and immerses himself in the medical texts, explaining the situation to others from a scientific viewpoint, and avoiding any mention of how he fees about it.

Suppression

The conscious attempt to prevent anxiety-provoking thoughts by trying not to think about them.

Example: A person is facing a potentially negative outcome for a situation, so he decides not to think about the negatives and only focuses on the possible positives.

Displacement

The unconscious attempt to gain gratification of impulses by shifting the focus to a substitute object.

Example: A person feels unable to control certain life-events, so engages in "spring-cleaning" the house and sorting out the external environment.

Sublimation

The unconscious attempt to gain gratification of impulses by shifting the nature of the impulse itself.

Example: A person who has strong needs to control and dominate channels his activities into becoming an expert in a certain field, thus demonstrating superiority and control but in a positive manner.

Reaction Formation

The conversion of an undesirable impulse into its opposite.

Example: A person who hates his spouse, yet is very kind to them to the extent that she feels smothered.

Regression

A movement towards immature behaviour.

This can occur in the presence of certain individuals, such as parents or authority figures, when the ego is threatened.

Example: A person is advised by his manager he has not been selected for promotion and he reacts by having a temper tantrum and claiming unfairness.

Undoing

A person who does an undesirable act seeks to nullify the effect by performing some other action. This can involve actions or thoughts.

Example: A person who rudely criticises a colleague then offers to help him with his work.

Compromise Formation

The use of contradictory behaviour to gain satisfaction for an undesirable impulse.

Example: A person who sees himself as kind and pleasant goes out of the way to show kindness to a person he dislikes.

References

Assagioli, R. (1967). *Jung and Psychosynthesis: Lectures 1-3.* Retrieved 2008 from http://www.synthesiscenter.org/articles/0119.pdf

Assagioli, R. (1975). *Psychosynthesis* (2nd ed.). London: Turnstone Books.

Assagioli, R. (2002). *The Act of Will* (2nd ed.). London: The Psychosynthesis and Education Trust.

Beebe, J. (2007). Type and Archetype, *Typeface,* Vol. 18 (2), 8-12.

Briggs-Myers, I. and Myers, P.B. (1995). *Gifts Differing* (2nd ed.). Palo Alto: Davies Black Publishing.

Campbell, J. (Ed.) (1976). *The Portable Jung* (2nd ed.). Viking Penguin.

Cook-Greuter, S. R. (1999). *Postautonomous Ego Development: A study of its nature and measurement.* Doctoral dissertation. Cambridge, MA: Harvard Graduate School of Education. UMI Dissertation Services #933122

Cook-Greuter, S. (2002). *A Detailed Description of the Development of Nine Action Logics.* Retrieved 2008 from www.cook-greuter.com .

Cook-Greuter, S. (2004). Making the Case for a Developmental Perspective. *Industrial and Commercial Training,* Vol. 36,(7), 275-281.

Delunas, E. (1992). *Survival Games Personalities Play.* Carmel: SunInk Publications.

Eigel, M. and Kuhnert, K.W. (2005). Authentic Development: Leadership Development Level and Executive Effectiveness. In Gardner, W. L., Avolio, B. J. and Walumba F.O. (Eds.). *Authentic Leadership: Theory and Practice.* Elsevier.

Ferrucci, P. (2004). *What We May Be.* New York: Tarcher/Penguin.

Flautt, T. and Richards, J. (1999), *Working With the Enneagram.* Retreived 2009 from

http://www.breakoutofthebox.com/flauttrichards.htm

Freud, S. (1946). *The Ego and the Mechanisms of Defense.* New York: International Universities Press.

Golden, J.P. (2005). *Golden Personality Type Profiler Manual.* Harcourt Assessment Inc.

References

Hogan, R. and Hogan, J. (1997). *Hogan Development Survey UK Edition Manual.* Psychological Consultancy Limited, UK.

Joiner, B. and Josephs, S. (2007). *Leadership Agility.* San Francisco: Jossey-Bass.

Jung, C.G. (1970). *Psychology and Religion.* Princeton: Princeton University Press.

Jung, C.G. (1978). *Aion: Researches into the Phenomenology of the self* (5th ed.). Princeton: Princeton University Press.

Jung, C.G. (1981). *The Structure and Dynamics of the Psyche* (5th ed.). Princeton: Princeton University Press.

Jung, C.G. (1990). *Psychological Types* (9th ed.). Princeton: Princeton University Press.

Kegan, R. (1982). *The Evolving Self.* Harvard: Harvard University Press.

Keirsey, D. (1987). *Portraits of Temperament.* Del Mar: Prometheus Nemesis Book Company.

Loevinger, J. (1976). *Ego development.* London: Josey-Bass Publishers.

Luft, J. (1984). *Group Process: An Introduction to Group Dynamics.* Mayfield Publishing Co.

Maddox, J. (2006). Linking Emotional Intelligence with Jungian Typology. *APT Bulletin of Psychological Type,* Vol. 29, (3), 8-12.

McCrae, R.R. and Costa, P.T. (1989). Reinterpreting the Myers-Briggs Type Indicator from the Perspective of the Five-Factor Model of Personality. *Journal of Personality,* 57 (1), 17-40.

McDowall, A. and Smewing, C. (2009). What Assessments do Coaches Use in Their Practice and Why?. *The Coaching Psychologist,* Vol. 5 (2), 98-103.

Parfitt, W. (2003). *Psychosynthesis: The Elements and Beyond.* Glastonbury: PS Avalon.

Quenk, N. (2002). *Was That Really Me?.* Palo Alto: Davies-Black Publishing.

Riso, D. and Hudson, R. (1996). *Personality Types: Using the Enneagram for Self-Discovery* (Rev. ed.). New York: Houghton Mifflin.

Ryckman, R.M. (2000). *Theories of Personality.* Belmont: Wadsworth-Thomson Learning.

Scoular, A. and Campbell, M. (2007). What Value do Psychometrics Bring to Business Coaching?. *Training Journal Magazine.* Retrieved 2008 from http://www.meylercampbell.com/pdfs/TrainingJournal.pdf

Sharp, D. (1987). *Personality Types: Jung's Model of Typology.* Toronto: Inner City Books.

Spoto, A. (1995). *Jung's Typology in Perspective* (2nd ed.). Illinois: Chiron Publications.

Stein, M. (2004). *Jung's Map of the Soul* (6th ed.). Illinois: Open Court.

Thomson, L. (1998). *Personality Type: An Owner's Manual.* Boston: Shambhala.

Torbert, B. (2004). *Action Inquiry.* San Francisco: Berrett-Koehler.

Whitmore, D. (2000). *Psychosynthesis Counselling in Action* (2nd ed.) London: Sage Publications.

Whitmore, J. (2009). *Coaching for Performance* (4th ed.). London, Nicholas Brealey Publishing.

Wilber, K. (2000). *Integral Psychology.* Boston: Shambhala.

Index

Action Learning, 217

Archetypes, 38, 39, 41

Assagioli, 10, 46-59, 202, 209, 210, 221

Beebe, 20, 28, 29

Best Fit
   practical applications, 198

Collective Unconscious
   definition, 53

Conflicting Functions, 217

Constellation technique, 196, 217

Cook-Greuter, 32, 61-66

Costa and McCrae, 23

Delunas, 26, 85

Differentiation, 72, 83, 217

Dominant function
   definitions of, 19
   working with, 193

"Egg" diagram, 50

Ego
   definition, 36
   practical applications, 202

Ego defence mechanisms, 37, 207

Ego development
   diagnosis, 64, 190
   stages, 62
   theory, 60

Eigel and Kuhnert, 61

Eight-function model, 28

Emotional intelligence, 31-33, 46, 66, 77, 81, 211, 214, 215

Empty Chair technique, 197, 204, 217

Enneagram, 1, 30

Entropy, 218

Equivalence, 218

Feedback - developmentally focused, 191

Field of Awareness
   definition, 52

Five-factor model, 23

Flautt and Richards, 30

Flow (in, state),55, 78, 83, 218

Free drawing, 196

Function-attitudes
   descriptions, 19

Golden Personality Type Profiler (GPTP), 24

Grip theory (Quenk), 24, 25, 28, 41, 85, 218

Higher unconscious
   definition, 52
   practical applications, 206

Hogan and Hogan, 31

Hogan Development Survey (HDS), 31, 214

Horizontal vs. Vertical Development, 32, 189

Hubris,80, 187, 219

The Shadows of Type

Imagination, 55, 56, 221

Impulse-Desire, 55, 56

Individuation, 43, 77, 79, 83, 219

Johari Window, 202-206,

Joiner and Josephs, 61, 62, 65

Jung, 4, 5, 10, 13, 14, 20, 24, 25, 33-36, 38-43, 46-58, 79, 200, 210, 218, 219

Kegan, 61, 62

Leadership Development Profile (LDP), 64, 190

Level of Considerate Individualism

   definition, 76

   practical applications, 214

Level of Determined Action

   definition, 73

   practical applications, 213

Level of Integration and Authenticity

   definition, 78

   practical applications, 214

Level of Personal Identity

   definition, 71

   practical applications, 213

Level of Power and Control

   definition, 67

   practical applications, 211

Level of Social Identification

   definition, 69

   practical applications, 212

Levels of development

   and field of awareness, 82

   practical applications 211-215

Light Shadow

   definition, 41

Loevinger, 60-62, 64, 66, 84

Lower unconscious

   definition, 51

   practical applications, 207

Luft and Ingham, 202

Maddox, 31

Magician Level

   definition, 80

   practical applications, 215

McDowall and Smewing, 21

Middle unconscious

   definition, 51

   practcial applications, 206

Mid-life, 219, 228

Myers and Briggs, 14

Mystic/Pragmatist model, 209, 214

NEO-PI™, 23

Neuroticism, 23, 24, 32, 33, 220

Parfitt, 49, 52, 57

Persona

   definition, 38

Polarities, 203

Practical applications

   summary, 185

Preferences

   definitions, 15

Index

Projection, 40, 222
Psyche
  Assagioli's map, 49
  definition, 36
  Jung's map, 37
Psychosynthesis, 1, 10, 46-59, 81, 82, 85, 201, 208-210
Quenk, 24, 25, 28, 40, 85, 218
Repeated Question, 200, 220
Riso and Hudson, 30
Scoular and Campbell, 21
Self/I
  definition, 43
  practical applications, 208
Shadow
  definition, 39
Sharp, 40, 41, 43, 45
Spoto, 33, 35, 36, 38, 43
Star diagram, 55
Sub-personalities
  definition, 53
  practical applications, 204
Superconscious
  definition, 52
Survival games, 26- 28, 86, 98, 103, 108, 114, 120, 125, 131, 144, 149, 156, 162, 169, 175
Thomson, 20, 28, 85
Torbert, 61, 62, 64
Transcendent Function, 41, 200, 220
  practical applications, 200

Transpersonal, 46, 48, 53, 55, 57, 58, 60, 79, 80, 81, 220
Transpersonal Self
  definition, 53
Type descriptions
  brief, 17
  developmentally levelled, 85
  ENFJ, 86
  ENFP, 91
  ENTJ, 97
  ENTP, 102
  ESFJ, 108
  ESFP, 114
  ESTJ, 119
  ESTP, 125
  INFJ, 131
  INFP, 137
  INTJ, 143
  INTP, 149
  ISFJ, 155
  ISFP, 162
  ISTJ, 168
  ISTP, 174
Type dynamics, 16
  practical applications, 194
Unconscious
  collective, definition, 39
  personal, definition, 39
Wilber, 32, 61, 62, 65
Will
  definition, 54
Witness Consciousness, 221

Printed in Great Britain by
Amazon.co.uk, Ltd.,
Marston Gate.